yes, you can!

Home repairs made easy

Meredith® Books
Des Moines, Iowa

Editor: Ken Sidey
Senior Associate Design Director: Ken Carlson
Assistant Art Director: Todd Hanson
Writer: Catherine M. Staub
Illustrator: Michael Burns
Photographers: Robert Jacobs, Scott Little
Copy Chief: Terri Fredrickson
Publishing Operations Manager: Karen Schirm
Edit and Design Production Coordinator: Mary Lee Gavin
Editorial Assistants: Renee E. McAtee, Kairee Mullen
Marketing Product Managers: Aparna Pande, Isaac Petersen, Gina Rickert, Stephen Rogers, Brent Wiersma, Tyler Woods
Book Production Managers: Pam Kvitne, Marjorie J. Schenkelberg, Rick von Holdt, Mark Weaver
Contributing Copy Editor: Wendy Wetherbee
Contributing Proofreaders: Janet Anderson, Kristin Bienert, Gretchen Kauffman, Stephanie Petersen, Paula Reece, Brenda Scott Royce

Meredith® Books
Executive Director, Editorial: Gregory H. Kayko
Executive Director, Design: Matt Strelecki
Senior Editor/Group Manager: Larry Erickson

Publisher and Editor in Chief: James D. Blume
Editorial Director: Linda Raglan Cunningham
Executive Director, Marketing: Jeffrey B. Myers
Executive Director, New Business Development: Todd M. Davis
Executive Director, Sales: Ken Zagor
Director, Operations: George A. Susral
Director, Production: Douglas M. Johnston

Vice President and General Manager: Douglas J. Guendel

Meredith Publishing Group
President: Jack Griffin
Senior Vice President: Bob Mate

Meredith Corporation
Chairman and Chief Executive Officer: William T. Kerr

In Memoriam: E.T. Meredith III (1933-2003)

All of us at Meredith® Books are dedicated to providing you with the information and ideas you need to enhance your home. We welcome your comments and suggestions. Write to us at: Meredith Books, Home Improvement Editorial Department, 1716 Locust St., Des Moines, IA 50309-3023.

If you would like to purchase any of our cooking, crafts, gardening, home improvement, or home decorating and design books, check wherever quality books are sold. Or visit us at: meredithbooks.com.

Note to the Readers: Due to differing conditions, tools, and individual skills, Meredith Corporation assumes no responsibility for any damages, injuries suffered, or losses incurred as a result of following the information published in this book. Before beginning any project, review the instructions carefully, and if any doubts or questions remain, consult local experts or authorities. Because codes and regulations vary greatly, you always should check with authorities to ensure that your project complies with all applicable local codes and regulations. Always read and observe all of the safety precautions provided by manufacturers of any tools, equipment, or supplies, and follow all accepted safety procedures.

Thank you

There are so many people I'd like to thank—without their help I would never have made it to where I am today. I should list every teacher I have ever had, but I don't have room, so please know that I think of you and thank you for your guidance and support. In particular, let me thank:

Maurice "Mo" Stroemel, for opening my eyes to "the dark side" of theater—technical theater—and showing me what fun it is to be a carpenter. **Scott Miller,** for the idea and for your incredible patience. You had faith this book was something I could complete. You were in it for the long haul. **Ellen Gray,** for helping me see the possibilities. You were the first one to really get me excited about this project and convince me it could be done. **Catherine Staub,** for your dedication to making my voice come to life on these pages. You have done an outstanding job. **Leigh Seaman,** for giving me my first big break and having confidence in my ability to get the job done. **Denise "D" Cramsey,** for helping me smile when I thought I couldn't and for understanding the importance of my priorities. **Tom Farrell,** for always being a friend first. You will always have my trust. **Steve Schwartz,** for always having a smile on your face. You made sure I always felt supported and had someone to turn to. **"The Stapler,"** for holding me together, helping me learn to be honest with myself and find my true identity. **Robert Jacobs,** for letting me play and be myself. You know even adults need a recess sometimes. **Ken Carlson,** for your generosity and creativity. You allowed me to express myself and made it look good in the process. **Todd Hanson,** for putting so much time and effort into making this book the best it could be and for giving me one of the most exciting rides of my life. **Ken Sidey,** for your persistence and commitment. Your phone calls and e-mails gave me the push I needed to not give up when I felt stuck. **Matt "Donkey" Strelecki,** for going above and beyond the call of duty. You were there to carry me through it all. **The cast and crew of** *Trading Spaces* **and** *Trading Spaces Family,* for helping me love my job and in turn love my life. You all help define teamwork. **My incredible friends,** for continually supporting me and calling, no matter how many times you get my voice mail. **My family,** for always encouraging me to follow my dreams. You are understanding and open minded, and you have taught me the most important lesson of all, that the best thing in life is to love and be loved. **My dear sweet Shaun,** your love and support inspire me to be my best. You have created a place where I always feel at home—no matter where I am on a map—right beside you.

Dedication

I dedicate this book to **my sister Heather.** Your faith in me gives me confidence to conquer any obstacle. Your work ethic inspires me to work harder and focus my priorities. Your guidance helps me find my way in a world that I don't always understand and that doesn't always understand me. Our growth as individuals has helped us become closer to one another, and for that I am truly grateful.

table of contents

chapter 1 working in your home 8

chapter 2 safe and secure 18

chapter **3** basic carpentry

40

chapter 4 wiring basics

146

chapter 5 plumbing basics 180

6 seasonal maintenance 230

working in your home

It's my hope you'll gain three things from this book: the confidence to begin a project, the information to complete that project, and the inspiration to move beyond basic repairs to create the home you desire.

I have found that when most people start a project, they find some way to finish it. This book will provide detailed information about common projects. It's also been my experience that once homeowners successfully complete a few projects, they're hooked and progress from home repair novices to weekend home improvement warriors.

Work basics

Working in your home should be empowering, enjoyable, and safe. This chapter provides the building blocks to achieve each. I'll walk you through the basics of working up to code and working safely. I'll help you assemble a starter tool kit that should enable you to complete most basic home repairs. Once you're ready to dive into more specialized repairs, check out the toolboxes in the carpentry, wiring, and plumbing chapters. I'll also discuss hiring and working with a contractor, because even as a professional carpenter, I sometimes need to call in another pro—a plumber or an electrician for example—for jobs beyond my expertise or comfort level.

If you have more than one repair on your list of things to do, carve out a workspace. I've taken over the garage at home for my workshop. Maybe you won't need that much space, but it's handy to have an established location to store your tools and a sturdy work surface.

working safe and smart

Staying safe while you work is the most important part of any home repair and improvement project.

Keep focused on your work. If you are getting distracted, stop. Keep your eyes on your work. Don't worry about being polite when it's a safety issue. Don't allow people to interrupt, particularly if you're working with power equipment. It helps to set expectations with others in your home. I do this with everyone around me when I'm working. Train them not to come up behind you and tap you on the shoulder. Instead they should stand in your peripheral vision until you acknowledge them.

Safety rules

Here are additional safety rules to follow:

- Before using a power tool, read its instruction manual and follow the manufacturer's safety cautions. Before you operate a tool, tighten any adjustments and check that any safety guards are installed and working.
- Keep power tools dry, and plug them into grounded electrical outlets. Take care not to cut the power cord.
- Keep fingers away from a blade or bit. Clamp small pieces of wood before cutting them, rather than holding them.
- Wear work gloves when handling rough materials, but take them off and roll up your sleeves if operating a power tool.
- Wear eye and ear protection when operating a power tool.
- Unplug any power tool before changing its blade or cutter.
- Support and clamp any material to be cut to prevent the saw from jumping out of the cut or the pieces from flying apart.
- When wiring, shut off the power to the circuit first, then use a tester to make sure the power is really off. Even then, work as if the circuit is live. When working with plumbing, shut off the water first.
- When working on a ladder, don't lean out to either side. Keep your body weight between the sides of the ladder.
- Wear a dust mask whenever you're generating dust and debris. When working with spray paint, work outside on a day when there is no breeze.
- Wear rubber gloves when working with solvents. Wash your hands thoroughly after removing the gloves.
- Wear shoes that cover your toes and feet when you're working and when you're in a shop area. Wear shoes with thick soles that will likely stop a nail or other sharp object before it cuts your foot.
- If you have long hair, confine it with a ponytail holder or dew rag anytime you'll be working with moving parts.
- Remove all jewelry and watches before you begin working.

MASK
Wear a dust mask when cutting, sanding, or taking on any demolition project. Check the packaging and match the mask to the type of work you are doing.

RUBBER GLOVES
Protect your hands by wearing the appropriate gloves when working with paints, stains, and solvents.

SAFETY GLASSES
Glasses or goggles provide protection from flying debris. The lenses are designed not to shatter. Find a comfortable pair and wear them—all the time.

WORK GLOVES
Heavy-duty leather gloves protect your hands from splinters and jagged, sharp edges. Do not wear them when operating power tools.

EARPLUGS
Exposure to the noise of power equipment can damage your hearing. Wear earplugs or earmuffs.

safety gear

Avoid physical strain

Though you probably wouldn't think about it until the next day when your muscles are aching, undertaking home repair and improvements can be quite a workout. Even if you work out regularly, you'll probably use different muscles working on your home. Follow these guidelines to avoid injury and minimize muscle pain:

• Get a helper to assist with some of the work, and take plenty of breaks.

• Don't overexert when lifting heavy objects, or when repeatedly lifting lighter loads.

• Lift with your legs, not your back. When picking up a heavy object, keep your back as upright and straight as possible. Bend your knees to reach the object.

• Working in an awkward position can put a strain on your back and other areas of your body. Take the time to move or to arrange things so that you are as comfortable as possible.

working to code

Building codes help ensure a safe home improvement.

Since most of the projects in this book are repairs, maintenance, and minor improvements, you probably won't have any need to visit the local building department for permits—yet. However, you're going to be inspired by the projects you successfully complete with the suggestions and steps in this book and will move on to projects that require adhering to building codes. Your local building department has comprehensive, detailed lists of regulations (codes) covering remodeling projects, including wiring,

you could be in legal trouble if it is found that significant work was done without being inspected. You may be required to have the work professionally checked, or you may be ordered to tear out the work and start again. Insurance companies may hesitate to pay a claim for damage done to your house if you have not followed codes.

In general, the building department and codes come into play whenever a new permanent structure is built, or when new electrical, plumbing, or gas service is installed. For instance, you probably do not need a permit to replace an existing toilet, sink, tub, or light fixture. If you run new electrical cable or new pipes in order to install fixtures where there were none

> " Building codes typically come into play whenever a new permanent structure is built, or when new electrical, plumbing, or gas service is installed. "

plumbing, roofing, structural framing, and the installation of permanent appliances (like air-conditioners), as well as new construction. If you're unsure whether a code governs the project you are planning, check with your local building department.

The regulations for home improvement and construction are based on decades of experience. A project that is built up to code will likely be safe and durable; a project built without benefit of codes may be dangerous and flimsy.

When it comes time to sell your home,

before, then you need a permit.

Working with a building department involves several steps. First, go to your local building department and ask for general guidelines for the project you are proposing.

Second, make a detailed, neat drawing. The inspector may ask for changes and clarifications. Finally, once your plans are approved, one or more inspections will be scheduled—typically, one inspection for the rough installation, and one for the finished project.

ADJUSTABLE WRENCH
An adjustable wrench firmly holds nuts, bolt heads, and hose connections far better than pliers and is less likely to damage them.

HAMMER
A 16-ounce framing hammer is a good all-around tool. It's a comfortable weight for most people. Select one with a synthetic neck and handle. Give it a couple of swings in the store (in a safe spot) to test if it feels balanced in your hand.

GROOVE-JOINT PLIERS
Extremely useful for tightening and loosening hardware, pulling nails, and gripping almost anything.

A well-stocked toolbox makes every task easier, quicker, and safer.

basic toolbox

METAL TAPE MEASURE
A 25-foot metal tape measure is an all-purpose length for most home projects.

basic toolbox

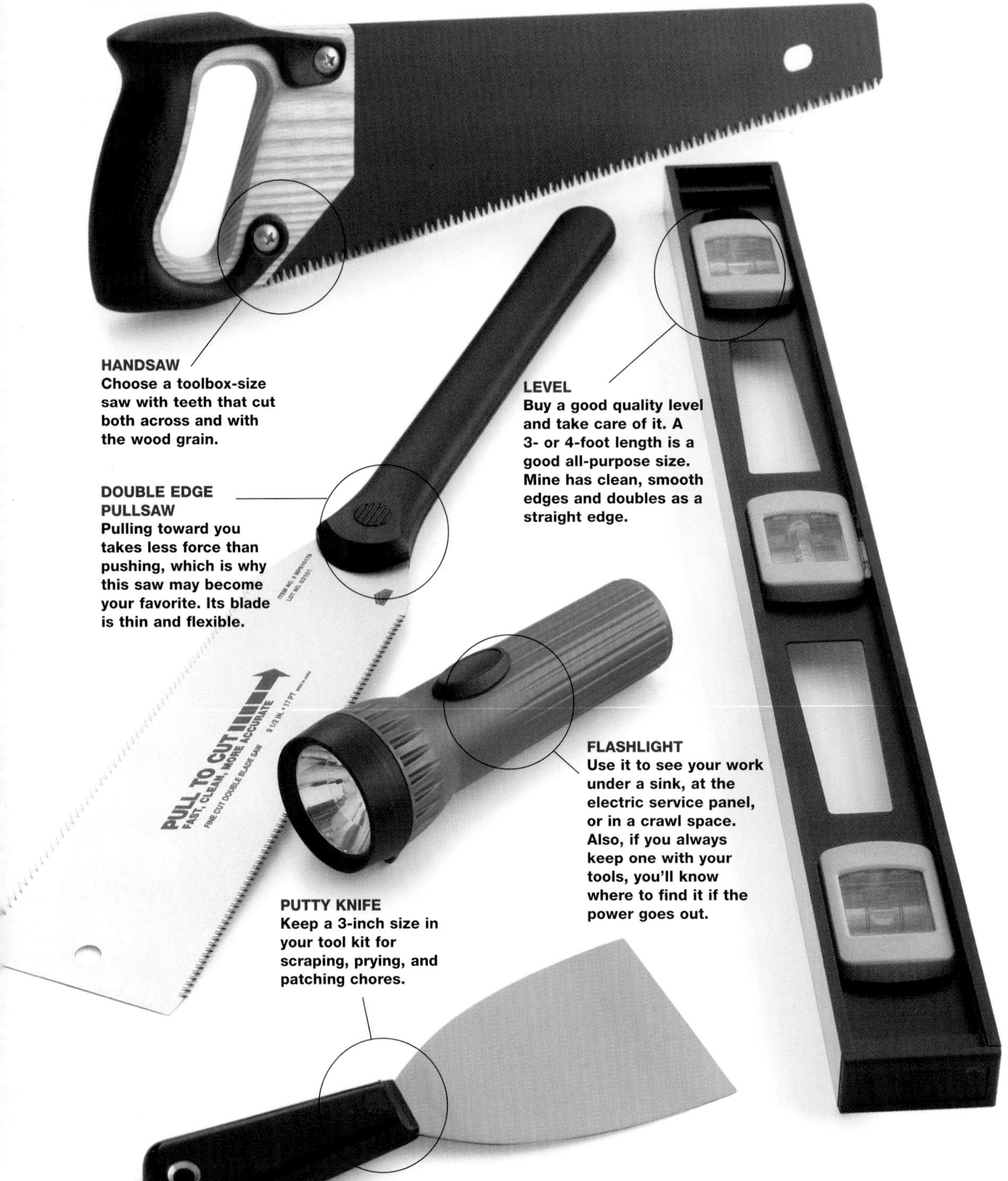

HANDSAW
Choose a toolbox-size
saw with teeth that cut
both across and with
the wood grain.

**DOUBLE EDGE
PULLSAW**
Pulling toward you
takes less force than
pushing, which is why
this saw may become
your favorite. Its blade
is thin and flexible.

PULL TO CUT
FAST, CLEAN, MORE ACCURATE
FINE CUT DOUBLE BLADE SAW

LEVEL
Buy a good quality level
and take care of it. A
3- or 4-foot length is a
good all-purpose size.
Mine has clean, smooth
edges and doubles as a
straight edge.

FLASHLIGHT
Use it to see your work
under a sink, at the
electric service panel,
or in a crawl space.
Also, if you always
keep one with your
tools, you'll know
where to find it if the
power goes out.

PUTTY KNIFE
Keep a 3-inch size in
your tool kit for
scraping, prying, and
patching chores.

PHILLIPS SCREWDRIVERS
A phillips screw is self-centering, so when you apply torque, the screwdriver won't slide out. Look for a set that includes a variety of sizes.

UTILITY KNIFE
Purchase one with a retractable blade that locks firmly into place.

SLOT SCREWDRIVERS
Look for a screwdriver kit that contains slot and phillips heads in a variety of sizes. A set that comes in a convenient pouch or case is a bonus.

EXTRA PENCILS
You'll need to mark spots to drive nails or screws and lengths for cutting wood. Keep pencils sharp to make distinct lines.

CHISEL
Select a framing chisel that is designed to withstand the strike of a hammer. Look for the metal blade to extend well into the handle. A set of sizes up to 1 inch wide covers almost any job.

basic toolbox

EXTENSION CORD
Stock a 25-foot 16-gauge ground-fault circuit interrupter cord for safe access to work areas that don't have outlets within short reach.

PRY BAR
Great for removing nails, though you need to take care not to damage the surface when applying pressure.

BLOCK PLANE
Use to shave wood along the length of a board to get smooth edges. Protect the blade when not in use; keep it sharp for best results.

CAULKING GUN
Use this to fill cracks with caulk and to apply adhesive to large areas.

SMALL PRY BAR
Handy for removing nails in tight areas and when completing demolition that requires a delicate approach.

yes, you can!

what if...

a project seems too daunting to tackle yourself?

ven though I'm convinced you can successfully complete every project in this book, there may be times you discover unforeseen problems on what you thought would be a simple repair. Read about one of my experiences like this on page 151. There may also be emergency repair situations that call for the tools and expertise of a professional. I've had a few of those—see page 214. So basically, though you can handle numerous repair and upgrades yourself, there are times when it makes sense to hire a contractor.

Shop around

- Unless it's an emergency, get the names of several contractors by asking for recommendations. Take a look at examples of their work to see if it meets your expectations.
- Get rough estimates. It will help you narrow the field of candidates.
- For a major job, get at least three bids. Give a contractor about three weeks to produce the bid. Read the bids closely; they should detail the materials that will be used. If one contractor is much lower, check to make sure she or he is truly capable and experienced.
- When accepting bids, find out how long the contractor has been in business—the longer the better. Ask who finances the

contractor's company (usually it's a bank).
- Ask the bank about the contractor's general solvency. You don't want a contractor to go bankrupt in the middle of your project.
- The contractor should carry insurance covering property damage, liability, and workers' compensation. If the contractor is not covered, you could be liable for hefty fees in case of an accident.

Get it in writing

Once you've chosen a contractor, get the details in writing before any work begins. The contract should:

- Itemize in detail all work to be done. Specify the type and brand of materials and finishes to be used. Include a specific timetable. You may want to work in a penalty for late completion.
- Fixed-price contracts should specify the total cost. Cost-plus contracts should specify the cost of materials and labor. Payments should depend on work completed.
- Include in the contract a warranty ensuring that the labor and materials are free from defects for at least a year.
- An arbitration clause delineates the method for resolving disputes.
- A release of liens clause ensures that you won't be responsible for liens filed against the contractor by suppliers or subcontractors.

safe and secure

Working safe isn't only about protecting yourself; it's also about protecting the people you love— and your home.

Your home is a place where you should feel safe and secure. Creating a safe home begins with identifying potential dangers so you can take steps to correct them. This book is about making your home safe and secure, because it shows you how to complete basic home repairs. When your home is in good condition, it becomes safer than if it's in disrepair. In this chapter, I'll discuss specific safety issues you can address by taking relatively simple steps, such as installing proper locks and latches, putting in smoke alarms, and knowing how to operate a fire extinguisher.

I'll also walk you through a basic home safety inspection. Certainly this is not meant to foster fear. Instead it's about being in control of your home so you can maintain an environment in which you feel comfortable.

Home safety

Some aspects of keeping a home safe simply involve common sense and attentiveness—keeping harmful chemicals out of reach of children and having fire extinguishers readily available in the kitchen. Do you know how to operate a fire extinguisher if you need it?

When faced with an emergency it's human nature to kick into overdrive— a response designed to save us if we're being chased by a lion, but not necessarily what we need to stay levelheaded during a home emergency. Review this chapter before you think you need it.

keeping your home secure

Begin by assessing two major areas of your home: the perimeter and the points of entry. Once you've examined them with a critical eye, you'll be able to take the steps covered in the rest of this section.

TOOLS AND MATERIALS:
• Paper and pencil

WYNN TIP:
Nothing deters a burglar more than a home that offers no assistance in entry. Pick up the lawn. Keep areas well-lit and clutter-free.

CHECK OUTSIDE

Walk around your home and consider the following:

1 Is lighting adequate at night? A well-lit home is less appealing to intruders. If you live in a neighborhood, note the effect of municipal street lights. Determine what, if any, supplemental lighting you need on your property. See pages 22–23 for more information about using lights for safety and security.

If you live in an apartment complex, are common interior areas such as hallways well lit? Are parking areas equipped with properly operating lights? If not, contact the building superintendent.

2 Are tools or ladders left out? If so, they could become keys for illegal entry. Leaving items out can also be a calling card for thieves—if you are careless with items outside, they'll think you might be just as careless about securing the inside of your home.

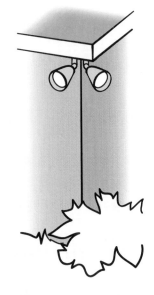

Step 4. Add lighting to areas where intruders could hide (see pages 22–23).

3 Do you keep tools in an unlocked shed or other outdoor storage compartment? Though not as tempting as tools left in plain sight, these also can be easily used to break in to your house. Add locks to exterior storage areas.

4 Do foundation shrubs and plantings obscure windows and offer convenient places for intruders to hide? Do large tree limbs stretch out as easy bridges to second-story windows? Consider trimming back trees and shrubs.

INSPECT ENTRY POINTS

Look at all windows, doors, attached garages, and crawlspaces. Consider the following:

1 Entry doors should be solid-core or made with heavy panels. A deadbolt lock with a bolt that slides deep into the door's frame is far superior to a handle lock or a rim lock (see pages 30–31). Equip the garage door with a solid lock as well. If an entry door hinge faces out rather than in, a burglar can easily pop the hinge pins and open the door. Install special hinges that make this impossible.

Installing a hasp with a padlock provides additional security against forced entry through basement windows.

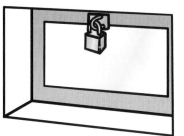

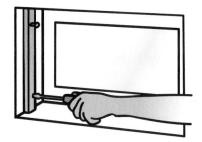

WYNN TIP:
An entryway intercom system lets you check the identity of anyone who visits without jeopardizing your safety. Look through a peephole for a first impression and use the intercom to ask questions.

2 Windows are the next most common point of illegal entry. Choose from a wide assortment of locking and securing options; see pages 24–25. Pay special attention to basement windows, and consider installing glass block. As you plan upgrades in window security, keep in mind that it may be necessary to exit through a window in an emergency, such as a fire. Though window bars, for example, keep most would-be intruders out, they also prevent you from making a quick escape.

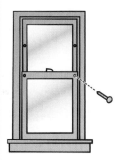

Nails prevent a window from being opened wide enough to allow entry.

using lights
for safety and security

Light provides a cozy warmth to your home, and you can use it to thwart burglars.

ight up your property to protect yourself and your family. External lights make it difficult for burglars to enter your home unseen, and internal lights set to a timer give the impression someone is home. Both deter burglars.

Take advantage of street lighting; trim trees to allow the light to reach your home.

When you're away from home, set timers on lamps in various rooms. Think about your evening movement patterns and set the timers to simulate these movements. If you have a radio, tune it to a talk show so it will also sound like people are in the house.

Landscape lighting

Install landscape lighting. Thanks to improved solar lights you don't need to be an electrician or even rent a trencher. The new lights have rechargeable batteries that store the energy of the sun during the day, so they don't need to be plugged in to your electrical system to run at night. When fully charged, most lights will stay activated for up to 15 hours. To ensure that the batteries charge to their full capacity, place the lights where they will receive the full light of the sun during the day.

Motion detectors

Set up lights on motion detectors on the exterior of your home. If you have an existing backyard light or a light over the garage, converting to a motion-detector light is simple. Most kits are preassembled for ease of installation. Once installed, the light turns on when the motion detector senses movement within its range and automatically turns off after a preset period of time when no motion is detected. The light stays on as long as there is movement. You might want to consider buying a wide-angle motion sensor. They detect an almost 75 percent wider area compared to standard detectors.

installing a motion-detector light

With a kit and a couple of basic tools, you can secure your home by replacing an outdoor fixture with a new motion-detector light.

WYNN TIP:
Point the bulbs slightly downward so water will not fill the fixture sockets.

WYNN TIP:
Some people just aren't comfortable working with electricity. If you're one of them, hire a professional. There are plenty of projects in this book you can successfully tackle yourself!

1 Turn off the power to the circuit at the service panel. Use a neon circuit tester to make sure power is off (see page 153).

2 Remove the old fixture. Align the screw holes on the fixture coverplate with the electrical box screw holes on the sensor.

3 Thread the motion-detector wires through the coverplate gasket. Use wire nuts to connect the motion-detector wires to the electrical box wires; fastening black wire to black wire, and white wire to white wire. A ground wire is not normally required, so fasten it on the house circuit to the electrical box.

4 Attach the new motion-sensor fixture with the screws provided.

5 Screw in lightbulbs recommended by the manufacturer.

6 Adjust and test the motion detector. Set the slide or switch to the "TEST" position. Turn the sensor adjustment dial halfway.

7 Turn the power on at the service panel. The lights typically come on for 30 seconds and then turn off. The lights may stay on longer if the detector senses motion.

8 Aim the detector head toward the area where you wish to detect motion. Walk across the detection zone at the farthest point you wish the lights to reach. Adjust sensitivity until the lights come on in the desired detection zone. Move the control switch to set how long the light stays on. If uncertain, read the manufacturer's instructions.

ADJUSTING SENSITIVITY

If the light comes on more than you want or blinks repeatedly, try reducing the sensor sensitivity. Turn the dial one-eighth of a turn at a time until the light stays off. Check to make sure the light comes on when you want by walking in the detection zone.

Use electrical tape to block off sensor lens areas where motion or light from lamps unnecessarily sets off the sensor.

Step 8. Adjust the lamps to illuminate the detection area.

what if...

you need to secure windows?

**TOOLS AND
MATERIALS:**
- **Drill and
  bits**
- **Screwdriver**
- **Pliers**
- **Hammer**
- **Key locks**
- **Nails**
- **Tape
  measure**
- **Screws**

Most homes have many windows, and securing all of them can be costly and time consuming. The best place to start is with sliding glass doors and windows accessible from ground level. Take into consideration which upper-level windows could be reached from a balcony, garage or porch roof, or tree.

Burglars usually enter homes through doors. But don't expect intruders to stand on tradition. If the doors are locked, they will concentrate on operative windows. If a burglar finds a window that can be easily forced open and allows access without calling attention, he or she will enter through it. If the window can't be forced open, a burglar may stick tape to a pane, break it, and quietly pull away the pieces to gain access to the latch. If a burglar decides the home is too secure, he or she won't bother with it and will opt to look for an easier target.

Intruders don't like to make noise, so a large expanse of fixed glass window presents less of a security problem than you may think. Smashing a picture window probably would call attention to a break-in.

Follow these steps to secure various types of windows in your home.

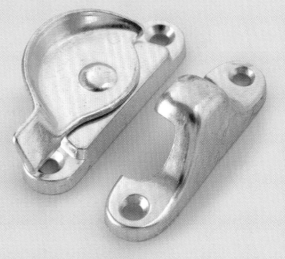

INSTALL HEAVY-DUTY SASH LOCKS

Ordinary sash locks offer little security because you can open most of them with a knife blade. A heavy-duty model that clicks shut offers more resistance.

WYNN TIP:

Make sure all windows work properly. Sashes that wobble when you crank them, rattle in high winds, or have to be propped open offer only token resistance to break-ins.

INSTALL A KEY LOCK

Key locks can't be jimmied, even if the glass is broken. Most will also let you lock the window in a partly open position. Drill a hole in the upper sash for every position you want to be able to lock.

USE NAILS AS LOCKS

With the sash closed, drill a hole on each side of the window, through the bottom sash and most of the way into (but not through) the top sash. Open the window halfway and drill again the same way. To secure the window in either position, insert nails into the holes.

SECURE A CASEMENT WINDOW

Many casement windows won't open enough to admit an adult. To check yours, open the window and measure from the inside edge of the sash to the jamb. Most adults will require at least 10 inches of clearance. If a fully opened window will admit a person, open the window partially so the opening is 10 inches or less. Then remove the operator crank and set it out of reach.

LOCK A HASP OR INSTALL A STOP ON A BASEMENT WINDOW

A hasp on a basement window can be secured with a padlock. Use a keyless combination lock or keep the key somewhere handy (but not on the sill). If your windows don't have hasps, drive long screws into a stop on each side. Leave a few inches to open the window for ventilation.

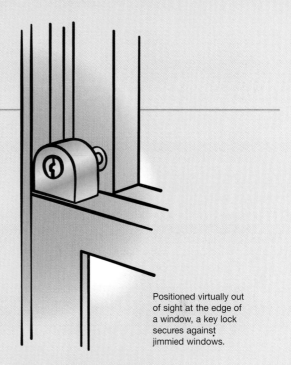

Positioned virtually out of sight at the edge of a window, a key lock secures against jimmied windows.

ADD A GRILLE OR GRATE

Custom-made grilles mortared into the foundation give basement windows a behind-bars look, but they provide peace of mind in a high-crime area. Just remember that if the grilles are mortared in, you won't be able to escape through the windows in case of an emergency. If these would be the only exit windows if a fire blocks the door, opt for scissors-type gates and hinged iron shutters that can be padlocked from the inside yet opened for escape.

AVOID INSTALLING SLIDING WINDOWS AT GROUND LEVEL, IF POSSIBLE

Thieves like sliding windows (and sliding glass doors) because some can be pried up and out of their tracks, even when the locksets are in the locked position.

securing exterior doors

Several projects in this book will help you secure the entrance doors to your home. Here's an overview of the steps you can take to make sure your doors are secure—without making your home feel like a bank vault.

WYNN TIP:
If it makes you feel better, install a chain lock, but don't rely on it as your only means of securing a door. Chain locks can be forced open fairly easily. To install, mount the hardware with screws that penetrate the door frame and the jamb studs. Select the heaviest chain available.

INSTALL A DEADBOLT

The locks that come with exterior door handsets are not enough to keep an intruder from entering your home through a door. A high-quality deadbolt lock with a bolt that slides deep into the door frame is the best door safety feature. Double-cylinder deadbolt locks employ special one-way screws that you can drive in but cannot be turned out; otherwise an intruder could simply remove the assembly. Fittings with a double-cylinder lock generally include an extra set of conventional, slotted screws. Mount the lock and strike plate with these, make any adjustments, then withdraw the slotted screws and replace them with the tamperproof versions. See pages 30–31 for more information on how to install deadbolts.

ADD A PEEPHOLE

Though solid doors provide a better measure of safety than doors with glass panes, you can't see who's at the door to determine whether you want to let them in. A peephole lets

A deadbolt offers security a knob lock alone can't provide.

you view who's visiting from behind the safety of the closed and locked door. See page 28 to install a peephole.

INCREASE HOLDING POWER

All door hardware, such as hinges, strike plates, and deadbolts, depends on screws for holding power. If the screws that came with the hardware don't penetrate at least halfway into the door or 3 to 4 inches into the doorjamb and wall studs, discard them and buy longer ones. Longer screws provide greater security with minimal expenditure. For added strength, coat the screws with glue before driving them into pilot holes.

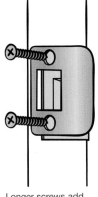

Longer screws add additional holding power to a door strikeplate.

Sliding door solutions

PROVIDE EXTRA SECURITY TO SLIDING DOORS

The locking mechanism that comes with most sliding door handles doesn't offer much security. Beef it up with additional measures. For quick and simple protection, insert a broom handle or other piece of wood into the track when the door is closed. Even if the lock is broken, the door can't be slid open from the outside. You can also secure sliding doors by drilling holes through both the track and the sash frames. Slip nails into the holes to prevent the doors from opening.

ATTACH A TOE LOCK

Toe-operated locks for sliding doors are convenient and unobtrusive. Mount the lock on

WYNN TIP:
Replacing all the locks in a home can be very expensive. Have locks rekeyed instead. Rekeying is an inexpensive way to make your home safe if you have recently moved in or have lost a key to your house.

WYNN TIP:
Think carefully before you buy and install safety accessories. Family members may need to exit the house quickly in case of fire. You don't want a family member trapped inside because he or she can't find the key to get out or because the deadbolt levers are mounted too high to operate.

WYNN TIP:
Mount any surface lock about 8–10 inches higher than the existing knob set so that you can see and operate it easily.

the casing and drill a hole in the sash where the locking rod will enter.

REINFORCE HOLES

When you drill a hole into a piece of wood, you create a structurally weak point. Adding a metal reinforcer gives you back the strength. When purchasing a reinforcer, make sure it fits the thickness of your door. Installing one is simple: Remove the lockset. Slip the reinforcer over the door's edge and align. Drive screws.

SECURE THE LATCH GUARD

Add a heavy-duty latch guard to provide added holding power to the strikeplate. Choose a guard with a flange that does not allow a pry bar under it. Mount the latch guard with screws long enough to enter the wall studs for added support.

A toe lock is easy to install on the inside of a sliding door.

installing a peephole

A solid door protects your home from intruders, but how do you know whether to open the door when you can't see who is on the other side? Installing a peephole solves the problem. You can complete this project in minimal time with a few tools.

TOOLS AND MATERIALS:
- **Drill and bits**
- **Slotted screwdriver**
- **Tape measure**
- **Peephole kit**
- **Dust mask**
- **Safety glasses**
- **Pencil**

1 You'll look through the peephole each time someone is at the door, so place it at a comfortable height. Mark the center of the door using a tape measure and pencil.

2 Double-check that the mark is centered at the predetermined height. Drill a pilot hole through the door at the mark. A small drill bit (⅛ inch) works best.

3 Read the peephole manufacturer's instructions to determine what size bit to use to bore the hole. Drill halfway through the door from the outside using the pilot hole as a starting guide. Go inside and finish drilling the hole. This method minimizes the chance of splintering, which can occur when a bit penetrates the door.

4 Insert the halves of the peephole into the hole. Check to make sure you put them in the correct way. Finish installing the peephole using a screwdriver that fits in the slots of the peephole rim to secure it to the door.

Step 3. Drill half way through the door, then finish the hole from the inside.

WYNN TIP:
Pay attention when you install the peephole. It's easier than you think to install it backward, which does no good unless you're outside wanting to look in.

installing a deadbolt

You want an entry door to welcome visitors to your home. But it's also essential that doors provide security. That's a job for a deadbolt, which provides the strength that a handle or knob lock alone can't. You can add just a deadbolt to a door, or you may want to replace the handle as well. For additional security, purchase a deadbolt with a metal strike enclosure, which extends deep into the doorjamb.

**TOOLS AND
MATERIALS:**
- **Drill with
  holesaw and
  bits**
- **Utility knife**
- **Awl**
- **Screwdriver**
- **Chisel**
- **Pencil**
- **Tape**
- **Lockset**

INSTALL A HANDLE SET

1 A lockset comes with a paper or cardboard template. Tape it or hold it against the door. If a hole for the handle set already exists in the door, or if a strike is already cut in the jamb, align the template with them so you won't have to cut a new hole for the handle or mortise (a shallow cutout) for the strikeplate.

2 With an awl or the point of a spade bit, mark for the holes for the handle set (if needed) and the deadbolt by piercing through the template.

3 Drill the larger hole through the face of the door using a holesaw. To avoid splintering the veneer, drill just far enough that the pilot bit of the holesaw pokes through. Then drill from the other side.

4 Use a spade bit to drill through the edge of the door, taking care to hold the bit parallel to the surface of the door. Some types of locksets require that you continue drilling into the rear of the large hole approximately ½ inch. Check manufacturer's instructions.

5 Insert the handle set bolt through the smaller hole. Temporarily screw it centered in the door and mark for its mortise with a sharp pencil or a knife.

6 Cut and chisel a mortise. Depending on the type of bolt, this mortise may be deeper near the center than at the edges.

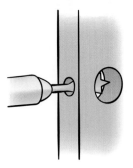

Step 4. Drill the hole for the bolt using a spade bit. Check the manufacturer's instructions for the proper size.

WYNN TIP:

A double-keyed deadbolt locks with a key on the inside as well as on the outside. It can be useful in situations where an intruder could reach through a window to the bolt. If you purchase a double-keyed lock, make sure the key is readily accessible inside (or in the lock) when the home is occupied, especially at night.

7 Install the bolt by setting it in the mortise, drilling pilot holes, and driving the screws provided to secure the plate.

8 Follow manufacturer instructions to install the handles or knobs. Tighten all screws.

9 Test the new knobs or handles from both sides of the door to make sure they operate smoothly. If not, you may need to clean out or widen the holes.

INSTALL THE DEADBOLT

1 Drill holes for the body of the lock and the bolt (described in Steps 1–4). Mark the position of the two mounting holes for the bolt and drill them. Insert the bolt and latch face, mark for the mortise, and cut it with a chisel. Screw the latch face into the mortise.

2 For many lock types, you'll need to use a screwdriver to partially extend the bolt. Insert the lock tailpiece through the slot in the bolt. Slip on the interior turn bolt or lock until the two pieces sit flush against the door.

3 Mark the location of the strikeplate on the doorjamb. Cut and mortise. Install the strikeplate and fasten with screws.

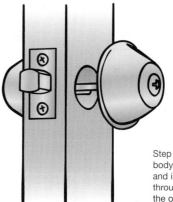

Step 2. Align the lock body on one side and insert the shaft through the bolt into the opposite part of the body.

WYNN TIP:

There is a reason deadbolt locks aren't designed to be spring-loaded. A spring-loaded latch retracts as it hits the strikeplate, allowing you to close a door with the latch extended. The problem is that someone can pry the door open. An extended deadbolt shaft has no give. Once set, it's locked in place and only an extraordinary amount of force will dislodge it.

what if...

you need a fire extinguisher?

hopefully you will never need a fire extinguisher. But you certainly can't wait until you need one to purchase it and figure out how to properly use it. If you don't have a fire extinguisher in the kitchen, another in the workshop, and one close to the fireplace, add fire extinguishers to this weekend's shopping list.

Home fires usually start small. Most can be brought under control by using an extinguisher of the correct type and size. Purchase extinguishers designed to put out the types of fires you are most likely to have. Check labels for specific information. Extinguishers are rated according to four types of flammables:

WYNN TIP:
Remember the word **PASS** when you need to use a fire extinguisher:
• Pull the pin.
• Aim the nozzle at the base of the fire.
• Squeeze or pump the handle.
• Sweep from side to side at the base of the flame.

Class A: ordinary combustibles, such as wood, paper, cloth, and rubber

Class B: flammable liquids, such as gasoline, cooking grease, and solvents

Class C: electrical equipment, such as wiring, fuse boxes, and electrical motors

Class D: combustible metals, such as magnesium and sodium

An "ABC" extinguisher will handle most any type of home fire. Kitchen fires typically involve burning grease or electrical equipment, so you may wish to purchase a "BC" extinguisher for the kitchen.

Spend a little more money for an extinguisher that has a high "UL" number, which indicates how much extinguishing agent it contains. The higher the number, the longer the unit will last, and the larger the unit will be.

Regularly check fire extinguishers. They should be under full pressure.

Most household extinguishers are disposable. If you use one for even a short burst, properly dispose of it and purchase a new one.

TO USE A FIRE EXTINGUISHER:

- Hold the extinguisher 5–6 feet away from the fire. Any closer could cause the fire to disperse, and any farther away might not be effective.
- Aim the spray at the base—the source— of the fire; hitting the flames in the middle won't do much good.
- Use a sweeping motion when spraying to cover the area thoroughly.
- Use short bursts or a long spray.

WYNN TIP:

Know when *not* to fight a fire and leave immediately. Only try to extinguish small fires. Don't attempt to put out a fire with the wrong type or size of extinguisher. If the fire could block your only exit or spreads quickly, leave. If the fire is out of control, get out. Closing the door behind you cuts off or restricts oxygen to the fire.

selecting smoke detectors

Most fatal fires occur at night while people are sleeping. Install smoke detectors to alert your family to danger.

moke detectors are a critical component of a home safety plan. If you live in an apartment or building where someone else is responsible for the detectors, check with the building superintendent to make sure they are working properly.

If you are responsible for your own smoke detectors, regularly check to make sure they are operating. In battery-operated units, replace the batteries twice a year on a set schedule.

If you need to install new detectors, you can choose between two types: photoelectric and ionization units. Combination units are also available but are more expensive. Photoelectric units use a beam of light and a photoelectric cell to detect smoke. When smoke enters the unit, it scatters the light, triggering an alarm. An ionization unit gives the air inside the detector an electrical charge. Smoke particles cut down current flow, which in turn sounds a warning.

Photoelectric smoke detectors react more readily to slow, smoldering fires; ionization detectors respond quicker to fast, flaming fires. Consider installing at least one of each—an ionization detector in the hallway outside of your bedrooms, plus a photoelectric unit in the living area.

Smoke detectors are typically powered by battery or electric current. Batteries must be replaced regularly, and plug-in units must be located next to a power source where they will not be unplugged. Install at least one detector on each floor of your home. Consider installing at least one battery-operated detector and one plug-in detector. That way you'll be covered if the power is out or if a battery dies.

installing a smoke detector

In the event of a fire during the night, you need to make sure everyone wakes up in time to escape. The most effective way to do this is to install and maintain smoke detectors in your home.

TOOLS AND MATERIALS:
- **Drill and bits**
- **Screwdriver**
- **Smoke detector**
- **Batteries**
- **Tape measure**

WYNN TIP:
In a single-level home with bedrooms clustered together, you can install one smoke alarm in a hallway between the bedrooms and living areas. If your sleeping areas are spread out or are on different levels, you should use at least two detectors to adequately cover all the sleeping areas. Mount one at the top of the stairway in a multi-level home.

1 Carefully read and follow the installation instructions that come with the smoke detector.

2 Determine where to place the detector. Knowing how smoke travels will assist in placement: Once smoke reaches the ceiling, it spreads horizontally. This makes the center of a room the optimum location for a smoke detector. If the ceiling is not an option, mount the detector high on a wall, about 8–10 inches below the ceiling. Ideally, you should have at least one detector on each floor in hallways leading to bedrooms and at the top of stairwells.

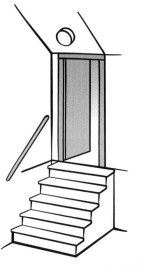

Since smoke rises, placing a detector at the top of the basement staircase provides early warning.

Place the detector in the center of the ceiling for optimal effectiveness.

Analyze your home's air currents and avoid dead corners where there is poor air circulation. If you have plug-in detectors, locate them near outlets. Also, to avoid frequent false alarms, position detectors away from the furnace, fireplaces, and smoky areas in the kitchen.

3 Use the drill and screws to mount the detector. Install new batteries for a battery-powered unit. Plug in an electric-powered unit. Test the alarm.

WYNN TIP:
Protect your family and home from basement and utility area fires as well. Because smoke and heat rise, install a detector at the top of the basement stairway, if possible.

making a home safe for children

Protecting your children in the home is simple and inexpensive.

arents become suspicious when the house gets quiet, because it usually means their children are into something.

Young children love to explore, climbing into new places, testing newly developed motor skills, and tasting anything in reach. Wanting to be big, they carefully watch everything adults and older siblings do, and try to imitate them. They go quickly from crawling to standing up, walking, and reaching—even grasping things that seem out of reach—so parents need to plan ahead. Fortunately it is easier than ever to child-proof your home.

Bathroom safety

A bathtub has hard and slippery surfaces. Cover the spout with an inflatable or foam spout cover. Apply slip-resistant strips to the bottom of the tub or buy a nonslip tub mat. Consider installing a grab bar or two.

Keep all electrical appliances far away from the tub. Never leave water in a bathtub. And never leave a child unattended in the tub.

Adjust the temperature on the water heater so it is warm enough for your shower, yet not so hot as to scald a child. Most experts recommend a setting between 100–120 degrees Fahrenheit. If faucet handles can be reached by a child, turn off firmly; a child who turns on the hot water could be scalded. Install faucets equipped with anti-scald devices or retrofit existing fixtures.

Many products found in a bathroom, such as aftershave and perfume, can be harmful if swallowed or if they get in a child's eyes. Keep them out of reach and out of sight.

Toddlers earn their name. They waddle around in a constant state of unbalance as fast as their feet can possibly carry them. It's no wonder corners of counters and tables pose a danger. Cover corners with bubble wrap.

Stair safety

At a certain stage, a child finds stairways irresistible. Use gates to keep the stairs out of bounds. Purchase only new gates, which meet modern safety standards.

Electrical safety

Electrical cords are a potential hazard, especially if a child handles the plug with wet fingers. A child also might pull down a household appliance by the cord. Position furniture such that the child cannot reach plugs. Cover unused electrical outlets with special plastic safety plugs or covers.

If you have heating units that get hot—a wood-burning stove, a kerosene unit, electrical baseboard heaters, or even steam radiators—take special precautions to keep the child away and never leave children alone in these areas.

Kitchen safety

Little hands love to explore, especially in the kitchen. Because kids grow quickly, they will be standing on their tiptoes trying to reach things on countertops before you know it, including stove burners. If you are cooking while a child is in the kitchen, use the back burners whenever possible. Purchase a guard about 4–5 inches high to fasten to your stove front. It will prevent burns to curious toddlers.

If a stove knob is left uncovered, a child can easily turn on a burner. Special covers are available to protect the knobs. When buying a new stove, look for one with the knobs on the top instead of the front.

Avoid scalding accidents in the kitchen by turning pan handles inward while cooking.

Bedroom safety

Throw out wire hangers and use plastic or wooden hangers. Many children have suffered serious eye injuries and loss of sight from playing with wire hangers.

Fasten bookshelves and dressers to walls to child-proof them. Dressers tend to fall over when all the drawers are opened or when used as ladders. Never place heavy objects that may fall off on top of them.

Tie back blind and drapery cords. Dangling cords pose a strangulation hazard. You can cut blind cords so a child cannot reach them. Set the height of your blinds so the bottom of the blind is below the window. Cut the cord as high as it is comfortable but no less than 4 inches from the top. Slide the cord through the plastic end and tie a knot.

While the child is in the putting-everything-in-the-mouth stage, move all knickknacks up and out of reach.

Teach and talk to your children about dangers around them. They will understand and avoid situations that present a danger. You might be surprised, in fact, to overhear your child warning a friend to stay away from a "danger."

A child should never be left alone in a walker, swing, exersaucer, or even a

> **Child-proofing your home takes only a few minutes and a few simple products—a small price compared to the potential consequences.** "

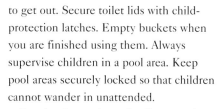

high chair. Your child may try to get out or move to follow you, incurring a head injury from a fall.

Toddler protection

Toddlers tend to tumble when they reach down because their heads are heavy. When they try to touch the water in toilet bowls, buckets, and especially swimming pools, they can fall in and are not strong enough to get out. Secure toilet lids with child-protection latches. Empty buckets when you are finished using them. Always supervise children in a pool area. Keep pool areas securely locked so that children cannot wander in unattended.

For the sharp edges of coffee or end tables, try placing pipe insulation over the edges. It's not exactly a designer statement, but you'll be thankful the next time your toddler bonks into it.

Poison safety

As children reach the age of two, you will probably find that they are attracted to shiny or interesting-looking containers and will want to open them to see what is inside. Because of this, they are at risk to poison, choke, and burn themselves. Stow all poisonous containers out of reach. Medicine may taste bad, but that does not deter a child from swallowing it. Place a lock on the medicine cabinet. Install a childproof latch on cupboards containing cleaning supplies.

preventing carbon monoxide poisoning

You can't see it, smell it, or taste it. These qualities make carbon monoxide (CO) one of the most dangerous poisons. Overexposure can cause headaches, nausea, dizziness, fatigue, blurred vision, and ultimately death. Its presence can be identified only by a carbon monoxide detector.

TOOLS AND MATERIALS:
- CO detector
- Pencil
- Drill and bits
- Screwdriver
- Wall anchors

WYNN TIP:
You may also want to place CO detectors next to your smoke detectors. Like smoke detectors, CO detectors are available in battery- operated and plug-in models. In either case, it is recommended to replace the CO detector every two years.

MINIMIZE THE LIKELIHOOD OF CARBON MONOXIDE IN YOUR HOME

1 Have the gas company inspect your home to check for proper ventilation.

2 Follow maintenance procedures for your furnace. A forced-air system is most likely to cause problems. Change the filters regularly, and check that air can flow freely through vents.

3 A fireplace may be a culprit. If the chimney does not draw well or if the chimney bricks are not well mortared, CO from burning wood can leak into living areas. This often occurs on upper floors, so install a CO detector there.

4 If tests show your home has high levels of CO, call in a contractor to make repairs. Meanwhile, open windows to provide ventilation. If that does not alleviate the problem, evacuate the house.

INSTALL A CARBON MONOXIDE DETECTOR

1 Install a carbon monoxide detector near but not in the room that contains the water heater and heating unit, main floor living room, and garage if used as a workspace.

2 Using the detector's base as a template, mark the screw locations on the wall. Drill holes and insert wall anchors.

3 Drive screws into the wall anchors. Leave the screw heads a bit away from the wall. Slide the mounting plate over the heads. Tighten the screws. Snap the detector into place.

4 In the event the alarm sounds, check to make sure everyone is OK. Open the windows to ventilate the house. Call your local utility company to examine your appliances. If anyone complains of headaches, nausea, dizziness, fatigue, or blurred vision, immediately leave your home and seek medical attention.

Since any appliance that uses flammable fuels can be the source of CO poisoning, position detectors throughout your home.

basic carpentry

I love the confidence, creativity, and freedom that come from completing carpentry projects. It's important to me to know I can keep my home in good running order.

y goal for this chapter is to show you how to be self-reliant in addressing minor annoyances—squeaky stairs, broken windows—and improve the way your home functions by adding simple upgrades, such as shelving. You could spend more time searching for an available, experienced carpenter than you would to complete the job yourself. The ability to handle small carpentry jobs can save you money while providing satisfaction that you did it. You can accomplish all of this with basic skills, a few tools, and materials.

Many of the projects in this chapter are basic home repairs. I admit it's more fun to undertake a home improvement project than a repair, but keeping up your home is essential. You'll also find simple improvement projects, such as building a closet organizer and installing recessed shelving, creating functional space to meet your needs.

I've found the hardest part of any project is getting started. Once you begin, you'll find a way to finish, and with this book, you don't have to go alone. The clear instructions and helpful tips that follow will guide you through to a successful completion. Now let's get started!

Assemble a toolbox with quality, basic tools

Each project in this chapter includes a list of the necessary tools and materials, but many of the projects require the same basic carpentry tools. In the next few pages, I'll walk you through assembling a carpentry toolbox, a handy addition to the basic tool kit we assembled in Chapter 1. This will allow you to tackle varied and complex projects.

Ask yourself four basic questions when determining the specific tools you want and need for your tool kit:

(1) What is your skill level?

(2) How complex are the projects you plan to take on?

(3) Do you have a large number of varied projects to complete?

(4) How much storage space do you have for tools and materials?

Depending on your answers to these questions, you may wish to add only a few

hand tools

LAYOUT SQUARE
Use this handy tool to check for square and other angles, and use it as a cutting guide.

TORPEDO LEVEL
Plumb and level small projects with this. Purchase a longer carpenter's level (page 14) for bigger projects.

FRAMING SQUARE
Use this to check corners for square. You can also use it to figure other angles, and it measures.

CHALK LINE
Snap long straight lines with a chalk line. It can double as a plumb bob to check for true vertical lines.

STUD FINDER
Indicates the location of wall studs behind wallboard.

COPING SAW
If you're planning any projects with angled molding cuts, you'll want a coping saw to cut away the back for a tight fit. Its thin blade also makes curved cuts easy.

tools to your current kit, or you may want to start collecting tools and materials to create a carpentry shop, envied by every do-it-yourselfer. When you decide to invest in a new tool, look for quality construction. If you are going to spend money on tools, you want them to last.

As you select tools, choose only those that are comfortable to use. Even if you are brand-new to carpentry, tools that fit your hand are vitally important. They allow you to make the most of your

strength without causing fatigue. Ergonomically designed tools are efficient and effective. The result will be finished projects that make you proud of your work.

When you select tools comfortable to you, learn how to use them properly. Give yourself an opportunity to practice. Hammer, drill, cut, and sand some scrap pieces before you start on a real project. Almost anyone is handy enough to use any item in this toolbox.

BACKSAW AND MITER BOX
This duo is essential for making accurate angled cuts. They are often used when working with door and window molding.

KEYHOLE SAW
If you only need to make one or two short, rough cuts, or you are working in tight quarters, grab this handy small saw. It fits easily in a toolbox.

COMBINATION SQUARE
You can check for level, square, and 45° angles with this multi-function tool. The blade slides and locks, so you can measure accurately and consistently.

hand tools

BAR CLAMP
Look for strong metal clamps with soft feet that won't damage the wood.

NOTCHED TROWEL
Use this to spread adhesive for floor or wall repairs.

TIN SNIPS
Handy for small cuts in wire or metal. Keep blades sharp for best results.

SANDING BLOCK
For quick, small sanding jobs, just wrap sandpaper around a scrap of wood. For larger projects, use a sanding block; it's more effective and easier on your hand. Purchase a package of sandpaper with a variety of grits (the higher number grit, the finer the surface).

NEEDLE-NOSE PLIERS
Use these for forming loops in wire; they double as a cutter.

SPRING CLAMP
Holds pieces while you fasten them together or while glue dries. Easy to operate with one hand.

LINESMAN PLIERS
Use these to firmly grab wires and twist them together for a solid splice; also cuts wires.

WOOD FILE
Also called a rasp, it removes wood faster than sandpaper; available in flat and curved shapes.

WIRE CUTTERS
Cut wires for electrical projects cleanly and accurately. It doubles as a prying tool to pull out nails.

COLD CHISEL
Use this to chip away concrete, masonry, or other hard materials. Strike with a baby sledge or hammer—be sure to wear eye protection.

MALLET
Look for one with a soft, gray head. The soft head will take some of the impact of the hit; I've found the gray heads aren't as prone to leave a mark. Use it to fit together or separate wood pieces.

NAIL SET
Use these to sink nails below the surface. Look for a color-coded set with three sizes. The colors make it easy to grab the correct size from the toolbox. Rubber-coated shafts reduce the discomfort of pounding.

BABY SLEDGEHAMMER
Heavier than a hammer but smaller than a long-handled sledge, this tool pairs with a cold chisel. Also helpful in demolition.

AWL
Use this to mark measurements, make pilot holes for small screws, or to punch holes in leather or thin metal.

SCRAPER
If you have lots of crusty old paint to remove before freshening up walls and woodwork, invest in a paint scraper and a few extra blades.

DRYWALL TAPING KNIVES
Even if you're not ready to put up drywall yourself, have these on hand for patching mid- to large-size holes. If you have 6-, 8-, and 12-inch blades, you'll be set.

PUTTY KNIFE
Add a 1-inch width to your tool kit for patching holes, repairing windows, and other jobs.

PLUMB BOB
Use this tool to establish true vertical lines. If you don't want to invest in this tool right away, a good chalk line can substitute.

DRYWALL SAW
The pointed tip enables you to jab into drywall; the large teeth cut quickly.

power tools

Stock your workshop with quality power tools. They're worth it.

One of the first questions beginning do-it-yourselfers ask when they dive into projects is "How can I do this faster and easier?" The answer, in many cases, is "With a power tool." And as more women than ever have gotten involved in home improvement, the market segment of women purchasing power tools has grown to the point that manufacturers are taking notice. Tool makers now offer models specifically designed for use by women. These tools are typically lighter and fit more comfortably in a smaller hand. Home centers often provide hands-on demos for how to properly use power tools. There is even a company that offers in-home tool demonstrations and "parties" to sell tools designed for women. But don't feel you have to limit yourself to "women's" tools. What's critical is selecting the best tool for you and the projects you plan.

Where to Begin

Not sure where to start? The power tool aisle of a home center or hardware store can be overwhelming, but it doesn't need to be. Start by looking at only one or two basic power tools, such as a cordless drill—tools that make everyday jobs easier and that you can use for multiple projects. When you're ready to take on bigger projects, look for a portable circular saw, and then maybe an orbital sander.

Whatever tool you need, look for quality—it's worth the investment. Today many medium-price tools offer features once available only on high-end lines. In general, quality tools feature metal rather than plastic parts, though some new high-tech plastic housings are very durable. Steel or aluminum parts should be smoothly milled and fit together precisely; controls

RECIPROCATING SAW
This saw makes cuts in tight places where most other saws can't. It is especially useful for cutting new openings in walls or ceilings. You can wait to purchase this tool until you're planning a big remodeling project or rent one.

JIGSAW
Not a necessity, but if I inspire you to exhibit your creative side with carpentry projects, this saw is handy for cutting curved lines. Look for a slow-start blade and a tight locking base to control the angle at which you cut.

POWER MITERSAW (ALSO CALLED A CHOP SAW)
If you're going to cut a lot of molding for trimwork, rent or investing in a power miter saw. A compound mitersaw (with a tilting head) produces a cut that is both mitered and beveled. Get a saw large enough to cut all the way through the material you are using (a 10-inch diameter blade handles most projects).

POWER DRILL AND BITS
Invest in a cordless power drill if you will be making lots of repairs in your home. A 14- to 16-volt variable speed reversing drill with a ¼-inch chuck covers most jobs. Look for a kit with a variety of bits. Each make of drill is weighted differently, so in the store pick up drills until you find one that is comfortable in your hand. Check for balance. Watch out for a light drill with a heavy battery; I find they tend to lean away from the wall as you work. An extra rechargeable battery is handy.

ORBITAL SANDER
This type of sander works best for fine work and in small areas. A 5- or 6-inch diameter model with a dust collector is a good choice.

power tools

should be user-friendly; ball bearings are better than bushings. Check out a variety of brands for each tool. Consider how often you will use a tool, and what features you need. Don't buy more tool than you need.

Hold a power tool in your hand at the store. Replicate the motions you will make when using it to make sure it is comfortable, balanced, and easily controlled. Don't go just by weight: You may find a larger, heavier version is more comfortable for you. If possible, try out a demonstrator model. Look for tools with safety features that prevent accidentally powering up the tool and cover blades or bits when not in use.

Once you make your selection and before you use your new purchase, take the time to read and understand how to safely use it. Purchase and wear recommended safety equipment, including eye and hearing protection. Don't operate power tools when children are present. Remove any potential distractions from the area. Keep focused and work safely.

Adding to Your Collection

As you take on more home repair and improvement projects, you'll probably want to add to your power tool collection. Check out the tool list that accompanies each project in this book. If you have several projects on your to-do list, see what power tools are common to each and shop first for those. Some of the bigger items—a tablesaw, chop saw, reciprocating saw, or pneumatic nailer, for example—you usually can rent from a home center or hardware store. That's a great option if you need the tool only for one project. It is also a good way to test a tool before making a major purchase. By renting first you can determine if you feel comfortable using the tool and if you think it will be useful for other projects. If so, add it to your list of future tool purchases. Find a secure place to store your tools, both to protect the tools and for the safety of others in your home.

PORTABLE CIRCULAR SAW
Many people think it's best to get a light circular saw so it's easier to lift. I disagree. Too light means it's too easy for the saw to get away from you. The weight of the saw can help keep your cut in line, and most of the weight is supported by the wood. Look for a strong locking base. Also look for a blade protector that wraps around the blade as soon as it's no longer in contact with wood.

TABLESAW
A tablesaw cuts material at almost any angle with unmatched precision. A good starter is a benchtop model with a 10-inch blade and a 15-amp motor. Check for a secure, locking fence that is parallel to the saw blade. A safety key that prevents the saw from operating unless the key is in place and a blade brake are good features. A base with locking wheels can be added to a benchtop model; roll it out of the way when not in use. Helpful accessories include a push stick to keep your fingers away from the blade and table extensions for handling long pieces of wood.

NAIL GUN AND COMPRESSOR
Make this investment if you're going to be doing lots of nailing—putting up molding or building furniture, for example. A pneumatic (air-powered) finish nailer and brad driver (shown) handle trimwork and basic furniture-building projects. They eliminate hammering and fumbling with individual nails, and countersink nails with one pull of the trigger.

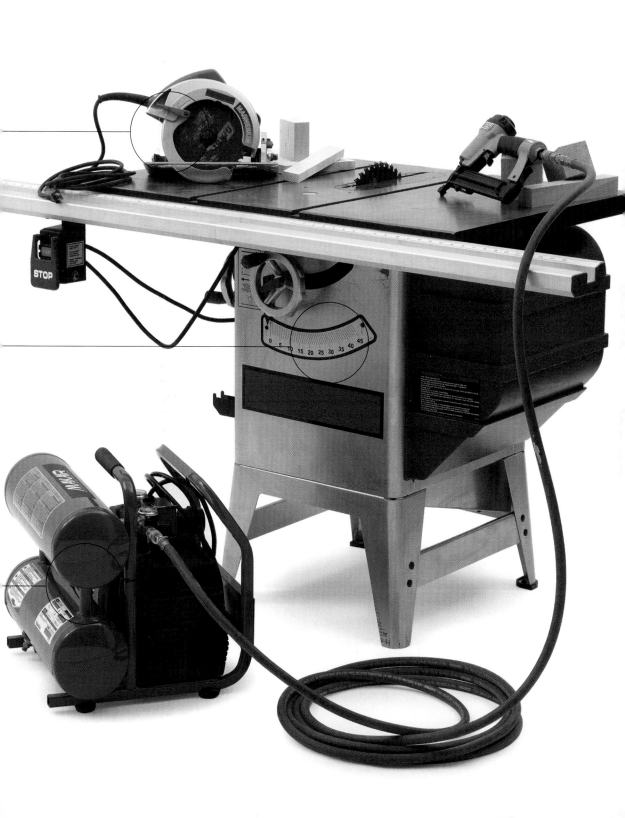

basic carpentry

1

Section One: Walls

No stud jokes, I promise. Studs—usually 2x4s or 2x6s— provide the framework for a wall. If you're hanging art and mirrors, or securing a tall bookcase, you'll want to locate the studs first.

I used to have a VERY easy method for finding studs: When I worked in theater, all I had to do was walk around the wall and look. I measured how far from the end of the wall the stud was located, then walked back to the front side and measured in from the same end to drive fasteners into the stud. I never missed!

Now that I work with the solid walls of real homes, finding the studs is a bit trickier. Check out the suggestions on the next page for some helpful hints. If you're still struggling to find the studs, you can always cheat a bit. No, you can't walk around to the back of the wall. But if you're planning to hang something that will cover a portion of the wall anyway, take a long, thin finish nail and hammer it into the wall where you think a stud is located. Just make sure you make this hole in an area where the nail will be concealed by the piece you're hanging. If you tap and the nail slides right in, you've missed the stud. Try again in a different spot. If the nail stops and you can't push it in all the way, you've found the stud.

working with walls

For many projects and repairs, you will need to locate the wall studs—the vertical 2×4s or other framing members that support a wall. You may also need to determine what's inside the wall, such as water pipes or electrical cables. Never cut or drill a large hole into a wall, ceiling, or floor unless you know what lies behind, above, or beneath it.

TOOLS:
- **Wire coat hanger**
- **Drill**
- **Stud finder**

FINDING STUDS

Studs are normally spaced at regular intervals—typically every 16 or 24 inches on center (OC). Studs in homes are usually 16 inches apart; in garages and outbuildings they are 24 inches apart.

Use your knuckles
Tap the wall with your knuckles. A solid "thunk" indicates a stud. Listen for the difference between the hollow sound between studs and the thunk when you're over a stud.

Look under coverplates
If rapping doesn't tell you anything, look for nails in the baseboard. They're usually driven into the studs. Remove the coverplate from an electrical receptacle to check: Wall boxes usually are nailed to the side of a stud.

Use a finder
Use an electronic or magnetic stud finder, which detects the density of the lumber or the nails or screws in it.

Once you locate one stud, measure 16 inches over and

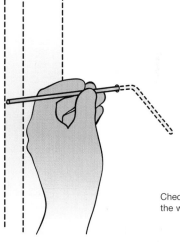

Check for utilities in the wall cavity.

check for another stud. If you don't find another, measure over 24 inches from the first stud and check.

CHECKING INSIDE A WALL

Know what's in a wall before cutting or drilling large holes into it. Some models of stud finders also detect wiring or plumbing behind wallboard. Look from above or below for utilities entering a wall cavity. Another method is to drill a small hole just through the wallboard. Insert a bent piece of coat-hanger wire and rotate the wire to see if you encounter any obstructions.

hanging objects on walls

Two things are key to hanging pictures and mirrors: creating a visually pleasing arrangement and using hanging hardware appropriate for the items and the wall surface on which you will hang them.

TOOLS AND MATERIALS:
- Tape measure
- Level
- Drill and drill bits
- Hammer
- Screwdriver or adjustable wrench
- Picture hangers
- Nails or screws, or hollow-wall anchors

WYNN TIP:
If you're going off to college, moving into your first apartment, or purchasing your first home, get a picture-hanging kit for your toolbox. These handy kits include multiple hangers for various weights of pictures, mirrors, and other hanging items.

PLAN THE ARRANGEMENT

Gather all of the pictures, photographs, mirrors, or other objects you plan to hang on one wall or in one area. Cut a full-size paper template of each item. Tape the templates to the wall, moving them around until you find a look you like. Determine the approximate weight of each item and select an appropriate hanger for each.

HANGING LIGHT TO MEDIUM-WEIGHT ITEMS

- Check the hardware packaging for recommended weight. Typically for items weighing less than a pound or two, use an ordinary picture hook. Secure it with a nail, anywhere on the wall.
- For heavier items, up to about 10 pounds, select a more substantial picture hook.

HANGING HEAVY ITEMS

Wherever possible, locate a stud and drive the fastener nail into the stud for better holding power.

A stud isn't always available where you want to hang a heavy picture. For those

occasions, you have several options, including hollow-wall anchors, toggle bolts, or plywood bridging. Hollow-wall anchors open behind the wall surface for an installation that won't pull out. Toggle bolts screw into wings that pop open inside the wall. These are great fasteners, but make sure of the location before installing because you can't remove them. (You can drive them completely into the wall and patch the resulting hole.) For heavy objects, attach a piece of lumber between two studs and attach hangers to the bridging.

Toggle bolts and hollow-wall anchors

1 Drill a hole through the drywall the width of the toggle wings or slightly smaller than the anchor shield.

2 Insert the fastener through the hole. If you are using a toggle fastener, take it apart, slide the picture hook over the screw and reassemble it. Pinch together the wings of the toggle and slide them through the hole. For an anchor fastener,

WYNN TIP:
Rather than scatter items across a wall, group them for greater impact. Draw an imaginary box around the perimeter of where you want to place the items, then arrange them close together within that box. Use similar frames, mats, colors, or subject matter to further connect the items.

slip the hook over the screw and turn the screw into the anchor shield. Then drive the anchor shield into the hole using a hammer.

3 Tighten the screw of the toggle fastener until it is snug. In similar fashion, tighten the screw of the anchor shield, which will draw the wings snug to the back of the wallboard.

Plywood bridging

1 Locate two studs. Measure the distance between them and add approximately 4 inches. Cut a 1×2 to that length.

2 Drive 2¼-inch screws through each end of the 1×2 into the studs. Locate wall hangers anywhere along the bridging.

HANGING HEAVY MIRRORS AND SHELVES

1 Measure and cut a 1×4 pine board approximately 2 inches shorter than the distance across the back of the heavy mirror or shelf.

2 Cut the length of the board using a table saw or circular saw with the blade set at a 45-degree angle. You now have two pieces: one will attach to the wall and the other to the object.

3 Drill pilot holes along the piece for mounting it to the mirror or shelf. Select flat-head wood screws or drywall screws that will go through the 1×2 strip and penetrate deep enough into the backing without cracking the mirror or going through the back of the shelf.

4 Apply a bead of wood glue to the back of the ripped strip and mount an inch or so below the top of the mirror or shelf. Make sure it is level horizontally. Carefully drive the screws, but not too deep. Allow the glue to dry following the manufacturer's directions.

5 Locate the wall studs. Have a helper hold the second mounting strip in position. Check for level and mark the locations of the studs on the strip.

6 Drill pilot holes in the second strip. Position the lip away from the wall facing upward so the two edges will overlap. Hold the strip in place and drive wood screws through the strip into the wall studs. Once the glue has dried, have a helper assist you with lifting and setting the mirror or shelf on the wall-mounted strip.

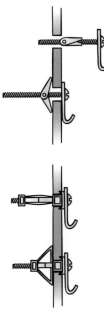

Anchor and toggle bolts expand to grip the wall to prevent the hardware from pulling out.

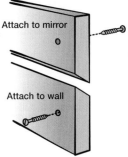

Step 4. Make sure the strip attached to the mirror angles downward; it will support the bulk of the mirror's weight.

Attach to mirror

Attach to wall

Step 6. Because mirrors are extremely heavy, the wall-mounted strip should be secured directly into studs.

building utility shelves and racks

As you gain confidence in your home repair abilities, you'll find yourself looking for additional projects—and accumulating do-it-yourself gear. These utility shelves and racks provide storage space for your growing assortment of tools and materials.

**TOOLS AND
MATERIALS:**
- Power saw
- Drill
- Chalk line
- Torpedo level
- Level
- Screwdriver
- Screws
- Square
- Tape measure•
  Unfinished
  plywood
- Ladder brackets
- Angle brackets
- Mending plates
- Screws
- 1× and 2×
  lumber
- Shelf brackets
- Rope

LUMBER RACKS

If floor and wall space is at a premium, hang lumber racks from ceiling joists.

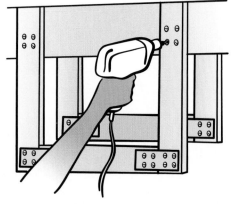

1 Cut six 3-inch-wide strips of plywood. The four side pieces should be the same length, and the two bottom pieces should be the same length.

2 Assemble the pieces into two U-shape hangers. Use mending plates and ¾-inch screws to join them. Snap a chalk line on the undersides of the joists so the racks will be in line with each other.

3 Attach the racks to the joists by driving four 2-inch screws through each of the plywood supports and into a joist.

4 Stack the lumber neatly, putting the widest pieces on the bottom to support the other boards and to help prevent warping.

Step 3. Overlap the hanger on the joist and drive screws for support.

Step 2. Mending plates provide a quick and easy method to join boards.

WYNN TIP:

The fastest way to assemble utility shelves is with store-bought ladder-style brackets available at most home centers. Have a helper hold the ladder brackets plumb while you attach ¾-inch plywood shelving with screws. Anchor the unit to the wall with angle brackets and screws driven into the studs.

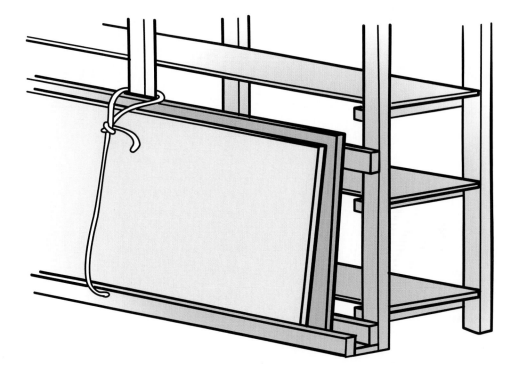

Get dual usage from a utility shelf by adding storage for scrap plywood and other sheet goods.

PLYWOOD STORAGE

1 Use store-bought ladder brackets to assemble the basic utility shelving unit described in my tip on the opposite page. Securely anchor one long side to the wall with angle brackets and screws driven into studs.

2 Cut two 1×2s and one 1×4 to the length of the unit. Drill pilot holes and drive screws to fasten them in a U-shape, placing one of the 1×4s on the bottom of the U.

3 Drill pilot holes and drive screws to attach the 1×4 side of the plywood channel to the long side of the shelving unit.

4 Drill a hole in the middle of the 1×2 and tie a rope to it. Use the rope to hold sheets of plywood securely in place.

WYNN TIP:
When storing lumber in an area where you can't control the humidity and temperature, such as a shed or detached garage, allow the wood to acclimate in the shop for a couple of weeks before working with it.

building utility shelves and racks *continued*

BETWEEN-JOIST RACK

Use the space between open joists in a garage or basement to store lumber, pipes, or other long objects.

1 Attach 1×2s to the underside of the joists—perpendicular to the joists—for an instant rack. Use 2-inch general-purpose screws.

2 If you need to store heavy objects, use 2×4s instead of 1×2s.

OVER-JOIST PLATFORM

Don't let open space above the joists in an attic or garage go to waste. Use it for storage.

1 Have a helper assist you in sliding pieces of ½-inch plywood up over the joists. Hoist enough plywood to create a roomy platform. You'll need space for stored items and space to easily access them.

2 Attach the plywood to the joists with 1¼-inch screws.

WYNN TIP:
When you need to purchase lumber for a project, try to pick out the boards yourself. Look for boards that are not heavily twisted, bowed, cupped, or crooked. Knots aren't a big problem, unless they are loose or mar the surface of a board that needs a smooth finish.

Take advantage of the space above joists for additional lumber storage.

HANGING JARS

This simple storage system is great for small items, such as screws and nails.

1 Determine the height at which you want to hang the jars. Use a torpedo level to mark a plumb line for the bracket. Drive screws to attach wall-mounted shelf brackets to studs. Make sure the next bracket you attach is level with the first.

2 Cut a 1×4 to the desired length for the shelf. Drive ½-inch screws to fasten the jar lids to the underside of the shelf. Leave clearance space so you can easily screw on the jars.

3 Lay the shelf on top of the brackets. Attach the shelf to the brackets by drilling pilot holes and driving ⅝-inch screws up through the brackets. Screw the jars onto the lids.

With the contents visible, you can quickly find what you're looking for.

WYNN TIP:
My garage is set up as a home workshop. In addition to these easy-to-construct storage racks and shelves, I have toolboxes to keep my tools and materials in order. To make it easy to find seldom-used but helpful items, use a label maker to create stick-on labels for all drawers.

At the end of every work session, take a couple of minutes to put things back in place. That way, you'll always know where to find things, and if young children slip into your work area, potentially dangerous items will be out of sight and reach.

Be careful when stowing and accessing items from overhead storage areas. It hurts when a short 2×4 that you forgot was on top of those sheets of plywood knocks you on the head.

installing wall-mounted open shelves

Shelves—both decorative and utility—can easily be attached directly to walls. Locate studs first so you can drive fasteners to form strong, secure connections.

TOOLS AND MATERIALS:
- Drill
- Torpedo level
- Straightedge
- Shelf brackets
- Screws
- Shelving

1 Determine where you want the shelf. Locate a stud (see page 51) and position the first bracket. Drive a screw through the hole in the bracket and into the stud, but do not tighten it completely.

2 Use a torpedo level to plumb the bracket, then drive a second screw, and tighten both screws.

3 Place a level on top of the first bracket and use it to find the height for the bracket at the opposite end of the shelf. Locate a stud and recheck the height for the second bracket along the stud. Drive a screw through the hole in the bracket and into the stud. Plumb the bracket and finish attaching it with screws.

4 Add intermediate brackets as needed. Place a straightedge on top of the outer brackets to determine the height for the additional supports.

5 Lay the shelf on top of the brackets. Attach the shelf to the brackets by drilling pilot holes and driving $\frac{5}{8}$-inch screws through the brackets into the shelves.

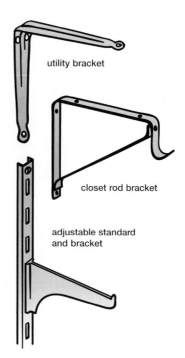

utility bracket

closet rod bracket

adjustable standard and bracket

WYNN TIP:
Over time you'll probably pile more and more stuff on utility shelves. Plan for plenty of support so shelves won't sag. A $\frac{3}{4}$-inch plywood shelf needs support about every 36 inches to prevent sagging; $\frac{3}{4}$-inch particleboard can span about 28 inches.

working with plywood

Here are a few tips to help you handle and finish this all-purpose material.

the utility shelves on the preceding pages are designed to be rugged, so they don't need to be painted or stained. But depending on what you want to store and how you use your basement, you may decide to finish the shelves. Plywood can soak up a lot of paint, making for a costly and time-consuming job. Consider covering the shelf tops with shelf paper and giving the other surfaces a quick coat of polyurethane. If you choose to paint it, birch-veneer plywood soaks up less paint than pine plywood.

When cutting across the surface grain of plywood, first score the cut line with a utility knife to prevent splintering. You do not need to do this when cutting with the grain.

Give exposed plywood edges a quick sanding with a hand sander to remove burrs and to prevent splinters.

When you use a tablesaw to rip (cut with the grain) a large sheet of plywood, have a helper stand to the side to assist you in positioning the sheet against the saw fence. Halfway through the cut, the helper should move behind the saw to support the portion of the sheet leaving the table.

installing decorative molding shelves

Making your own decorative molding shelves is a terrific way to add style to your home. If you plan to place heavy items on the shelf, make sure you drive fasteners directly into the studs.

TOOLS AND MATERIALS:
- Drill
- Torpedo level
- Clamps
- Miter box and backsaw or power miter
- Straightedge
- Nailset
- Stud finder
- Paintbrush
- Shelf boards
- Crown molding
- Wood glue
- Finishing nails
- Screws
- Wood filler
- Sandpaper
- Primer and paint, or stain and sealant

These decorative shelves are constructed from shelf boards and crown molding. Select boards that are as deep as you want (6–10 inches) for displaying objects.

1 Cut the shelf boards to length. Typical lengths are 2, 3, or 4 feet for a shelf. A set of three makes a nice grouping.

2 Cut the molding to length; the ends are cut at opposing 45-degree angles. Use a miter box and backsaw or power mitersaw. Measure and cut the end (side) pieces to join the front molding. The part of each end piece that fits against the wall should be a 90-degree cut; the other end is a 45-degree cut to match the front piece.

3 Apply wood glue to the adjoining surfaces of the molding and the shelf. Attach the front length of

Step 2. Hold the molding firmly so it doesn't move while cutting.

crown molding to the shelf with glue and secure with clamps.

4 Drill pilot holes to reduce the chance of splitting and drive finishing nails through the crown molding into the shelf piece. Apply glue to the end pieces and attach them to the front molding using finish nails. Set the nails using a nail set.

8 To install the shelf, locate wall studs with a stud finder. Attach a cleat (board such as a 1×1) to the wall and fit the shelf over the cleat. Drill pilot holes and secure with countersunk screws down through the shelf into the cleat.

Step 5. Filling the nail holes adds a professional finishing touch.

5 Fill the nail holes with wood filler and allow it to dry. Check for shrinkage and apply more wood filler, if necessary.

6 Sand to finish. Start with a medium-grit (120–200) sandpaper and gradually work to a fine-grit paper for a smooth finish. Remove all dust.

7 Apply primer and paint, or stain and a clear-coat sealant. Allow the finish to completely dry.

WYNN TIP:

For decorative displays, group several shelves. Before you start drilling holes, plan the placement. Cut strips of paper to the size of the shelves plus the items you plan to display. Tape the strips to the wall. Rearrange them until you like the look. Leave the paper on the wall while you locate studs and drill pilot holes.

building the basic box

Many of the projects in this section require you to create and join right angles to make a basic box or cube. From there you can add fixed shelves, adjustable shelving supports, decorative detailing, drawers—or almost anything else to transform a basic cube into the specific item that you want.

TOOLS AND MATERIALS:
- **Power saw**
- **Drill and bits**
- **Hammer**
- **Screwdriver**
- **Tape measure**
- **Framing square**
- **Nails**
- **Finish screws**
- **Plywood or particle board (¾-inch thick)**

Step 2. Pilot holes reduce the chance of splitting the end.

1 Determine the dimensions of the box to meet your needs. Measure and mark the two sides. Next measure and mark the top and bottom. Double-check the measurements to ensure the parallel boards are the same size—it's better to check twice and cut once, avoiding expense and frustration.

2 Join two adjacent pieces to form a right angle. Check for square using the framing square. Use a power drill and bit to make pilot holes to prevent the wood from splitting. Drive 2-inch screws to hold the pieces in place. (For a stronger joint, add glue. After drilling pilot holes, spread glue, then drive the screws.) Continue creating right angles with the adjoining pieces until you have created a box. Check each corner for square; then fasten. Clamp the sides in place and check again for square.

3 For a back, cut a piece of ¼-inch plywood ¼ inch shorter and narrower than the box. Center

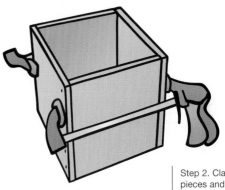

Step 2. Clamp the pieces and check for square.

it on the back so there is a ⅛-inch reveal all around. Drive 4d box nails every 6 inches to fasten.

4 That's it! You've created a basic box that serves as the basis for numerous other projects. Take a look at the next several projects for ways to upgrade the box.

WYNN TIP:
For this basic box you'll use a butt joint—a simple joint that requires 90-degree cuts. This clean-looking joint is easy even for beginners, and it is strong and stable when fastened with screws. If you want, add shelves to your basic box to hold heavy items. Add a cleat under the shelf for additional support.

installing adjustable shelves

Install adjustable shelves for easy, flexible storage. Choose from several variations for shelf support; it's only a matter of personal preference, all serve their purpose equally well. The key to constructing solid shelves is to make sure all the supports are level with one another. The first two options presented here use a basic box frame (see page 63).

TOOLS AND MATERIALS:
- Drill and bits
- Hacksaw
- Tape measure
- Level
- Framing square
- Pegboard
- Metal shelf support strips and clips

WYNN TIP
You may need to attach a support strip and clips in the middle of long shelf spans to prevent them from sagging. See page 58 for recommended shelf spans.

Step 3. Mark for level so your shelves don't rock.

METAL SUPPORT STRIPS INSIDE A FRAME

1 Measure to determine the length of one strip. They don't need to run the full height of the unit, just a notch or two beyond where you want to place the top and bottom shelf.

2 Cut the first strip to the desired length with a hacksaw. Use this piece as a guide for cutting the others. You will need a minimum of four strips. Before cutting, make sure the slots line up. Some strips have numbers stamped on them to help position the clips. If you have strips with numbers, align them.

3 Mark with a pencil where you will attach the strips. Remember it is very important to make sure all the supports are level with one another before drilling pilot holes.

4 Drill pilot holes. Use a depth guide so you don't go through the sides of the frame or wrap a piece of tape around the drill bit to indicate when to stop drilling. Drive screws to attach each strip. Insert support clips.

PIN SYSTEM INSIDE A FRAME

1 Cut a piece of pegboard to use as a template for drilling regularly spaced holes in the sides of the frame box. Mark one end of the template as the top, so you'll always align it the same way. An alternative method for marking is to use a framing square. First draw vertical lines about an inch in from the front and rear edges of the unit, parallel with the edges. Measure with a framing square and mark evenly spaced, short horizontal lines along one of the vertical lines. Then use the square to copy the horizontal measurements to the other vertical line.

2 Drill only as many support holes as you'll need. Use a drill bit depth guide so you don't drill through the side of the frame.

Step 1. A pegboard template allows for quick work when drilling multiple support holes.

Step 2. If you don't have a depth guide, wrap a piece of tape around the bit to mark the proper depth.

3 Insert bracket pins or flat pins in the holes to support the shelves.

METAL SUPPORT STRIPS ON A WALL

To display light objects, you can attach metal support strips directly to the wall and use shelf brackets to support the shelves.

1 Determine the length of the strips. Cut the first one with a hacksaw. Then use this piece to measure the others. Line up the slots. To help position the shelf brackets later, line up the numbers (if stamped on the strip) on each strip.

2 For the best holding power, locate each strip over a wall stud. Use a stud finder and mark the locations with a pencil. Make sure all the supports are level with one another and mark where you will attach the strips. Use a level to double-check the placement before you attach the strips.

3 Drive screws through the drywall into the stud to attach each strip.

4 Place shelf brackets where desired. Add shelves.

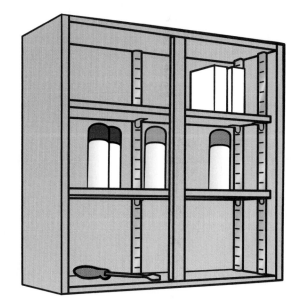

building a fixed shelf unit

Here's another adaptation of the basic box described on page 63. This one adds fixed shelves for durable, solid storage. Depending on the finished size, this fixed shelf unit can be freestanding or wall-mounted, or you can stack the boxes.

TOOLS AND MATERIALS:
- **Circular saw or tablesaw**
- **Chisel**
- **Tape measure**
- **Speed square**
- **Framing square**
- **Drill and bits**
- **Rubber mallet**
- **Hammer**
- **Wood glue**
- **Clamps**
- **Screws**

WYNN TIP:
The shelves are simple to make but require precise cutting. Give yourself time to practice cutting perfectly straight and square on scrap lumber. This will also allow you to test your power saw. If the blade is raising splinters along the cut, it's dull. Replace it.

1 Determine the dimensions you want for the unit. Measure and mark wood for the two sides, then for the top and bottom. Practice sawing on scrap lumber until you can make straight, square cuts. Cut the box pieces. Check that the sides are the same and that the top and bottom are identical.

2 The shelves will be held by a dado, a groove cut into the sides. Draw layout lines for each shelf. To help ensure the dadoes match exactly, clamp the side boards next to each other and mark at the same time. Use a piece of shelf board to mark the width. Mark precisely; you want the shelf to fit tightly.

3 Cut the dadoes ⁵⁄₁₆-inch deep using a circular saw, radial-arm saw, or tablesaw. Make several parallel cuts. Clean out the dadoes by chiseling out the waste. Then use the chisel to smooth the bottom of the groove.

4 Assemble the box by drilling pilot holes and driving 2¼-inch screws. You may also want to glue the joints. Check for square with the framing square as you fasten the pieces.

5 Measure from dado to dado for the lengths of the shelves before cutting. Cut the shelf pieces to length.

6 Spread wood glue in the dadoes. Slip a shelf into matching dadoes. Tap the shelf into place with a rubber mallet to prevent marring. Avoid tapping one end down farther than the other; alternate between ends every inch or so, or gently tap the middle of the shelf to work it into place.

7 When the shelf edges are flush with the edges of the outside pieces, check for square. Drill pilot holes and drive screws to reinforce and tighten the joints.

8 Add a back to the unit to increase stability (see page 70).

Step 1. A straight cut is important, so use a speed square or cutting guide.

Step 3. A solid and professional looking fit requires a clean dado.

WYNN TIP:
As you plan the overall width and height of a fixed shelf unit, consider what you want to store on the shelves and how many shelves you want. Shelves do not need to be spaced equally, but you probably don't want a very small space at either the top or bottom. Most likely it will be wasted space and appear the result of poor planning.

using decorative molding

Add character to your home by installing decorative molding

If your eclectic mix of furniture is looking like a hodgepodge of mismatched pieces rather than a planned grouping, consider how decorative molding might function as the unifying theme. Decorative molding applied to several pieces of furniture visually ties together the look of the room. It can also lend a traditional look to pieces that may feel devoid of style. Basic shelving units, bookcases, and plain tables are good candidates for a carpentry makeover. Most moldings, particularly those with a flat back, neatly wrap around a 90-degree angle with just a 45-degree cut on each piece of adjoining molding.

Crown molding, however, can become a nightmare because of its angled back and the compound angles required to join it. I'll admit it's caused me headaches in the past. But don't be afraid to give it a try, and don't feel bad if you make a mistake. Practice cutting on scrap pieces. And be prepared to waste material as you learn. Don't get me wrong: If you love the look of crown molding, give it a try. Just buy extra.

> " Decorative molding applied to several pieces of furniture visually ties together the look of the whole room. "

organizing closets

Upgrade a closet with this simple project that divides the space into sections tailored to suit your storage needs. To make installation easy, invite a friend to help and then go to his or her house to return the favor.

TOOLS AND MATERIALS:

- Circular saw
- Tape measure
- Framing square
- Stud finder
- Chalk line
- Hammer
- Nail set
- Drill and screwdriver bit
- Pencil and graph paper
- ¾-inch plywood
- ¾-inch edging
- 1×2
- 1¼-inch dowels
- Metal standards
- Metal clips
- Closet rod cleats
- Pole brackets

1 Divide your hanging clothes into two or three groups according to height. Determine how much width each group requires; you don't want to build a great closet system that crams the clothes. Also figure out how much shelf space you need for sweaters and how much rack space for shoes.

2 Draw a diagram of the shelf system on graph paper. Make a materials list with specific measurements for the shelves and hanging rods. Use ¾-inch plywood and solid wood edging for the shelves and upright supports. You'll need 1×2s for cleats and heel stops, 1¼-inch dowels for hanging rods, metal strips and clips to support the shelves, and hardware to hold rods.

3 Measure and mark the location for the top and bottom shelf supports on the back and side walls of the closet. A good approximate height for the top shelf is 76–84 inches above the floor. This provides plenty of storage room without making the top shelf unreachable.

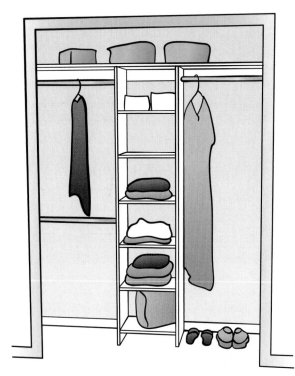

4 Locate and mark the wall studs using a stud finder. Attach supports to the studs for the best hold.

5 Cut two pieces of 1×2 to the width of the closet to use as cleats to support the shelves. Drive 8d finish nails through the supports into the wall studs.

Organizing your closet provides more storage space and greater accessibility.

6 Cut ¾-inch plywood to height for the sides of the center shelf unit. Plan the cuts so the top of the shelf unit is flush with the top of the bottom support cleat installed in Step 5.

7 Use metal strips and clips or holes and pins for adjustable shelves (see page 64). Or use 6d finish nails to attach the shelves. Space these shelves for sweaters and other folded items according to your plan.

8 Position the central shelf unit according to your plan. Mark the location. Mark the top of the unit for notches so it fits over the support cleat. (You may also need to cut notches for the baseboard.) Cut the notches using a jigsaw or handsaw. Place the center shelf unit in position. Check for level. Have a helper hold the unit in place while you set the long top shelf.

9 Drive 6d finish nails through the long shelf into the center shelf unit to hold it in place.

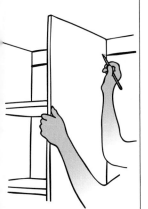

Step 8. Make a pencil line where you need to cut the center shelf unit.

10 Measure for the location of pole brackets on shelf unit and walls and mark. Attach pole brackets to center shelf unit with screws. Attach a pole bracket to a stud in each side wall of the closet. Cut the poles to length and set in place. Place the shelves in the center unit.

Step 9. Secure the center unit by fastening to the top shelf.

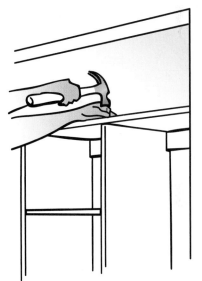

WYNN TIP:

Hate hitting your fingers with a hammer when starting a nail? Here are a couple of alternatives: Hold the nail with needle-nose pliers; or push the nail through a strip of thin cardboard and hold the other end as you start the nail.

building a traditional bookcase

Don't be fooled by the elegant look of a traditional bookcase. It's just another variation of the basic box on page 63. Here you simply add decorative trim to create a finished piece worthy of pride.

TOOLS AND MATERIALS:
- **Drill and bits**
- **Framing square**
- **Miter box**
- **Tape measure**
- **Hammer**
- **Birch plywood if painting or hardwood if staining**
- **Molding of your choice**
- **6d finish nails**

1 Determine the box dimensions. Measure and mark plywood to cut the sides, top, and bottom. Check to make sure the side pieces are the same size, and that the top and bottom pieces are the same size. ut top and bottom panels from hardwood, about 1 ½ inches wider and longer than the top and bottom of the box. Cut a piece of hardwood for an arched top piece. Do not assemble the box until you've drilled holes (page 64) or cut dadoes (page 66) for shelves.

2 Use a piece of pegboard as a guide to drill holes for shelf supports. Note which end goes up so you will be able to align it the same on both sides of the bookcase to ensure the shelves are level.

3 Drill only as many support holes as you think you'll need. Use a drill bit depth guide so you don't drill through the side of the pieces.

4 Join the side, top, and bottom pieces to form a rectangle by drilling pilot holes and driving 2¼-inch finish screws. You may also glue the joints. Check for square as you fasten each corner.

5 Cut a piece of ¼-inch plywood ¼ inch smaller than the shelf unit in both dimensions. Center it on the back so there is a ⅛-inch reveal all around. Drive 4d box nails every 6 inches. Check carefully for square as you work: this back piece will hold the shape of the case.

WYNN TIP:
If the bookcase is tall, use screws to secure the top of the unit to a wall stud so it won't tip over.

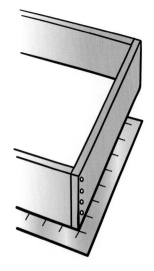

Step 4. A framing square allows you to quickly check for square.

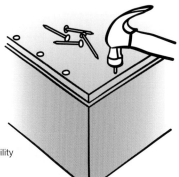

Step 5. The back adds greater stability to the basic box.

8 Attach the front and side molding pieces to the box using 6d finish nails. You may want to drill pilot holes first.

9 Measure the length for the two side front pieces. Cut them to length with a square, even cut. Attach the side molding pieces with 6d finish nails.

6 Attach the top and bottom panels with glue and screws, flush to the back and extending evenly on the sides and front. The screws must be short enough so they do not poke through the panels; drive them from inside the box.

7 Select decorative molding. Miter cut a 45-degree angle at the outside corner of each end of a piece of molding for the bottom front. Miter cut the adjoining end of each bottom side piece. Make sure the joints align. (See page 60 for more information about cutting molding.)

basic carpentry **71**

installing recessed shelving

Tucking narrow recessed shelves between studs in a wall is an ideal way to gain storage space. Before you begin this project, make sure the spot is free of electrical and plumbing lines (see page 51). After you cut the opening, finishing this project is as simple as building a box (yes, another project involving that easy-to-make basic box!) and inserting it into the wall.

**TOOLS AND
MATERIALS:**
- **Jigsaw or
  keyhole saw**
- **Circular saw**
- **Knife**
- **Drill and bits**
- **Hammer**
- **Tape measure**
- **Level**
- **Stud finder**
- **Coat-hanger
  wire**
- **Nails**
- **Finishing screws**
- **Plywood or
  particle board**
- **Clamps**

1 Locate studs by rapping on the wall, drilling test holes, or using a stud finder. Drill holes and insert a piece of coat hanger wire to explore behind the opening (some stud finders also detect plumbing and electrical lines). Do not cut the wall if utility lines are between the studs.

2 Cut the drywall with a drywall or keyhole saw. Be careful not to cut through to the other side of the wall. If the wall is plaster, cutting may be difficult. To prevent cracking the surrounding area, first score lines deeply with a knife. Cut alongside the studs for vertical lines; mark horizontal cut lines with a level.

3 Cut a 2×4 sill the width of the opening. Level the sill. Drive wood screws at an angle through the sill into the studs to form the bottom of the opening.

4 Build a basic box shelf unit using butt joints (see page 63). Rip-cut

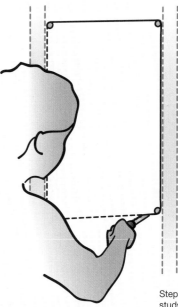

Step 2. Cut along studs with a drywall or keyhole saw.

the boards to the depth of the opening, minus ¼ inch for the back piece. Make the unit ⅛ inch smaller than the opening on all sides.

5 Decide what type of shelves you want to add. For adjustable shelves, drill holes for pins or measure, cut, and attach support strips (see pages 64–65). For fixed shelves, measure and cut shelf boards, which can be nailed into place.

6 Use bar clamps to hold the pieces together while joining. Remember to check for square. Set fixed shelves in place and hammer 4d or 6d nails through the sides into the shelves.

7 For the back, cut a piece of ¼-inch plywood the size of the shelf unit in both directions. Attach it by driving 4d box nails roughly every 6 inches around the edge.

WYNN TIP: Create a formal display niche for your prized collectibles using glass shelves— you can have them cut to size at a glass retailer.

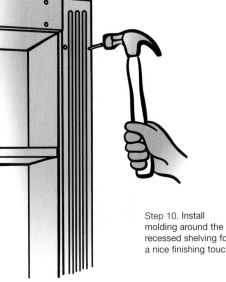

Step 10. Install molding around the recessed shelving for a nice finishing touch.

8 Set the unit in the wall hole. Check for level and plumb. Make sure the front edge is flush with the wall surface. Use shims (wooden wedges) to help level and plumb if necessary.

9 Drill pilot holes and drive 6d finish nails through the sides into the adjoining studs. Also drill pilot holes and drive 6d finish nails through the bottom into the sill.

10 Install molding around the perimeter. Butt-jointed casing is the simplest. Drill pilot holes to avoid cracking the wood and drive 6d nails into studs. Attach the molding to top and bottom of the box using 4d nails.

building under-stair shelves

If you have open space under the stairs leading to an unfinished basement, don't let it go to waste. To convert it to storage, you'll use a simple technique of measuring and cutting a triangular backing piece, then fitting the shelves.

TOOLS AND MATERIALS:
- Power saw
- Drill
- Plumb bob
- Level
- Framing square
- Chalk line
- Screws

1 Place a piece of ¼-inch plywood against the stairway, resting it on top of a 2×4. The plywood will serve as a quick way to outline the size and shape of the storage boxes. Later you'll cut it to form the back of the storage boxes. Check for plumb before measuring and marking. Mark on the plywood where the stairs meet the plywood, snap a chalk line, and cut. Do the same for the other backing pieces.

2 Test to see that the backing pieces fit under the stairs. Then lay them down and draw layout lines indicating shelves and uprights. Avoid making unusable small triangular boxes. Make several tall boxes. Be sure to allow for the double thickness of the uprights on the layout. The shelves will be wide; use ¾-inch plywood for the boxes so they won't sag.

3 Measure the layout lines and cut all shelves and uprights to length.

Step 1. Since the finished shelves will rest on 2×4s, place the plywood on a 2×4 before measuring.

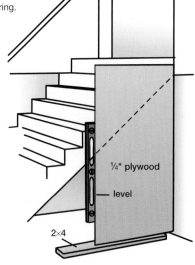

¼" plywood

level

2×4

Step 2. After you test-fit the back pieces, use them as a template for laying out the shelves.

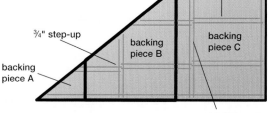

shelf layout

¾" step-up

backing piece B

backing piece C

backing piece A

upright layout

WYNN TIP:
Because basement floors may become damp, the bottom shelf of this unit should be raised a bit by resting it on pressure-treated 2×4 sleepers, which will not rot even if they occasionally get wet.

4 Assemble each box, checking for square. Drill pilot holes and fasten with 2-inch general-purpose screws every few inches along each joint.

5 Cut two pieces of pressure-treated 2×4 to fit along the bottom of the shelf system. Attach them to the floor. If working on a concrete floor, use 2-inch masonry nails every foot.

6 Cut the ¼-inch plywood for the backs of the boxes. Use your initial layout lines as a guide, but cut each approximately ¼ inch smaller than the box in both directions.

7 Center each back piece on the corresponding box. Drive 4d box nails every 6 inches.

8 Slide the tallest box onto the 2×4s. Place the next box beside it, then the next. For extra stability, fasten the boxes together using 1-inch screws.

WYNN TIP:
Label the parts of each box before you begin cutting so you'll quickly be able to identify which ones go together.

building entertainment shelves

Show off your creativity—and carpentry skills—while stylishly stowing your entertainment gear. The overall look of this set of shelves is informal, but you can adapt it with paint or stain to fit the decor of your home. Assembly is a snap.

TOOLS AND MATERIALS:
- Jigsaw
- Drill
- Hammer
- Framing square
- Hacksaw
- Plywood
- Veneer tape
- 2-inch conduit
- Couplings
- Carpenter's glue
- Pencil
- String
- Sandpaper
- Masking tape
- Primer and paint

1 On a sheet of plywood, use a framing square and pencil to draw a grid of 6-inch squares to use as a guide for drawing curved lines. The lines will span 6 feet, spaced 14 inches wide. First draw the top curve with a pencil, following the illustration below. Experiment until the line looks smooth and even. Draw the second line parallel with the first line and mark for a square cutoff.

2 Cut the first curved shelf with the jigsaw and sand the edges.

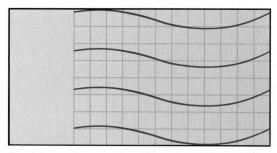

Step 1. Lay out the curved shelves to minimize lumber waste.

WYNN TIP:
To prevent chipping when cutting holes in plywood, clamp a piece of scrap wood to the underside of the piece you are cutting.

3 Use the first shelf as a template and draw the next two shelves. Use a framing square to draw a line dividing one of the shelves in half. Cut the remaining shelves and sand their edges.

4 On one of the shelves, mark the center of holes 3 inches in from each corner. Mark for another hole in the center of the shelf's width and 33 inches from one end. Drill with a holesaw that is the same diameter as the conduit. (Be sure to check the actual outside diameter of the conduit, not its nominal size.)

5 Use the first shelf as a template to mark holes in the other shelves. Drill the remaining holes.

6 Cover the plywood edges with iron-on veneer tape. Trim the tape to length, hold it in place, and use an iron to adhere the heat-activated glue to the edge.

7 Using a hacksaw or a tubing cutter, cut five pieces of 2-inch nonthreaded conduit to 54 inches or so, depending

WYNN TIP:
If the entertainment unit wobbles a bit, anchor it to a wall with angle brackets and screws.

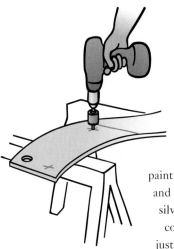

Step 4. Cut holes perpendicular to the surface for a clean, strong fit of the legs.

WYNN TIP:
If you've never used a jigsaw, practice before you start this project. Don't give up if your cuts aren't as smooth as you like the first time. Plywood isn't that expensive, so you can always start over. Or work those arm muscles by sanding out uneven areas. Another option is to make any irregularities part of your unique design. With these free-form curved shelves, no one will know that you strayed from the line unless you tell.

on how tall you want the unit to be.

8 Sand the shelves smooth. Apply a coat of primer and two coats of enamel paint to conduit, couplings, and shelves. If you like the silvery look of galvanized conduit and couplings, just leave them unpainted; the finish will last. If you want to paint the conduit and couplings, first sand them with a loose sheet of medium-grit sandpaper, then apply primer and paint. Let dry.

9 At the bottom of each leg, slip on a coupling and tighten the setscrews.

10 Slip the bottom shelf onto all five standards, and slide it down until it rests on the couplings.

11 Slip on couplings for the next shelf, and measure to see that they are all at the same height. Slip on the next shelf. Repeat for the third shelf. If the standards fit tightly into the holes, the unit will be stable.

WYNN TIP:
Look in the electrical department at a home center for a 2-inch galvanized conduit. It's typically used for heavy-duty outdoor wiring installations, but it creates a great industrial look for this piece of furniture.

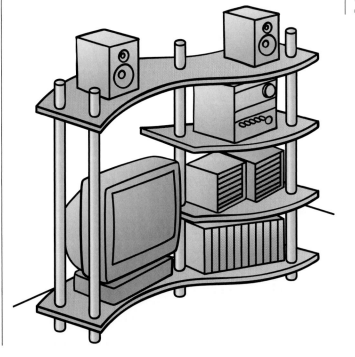

Prepping walls

Do you have a painting or picture on your wall you know belongs in just that spot and you can't imagine putting it anywhere else? Are you planning on painting the wall but figure it's not worth filling the hole of the nail holding your picture because you know the picture will go right back? Think again. Once you get a new color on the wall, you might find the picture that worked so well before doesn't really strike you with the same emotion. It takes less time and is more efficient to fill the hole with joint compound before you paint than to apply it over the painted area and paint again. If you want to put the picture exactly where it used to be, driving a nail in the same place is not a difficult task.

A money-saving tip to avoid

I'm all in favor of money-saving tips and tricks when they work. Here's one that doesn't. When my sister was moving out of her first dorm room in college, a friend suggested that she fill nail holes in the wall with toothpaste. My sister, a brilliant woman but not very street smart, tried the trick and failed. All of the holes were bright green spots! Minty fresh breath is fine for your mouth but doesn't freshen a white wall. Toothpaste has no place in home repair. Using joint compound is simple and inexpensive.

repairing small holes in drywall

Don't try to disguise a problem wall with paint. The flaws will show through and you'll have wasted time, money, and effort. Instead, take a little time to patch all holes and cracks, set any popped nails, and clean and prime the surfaces before painting. The results will look far better in the long run.

TOOLS AND MATERIALS:
- **Taping knife**
- **Joint compound**
- **Putty knife**
- **Sanding block**
- **Sponge**
- **Pegboard**
- **Wire**
- **Drill**
- **Pencil**

Apply joint compound to a small hole with a putty knife.

TO FILL A NAIL HOLE

Apply joint compound to the hole with a putty knife. Allow the compound to dry. If it shrinks, apply a second coat. To smooth the patch, either sand it or wipe it gently with a damp sponge.

TO PATCH A SMALL HOLE

1 Cut a piece of pegboard that is slightly larger than the damaged area but small enough to slip through the hole. Loop a wire through the holes. Or use a piece of wood into which you have partially driven a screw.

2 Smear joint compound on the perimeter of the pegboard or wood and slip the patch into the wall. Pull gently on the wire or screw until the patch clings tightly to the back of the wall.

3 Tie the wire on the patch to a pencil or small stick and twist it to pull the patch tight. After the compound dries, cut off the wire or remove the screw. Use a taping knife to fill the recess with joint compound.

4 Allow the joint compound to dry. Apply two or three more coats until the patch looks and feels level with the surrounding wall. Sand smooth or use a damp sponge to level the repair. Prime the patched area.

Step 2. Insert the patch into the hole with the joint compound facing out.

WYNN TIP:

Drywall patching kits are available from most home centers. Typically these are best suited for small holes, though some kits are available for medium-size holes. One style of kit includes a screen that adheres to the front of the drywall; you apply joint compound over the screen. Other kits have clips that clasp the patch to the surrounding drywall. For both, you need to apply mesh tape and drywall compound. If you have the materials to make your own patch, that can be just as easy as purchasing a kit for this type of repair.

patching larger holes in drywall

If your grade-schooler brought baseball practice indoors and you now have a large hole in the family room wall, don't despair. The hole can be patched—perhaps with some assistance from its creator. If the wall is damaged due to a doorknob that knocks against it, install a stop at the bottom of the door to prevent further damage.

TOOLS AND MATERIALS:
- **Keyhole saw or drywall saw**
- **Sanding block**
- **Drill**
- **Taping knife**
- **Drywall**
- **2×2s**
- **Joint compound**
- **Sponge**
- **Mesh tape**
- **Nails or screws**
- **Paint and primer**

REPAIR A MEDIUM-SIZE HOLE (UP TO 8 INCHES)

1 Mark a rectangle around the hole. Cut it out with a keyhole saw or drywall saw.

2 Cut a drywall rectangle patch 4 inches longer and wider than the hole. Turn the patch upside down. Carefully use a utility knife to remove 2-inches of wallboard along each side, while leaving the face paper intact.

3 Test the patch to ensure it fits snugly into the hole. If it is too big, trim as needed. If it is too small, start over and cut another one.

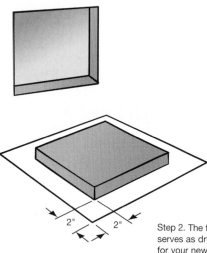

Step 2. The face paper serves as drywall tape for your new patch.

4 Spread a medium-thick bed of joint compound around the perimeter of the damaged area using a taping knife.

5 Insert the patch and smooth the face paper against the wall. (The face paper takes the place of drywall tape.) Blend the patch with the surrounding surface by feathering the edges with coats of joint compound.

6 Sand the patched area or smooth it with a damp sponge. Prime and paint.

WYNN TIP:
You have two basic choices when selecting joint compound: ready-mix and dry-mix. Ready-mix comes in buckets. Just scoop it out and apply it. Dry-mix comes in bags of powder that must be mixed with water before applying. Bags typically are labeled 90, 45, or 20; the mix will harden in approximately that many minutes. This compound sets, rather than dries, which adds strength.

Ready-mix is convenient and easy to sand, but dries slowly and is not as strong. Use ready-mix only for small repairs, such as filling nail holes. For larger repairs, apply one coat of dry-mix for its strength, and then use ready-mix for the top coats.

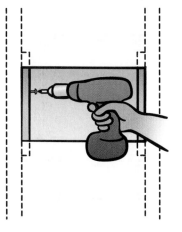

Step 2. The 2×2s are flush against the back of the drywall so the patch will be flush.

4 Apply fiberglass mesh tape over the perimeter of the patch. Cover with three coats of joint compound. Feather the edges to blend the patch with the wall. Allow each coat to dry before applying the next coat.

5 Sand the area or smooth it with a damp sponge. Prime and paint.

REPAIR A LARGE AREA (WIDER THAN 8 INCHES)

1 Cut a rectangle around the hole. The rectangle needs to span from stud to stud because you will attach bracing to the studs.

2 Cut 2×2 boards slightly longer than the opening's height. Insert the boards into the hole and position them against the studs as shown above. Attach by driving nails or screws.

3 Cut a drywall patch slightly smaller than the rectangle opening. Nail or screw the drywall patch into place, driving the fasteners into the 2×2 boards.

Step 4. The mesh supports the compound, giving it greater strength.

WYNN TIP:
For chronic cracks, try using paper reinforcing tape and a setting-type joint compound. It's a little trickier to mix and use, but it provides a more durable bond.

fixing popped nails

Nails can work out from a wall or ceiling stud over time and create a bulge or "pop" in the finish. Hammering a popped nail back into place is a short-term fix at best. Follow these steps instead to keep nails from popping back out again.

TOOLS AND MATERIALS:
- **Drywall taping knife**
- **Sanding block**
- **Sponge**
- **Putty knife**
- **Paintbrush**
- **Hammer**
- **Drill**
- **Joint compound**
- **Nails or screws**
- **Primer and paint**

Step 1. Drive the new fastener into the stud near the popped nail.

1 If a popped nail seems loose, it may have entirely missed the stud; pull it out and drive a new nail or screw into the stud. If it feels fairly firm, it either wasn't driven all the way into the stud or barely caught the stud. Drive new ringshank nails—nails with ridges to help them hold better—or drywall screws above and below the popped nail.

2 If using nails, set them slightly below the surface—called dimpling—by tapping with a hammer. Take care not to break the drywall paper. Drive screws slightly below the surface too. Run a taping knife over the area to make sure the fastener heads are recessed.

3 Use a putty knife or taping knife to fill the dimples or holes with joint compound.

4 After the first coat of compound has dried, apply a second and perhaps third coat. When the area is the same level as the surrounding wall, you can stop adding compound.

5 Sand the surface flush with the surrounding area. Prime and paint.

Step 2. A dimple should not break the paper, nor should the nail or screw head stick out above the surface.

WYNN TIP:

Though you can easily remove nails from wood, removing a nail firmly embedded in drywall may damage the drywall. Rather than remove a stuck nail, drive the nail slightly below the surface and cover it with joint compound. Sand the surface so it is flush with the surrounding area. After the compound dries, prime and paint.

making minor drywall repairs

Drywall repairs are pretty simple. Plus they're an easy way to quickly improve the look of a heavily used room. The most time-consuming part is not the patching but the priming and painting after you complete the repair. Save leftover paint for this purpose. Trying to have new paint mixed to match later is tough.

TOOLS AND MATERIALS:
- **Drywall taping knife**
- **Sanding block**
- **Sponge**
- **Putty knife**
- **Paintbrush**
- **Joint compound**
- **Mesh tape**
- **Primer and paint**

FILL DENTS

1 Brush away loose material. Use a taping knife to pack the dent with joint compound and level it off. Allow the compound to dry.

2 If the patch shrinks after drying, apply a second coat. Allow the second coat to dry. If necessary, apply a third coat. Allow to dry.

3 Sand the surface lightly, or wipe it with a damp sponge to smooth and blend the patch with the wall.

4 Prime the spot before painting. Just about any primer will do the job.

REPAIR LOOSE TAPE

1 If drywall tape is peeling, gently pull it off; you may need to pry it up with a putty knife. Use a sharp knife to make a clean break at the point where the tape becomes firmly embedded. If the tape has a bubble, cut around the area with a utility knife and pry off the damaged tape.

2 Wipe away dust and debris. Cut a piece of fiberglass mesh tape to roughly fit the spot where you removed the old tape; it's alright if it's a bit short at either end. Press the tape into place.

3 Apply joint compound over the tape using gentle strokes with a 4-inch taping knife. Cover the tape completely. If you are applying ready-mix, or "easy-sand" compound, mound the compound up a bit. If you reapply regular dry-mix compound, level it with a 6-inch taping knife. Let it dry.

4 Apply one and perhaps two more coats, feathering the edges. The patch should look and feel even with the surrounding wall. Let it dry. Sand, prime, and paint.

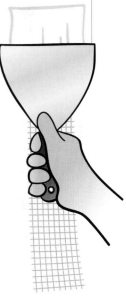

Step 3. Apply enough joint compound to completely cover the edges of the tape.

filling cracks in plaster

Plaster walls enhance the charm and character of older homes, but not when they are marred with cracks. Filling small cracks is well within the realm of a do-it-yourself repair project.

TOOLS AND MATERIALS:
- Chisel or old screwdriver
- Putty knife
- Taping knife
- Old toothbrush
- Sanding block
- Sponge
- Compound
- Vacuum
- Brush
- Mesh tape

WYNN TIP:
For small cracks, try aerosol crack seal. Spray it on just before priming the area.

Step 1. Widen the bottom of the crack to seat the patch properly.

FILL SMALL CRACKS

1 Counter-intuitive as it may seem, start by widening a small crack to at least ¼ inch with a chisel or old screwdriver. This allows you to work compound into the crack. Blow out and remove any loose plaster.

2 Apply vinyl spackling compound, which retains some flexibility. Work it into the crack and let it mound. Allow the compound to dry. Sand or sponge the compound smooth.

3 Seal the patch with primer before painting or the patch may "bleed" through and change the color of the paint.

FILL WIDE CRACKS

1 Use a chisel or screwdriver to make the crack broader at the bottom than it is at the wall surface.

2 Clean the debris and dust out of the crack with an old toothbrush or a wire brush. Use a vacuum to clear any remaining debris.

3 Use a small brush to wet the crack before patching. Pack joint compound, surfacing compound, or patching plaster into the crack with a putty knife or a wide-blade taping knife. Really force the material into the crack, then level it off.

4 Apply fiberglass mesh tape over the crack to help prevent recracking. The mesh will make the repaired area bulge a bit, so feather the compound out on each side.

5 Let the compound harden, then level off the repair with a second and perhaps a third application.

6 Allow the patch to dry. Sand the patch smooth or rub it with a damp sponge. If you have not embedded mesh tape in the patch, spray the area with aerosol crack sealer.

7 Seal the patch with primer, then paint it.

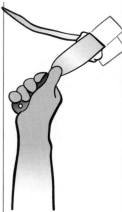

Step 4. Force joint compound into the crack to fill the channel.

WYNN TIP:
If the wall surrounding the crack feels spongy, you probably have more substantial problems than just cracked plaster. The plaster and perhaps the lath may have come loose. If it is a large area, it's time to call in the plaster pros.

repairing holes in plaster

Holes in plaster can indicate a larger problem. Unless you know how the hole was created, investigate to find the cause. You may discover a water problem that needs to be solved before repairing the plaster. Or you may find that a large area around the hole is spongy because the plaster has pulled away from the wall. In the case of major problems, call in a professional plasterer.

TOOLS AND MATERIALS:
- **Masonry chisel**
- **Utility knife**
- **Taping knife**
- **Pry bar**
- **Sanding block**
- **Sponge**
- **Painting tools**
- **Drywall**
- **Screws**
- **Compound**
- **Mesh tape**

WYNN TIP:
It's important to remove all loose plaster before patching. Otherwise you won't be able to create a solid patch and your repair efforts will be wasted.

1 Remove all loose plaster. Dig back with a masonry chisel, flat pry bar, or old screwdriver until you encounter solid plaster. (Potentially you could create a larger hole.) Brush out any remaining debris.

2 Scrape with a chisel or utility knife to undercut the edges of the hole. This allows you to make a stronger repair.

3 Cut a piece of drywall—the same thickness or thinner than the plaster—to roughly fit the hole. It's OK for the patch to be thinner than the surrounding plaster, however it should not stick out past the plaster. Attach it to the lath with 1¼-inch drywall screws.

4 Blend a stiff batch of dry-mix joint compound. Use a taping knife to press the compound into the spaces between the patch and the wall. Smooth the surface.

5 While the compound is wet, cut pieces of fiberglass mesh tape. Embed them in the compound. This bonds the compound to the surrounding wall and protects against cracks.

6 Apply additional joint compound, spreading it over the mesh. Cover the mesh but avoid applying too much compound so it doesn't blend with the surrounding wall. After it has dried, apply two more coats of ready-mix compound or surfacing compound.

7 Once the compound has dried, sand it smooth or rub lightly with a damp sponge to level the area. Apply primer and paint.

WYNN TIP:
For small holes, you can use plaster patching compound to make the repair. Plaster patch is designed not to sag.

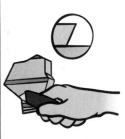

Step 2. Cut to create a channel for a patch that won't pop out.

Step 6. Apply enough compound to cover the mesh tape.

choosing paint color

High-quality paint is more economical in the long run.

many sensible, cost-cutting measures for home repair are available. Buying cheap paint is not one of them. You'll actually save money over time by purchasing high-quality paint. High-quality paint is more likely to cover in one coat—especially if you first apply a good primer tinted with the color you select. Quality paint will also prove to be more durable over time.

Latex or solvent-thinned

Latex is the most common choice for interior paint projects. It cleans up with water, has less of an odor than solvent-thinned paint, is environmentally friendly, and dries to the touch quickly.

Don't apply latex paint over solvent-thinned paint because it will peel. If you're not sure what type of paint you're covering, cover it with primer—a good idea anyway. Or go with a solvent-thinned paint if you suspect the base is a solvent-thinned paint.

Solvent-thinned paints require a solvent such as paint thinner for cleanup. This type of paint and its cleaners have a stronger odor than latex. The benefit of a solvent-thinned paint is greater durability.

Choosing a sheen

Sheen describes how glossy or dull a dried paint surface appears. Typical paint sheen designations are flat, eggshell, satin, semigloss, and gloss or high-gloss. The glossier the finish, the more surface imperfections will show. However, glossy paints provide a harder, more durable finish.

Thanks to new paint developments, some paint companies are now offering top-quality scrubbable latex paints in a flat sheen. High-gloss paints work better for trim because of the wear associated with vacuuming and cleaning floors.

Choosing color

With thousands of options available, selecting paint color can be overwhelming. Remember it's only paint—if you can't live with the color, just paint over it. That said, you do want to try to choose a color you like. Colors vary under different lighting. Don't rely on the tiny chip in the store to make your decision. Bring a variety of chips home. Tape them up in the room you will be painting, and look at them at various times of day. Once you've narrowed your choices, purchase the smallest sample size can and paint large boards or areas on the walls with different lighting exposure. Place the boards along the walls. After viewing them a couple of days, make your choice.

choosing brushes

Select a brush that matches your paint task.

natural-bristle or synthetic-bristle brushes? In general, use natural-bristle brushes with oil-based paints and synthetic-bristle brushes with water-thinned paints. Natural bristles soak up water, resulting in a streaked finish if used with latex paint. Many paintbrush manufacturers label the brush package or handle with the type of finish for which the brush is designed.

Brush quality

To test a brush for quality, spread the bristles and inspect their tips. Quality natural-bristle brushes will have little "flags," like split ends, on the bristle ends. The more the better. Better-quality synthetic brushes have fuzzy-looking tips. Next, check the brush's ferrule, the aluminum or stainless-steel band near the handle. It should be wrapped tightly and neatly around the brush and solidly secured to the handle.

As for whether to spend more money for a high-quality brush depends on whether you're going to take the time to thoroughly clean the brushes. If you are, invest in a better brush. But if you're not going to paint very often,

and you know you really won't do a good job cleaning the brushes, a less-expensive one makes more sense. If you think this is your one and only paint job, or you know you don't want to bother with cleaning brushes at all, grab a disposable brush. They're inexpensive, so they can be tossed when the job's done, saving considerable cleanup time.

However, painting with a disposable brush means you might have to apply two coats of paint, where a high-quality brush would cover with one coat. Also, a cheaper brush may shed bristle hairs, which are tedious to remove from the paint.

Brush type

For a basic room paint job, choose a 4-inch wall brush, a 2-inch trim brush, and a 2-inch sash-trim brush. Foam brushes are handy for covering small patch areas and inexpensive enough to throw out when finished.

Brush spinners

If you've just moved into your home and are planning to update every room with a fresh coat of paint, purchase a brush spinner to speed brush cleanup. After you've washed the brush, insert the handle of the brush into the spinner. Position the brush in a large bucket to contain splatters and pump the handle of the spinner until the brush is dry. It also works with roller covers.

FOAM BRUSH
Some people prefer a foam brush for cutting in along trim. Plus it's cheap and disposable; use it and toss it.

FOAM BRUSH 8505 3"

BRUSH SPINNER
Place a brush in the holder, pump the handle, and the brush will spin dry.

2" TRIM
Make this one of your first purchases. Use to cut in along trim for a clean line.

SHUR-
Makes Pain

Brush &
Applicato
Chassis
Limpiado
Y Rodillo

05200

2"
50.4mm

4" BRUSH
Its larger size makes this a good choice for large, flat areas.

4"
101.6mm

2" SASH
Angled bristles make this brush ideal for painting trim. If you can buy only one brush, get this for all-around painting duties.

2"
50.8mm

ROLLER AND COVER
Standard roller with cover is perfect for applying paint to walls.

TRIM ROLLER
Enables you to reach into small areas.

PAD
Ideal for painting straight edges and "cutting in" next to trim.

EXTENSION HANDLE
Extend your reach to paint ceilings or the tops of walls.

DONUT-STYLE ROLLER
Designed to paint moldings and other fine work.

yes, you can!

choosing rollers and pads

Rollers and pads provide for efficient paint application.

You'll find it most efficient to "cut in" the edges of a wall or ceiling with a brush and then paint the rest of the surfaces using a roller.

Roller quality

It's worth spending more when it comes to rollers. Purchase a professional-quality roller frame that rolls smoothly and holds the cover securely. Inexpensive frames can make loading the roller messy and difficult.

High-quality roller covers are a must! They have lint-free pile that is uniform in texture and fasten securely. Cheaper covers tend to apply paint unevenly or shed fibers.

Roller type

The roller you'll use most for painting walls and ceilings is 9 inches wide. Trim rollers are available in 3- to 4-inch widths suitable for small and hard-to-reach areas. If you've never used a trim roller, take time to practice. Soon you'll find them as easy to control as a brush.

If you have a lot of painting projects on your to-do list, you may want to invest in specialty rollers. Cone-shaped types are used for inside corners, around door and window casings, and almost any point where two surfaces intersect. Doughnut-style rollers are handy for painting moldings and trimwork.

Roller covers are available in a variety of materials and thicknesses. To paint rough surfaces, use a thick nap—approximately ¾ inch. A thick nap will produce a slightly pebbly stipple. Because thick-nap rollers can hold more paint, you may be able to achieve one-coat coverage with a thicker nap. Use a short-nap cover, either ⅜- or ¼-inch, to produce a smoother surface.

Paint pads

Paint pads are handy to use for cutting in along trim on flat walls. Since the pads have very short nap, novice painters can often produce a cleaner line with a pad than with a brush. Pads are also less prone to drips, while holding a good amount of paint for application.

Other accessories

Buy an extension handle that allows you to easily reach the ceiling—it will save time and energy. Make sure it fits the roller.

Paint trays are essential when painting with rollers. Look for a sturdy tray that won't collapse when you fill it with paint. If you'll be painting from a stepladder, buy a tray that has ladder hooks to keep the tray secure.

WYNN TIP:
Buy a few plastic tray inserts to save on cleanup time. Insert one inside a sturdy paint tray. Once you're finished painting, throw away the liner.

using and cleaning brushes

Though using a paintbrush may seem like a "duh" activity, following these tips will help brushes perform their best, and that means your paint job will look its best.

TOOLS AND MATERIALS:
- Brushes
- Water or paint thinner
- Foil or plastic
- Wire
- Newspaper
- Drill
- Cardboard brush holder or paper towels

PREPPING A NEW BRUSH

Remove any loose bristles by spinning the brush by the handle between your hands and slapping it against the edge of a table or counter. Better now than in your paint.

Soften the ends by working the bristles against a rough surface such as a brick patio or concrete wall. Remove any stray bristles that stick out from the ferrule at odd angles. Condition natural brushes by soaking overnight in linseed oil.

LOAD PAINT

Dip the brush into the paint to only one-third the length of its bristles. If you go deeper, you'll waste paint and create a mess. Squeeze excess paint from the bristles by lightly scraping it against the side of the container as you remove the brush.

STORE THE BRUSH WHILE YOU TAKE A QUICK BREAK

If a break will last less than an hour, leave the brush in the paint. Position the brush so only the bristles are covered. Drill a hole in the handle and thread wire through. Secure the wire to the sides of the container so only the bristles are submerged. Cover the container with foil or plastic wrap. For longer breaks, wrap the brush in foil or plastic. Seal tightly to prevent the paint from drying on the bristles.

If you're done painting for longer, clean the brush in solvent or water.

CLEAN AND STORE

Work out as much of the paint as you can by brushing back and forth across newspaper. Remove remaining paint with water or paint thinner, gently working the bristles to remove paint between them.

Wash the brush in soap and water. Reshape the bristles to their original shape and hang the brush to dry.

Wrap the brush in its original cardboard cover, or wrap it with several layers of paper towel to hold the bristles in shape but not squeeze them.

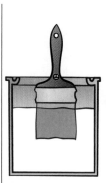

Secure the brush so only the bristles are submerged.

WYNN TIP:
Cleaning a brush in paint thinner can be hard on the bristles. Try wrapping them with a thick rubber band after cleaning. This will help hold the bristles in place.

using and cleaning rollers

Rollers are easy to use, but there are still a few tricks to smooth the process and help your finished paint job looks its best.

TOOLS AND MATERIALS:
- Roller frame
- Roller pad
- Paint tray
- Water or paint thinner/solvent
- Newspaper
- Aluminum foil or plastic bags

1 Cover the floor and any furniture you can't remove from the room with heavy drop cloths. Even when used carefully, rollers scatter paint speckles.

2 Fill the well of the paint tray with paint, but not the slanted portion. Push the roller into the paint, pull it back, and repeat until paint covers the entire roller. Even out the paint on the roller using the slanted portion.

3 Minimize dripping by starting the roller on an upstroke.

4 For the best coverage, apply the paint in two or more directions because most surfaces are irregular to some extent. Roll slowly, especially when the roller cover is loaded with paint. Otherwise you'll splatter, which wastes paint and makes a mess.

5 After applying paint to an area, go over it again with light vertical passes to even out any thick spots.

6 When you are done painting, clean excess paint off the roller by rolling it over a newspaper. For latex paint, run water over the roller. Squeeze the roller to help force out the paint. Continue rinsing until the water runs clear. For solvent-thinned paint, pour solvent into a clean tray and work the roller back and forth until the solvent remains clear. Allow the roller to dry, then wrap clean, dry roller covers in aluminum foil or plastic bags.

WYNN TIP:
If you get too much paint on a roller, it tends to slide across the wall rather than roll, which can leave small tracks in the finish when the paint dries. Periodically look over the area you've painted and even out areas where the finish is not even. Also keep a fairly constant amount of paint on the roller—the finished surface will look more consistent too.

Step 2. Don't fill the slanted portion with paint. Use this area to even out the paint on the roller.

prepping surfaces for paint

It's amazing how a fresh coat of paint can transform a room—but not if you don't prepare the surfaces first. Paint applied to an unprepared wall may peel, may not cover evenly, or may not go on at all, wasting time and effort. Inspect all surfaces. See pages 79–85 to repair holes and cracks, then follow these steps before you open the paint can.

TOOLS AND MATERIALS:
- **Portable light**
- **Screwdriver**
- **Sandpaper or liquid sander**
- **Sponge or mop**
- **Bucket**
- **Drop cloths**
- **Dish soap**
- **Primer**

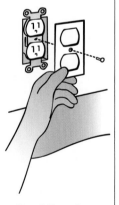

Step 4. Removing coverplates is easier and faster than masking or painting around them.

1 Remove all furniture from the room. If that's not practical or possible, group items in the middle of the room and cover with drop cloths. Cover the floor completely—unless you'll be replacing the flooring after painting.

2 Set up portable work lights so you can see what you're doing. Continue to reposition the lights when you begin to paint so you can see the corners.

3 If you are painting a ceiling, and there is a ceiling light, shut off the power, then disconnect it. Cover the globe to protect it from paint splatters, or remove it completely.

4 Remove all electrical coverplates to achieve a professional finished look. Don't try to paint over or around them.

5 Check the wall again for any holes and cracks you missed earlier. See pages 79–85 to fix these before painting.

6 Sand all rough spots and runs or drips from previous paint jobs.

7 Remove all dirt and dust. Pay particular attention to the tops of baseboards and moldings.

8 Wash the ceilings and walls with a sponge or mop, using water with a couple of drops of dish soap. Make sure to rinse all soap off the walls, and allow them to dry completely before painting.

9 Prime all surfaces with a quality primer. See page 96 for painting techniques that should be used for applying primer as well. Have the primer tinted with the color of the new paint to save on the number of coats needed.

WYNN TIP:
You can paint over clean, properly applied wallpaper, but I don't recommend it. I know stripping wallpaper is no fun, but you'll end up with a better surface and a finish that will last. If you can't stand the thought of removing wallpaper, apply a primer over the wallpaper. If any of the paper begins to peel, curl, or release from the wall, you'll have to remove it. If not, apply paint over the primer after it dries.

painting ceilings

The best way to paint a room is to start at the top and work down. I recommend painting the ceiling, even if you don't think it looks too bad. If you don't paint it, once you finish the walls and trim, you'll be amazed at how dingy it looks.

TOOLS AND MATERIALS:
- **Ceiling paint**
- **Roller with extension handle**
- **Brushes**
- **Paint tray**

1 Set up extra work lights so you can see what you're doing.

2 Use a trim brush or trim roller to paint a strip on the ceiling along the walls, called "cutting in." If you will only be applying one coat to the ceiling, you can allow the paint to lap onto the wall. If you think you'll need to apply two ceiling coats, don't overlap paint onto the wall; the paint buildup leaves a ridge.

3 Pour ceiling paint into the well of the paint tray. Attach the extension handle to the paint roller. Roll paint onto the ceiling with a series of diagonal swaths.

4 Cross-roll to even out paint and fill in any open areas.

5 Continue spreading the paint from wet areas into dry areas. After finishing a small section, check to see whether you've created any visible lap marks. If so, even them out by lightly going over them with a fairly dry roller.

WYNN TIP:
Buy ceiling paint. It has a flatter sheen than wall paint and is designed to help hide imperfections.

WYNN TIP:
Most people paint ceilings white, and when you repaint white over white, it's tough to tell if you've missed any spots—until the paint dries and everything is put away. Several paint manufacturers have come up with a solution: ceiling paint with a temporary colorant that fades to white after 30 minutes.

Step 2. Cut in the edge along the wall before you paint the center.

painting walls

Now begins the exciting transformation—adding color to the walls. Painting walls is not difficult, but doing the job right does require attention. The nice thing is that if you don't like the finish color, you can just repaint until you get what you want. All you've lost is a little time, but you've gained a satisfying environment.

TOOLS AND MATERIALS:
- Drop cloths
- Ladder
- Brushes
- Trim brush or trim roller
- Roller
- Extension handle
- Paint
- Paint tray
- Painter's tape

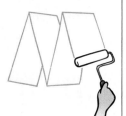

Step 4. A diagonal application of paint provides the base for even coverage.

WYNN TIP:
When you're ready for a break, cover the paint tray with plastic wrap. When you get back to work, stir the paint lightly with the paint stick. When left untouched, paint skins over.

1 Use painter's tape to mark off the trim, unless you plan to paint the trim after finishing the walls. (If so, wall color can lap the trim slightly, but take care not to get too much wall paint on the trim; the paint can build up and leave a ridge.)

2 Open the paint and stir it with a paint stick. Even if you just brought the paint home from the store, it may have separated.

3 Use a trim brush or trim roller to cut in the corners and around all of the woodwork. Paint about 3 inches out from the edges to make the next step—rolling the large sections—easy.

4 Pour paint into the well of the paint tray. Load the roller and apply paint in a large "M" shape. Start the roller going up, then pull it down.

5 Cross-roll to fill in the M with paint. You can work horizontally or vertically; it's up to you.

6 Determine what size area one loaded roller can fully cover. Work in sections of this size. Don't attempt to "stretch" the paint, or you'll have noticeably uneven coverage. After each section, check for drips, runs, and skid marks from the roller. Even these out before working on the next section.

7 Continue to work around the room in small sections. Always work from wet edges so you don't have lap marks.

8 Remove the painter's tape before the paint is completely dry to avoid peeling off the new wall paint. If you have to wait a day or more to paint a second coat, remove the tape after the first coat, then retape before you paint the second coat.

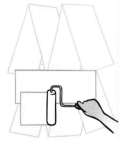

Step 5. Overlapping when applying paint provides an even finish.

WYNN TIP:
If you are using a dark, saturated color and will be using more than 1 gallon of paint, get a 5-gallon bucket and mix the individual gallons together. Even if all of the gallons were mixed at the same time at the same store, colors can differ slightly from gallon to gallon. The differences will be particularly noticeable with dark colors.

painting cabinets

Painting is an inexpensive way to make a dramatic difference in the appearance of your kitchen. When spiffing up cabinets, use paint made especially for them. Cabinet-rated paint stands up to the constant wear and tear of daily use and protects against grease and oils in the air from cooking.

TOOLS AND MATERIALS:
- **Screwdriver**
- **Drop cloth**
- **Roller pad or brush**
- **Cabinet paint**
- **Wood scraps**

1 Place a drop cloth on the floor. Give yourself as much room as possible to lay out all of the drawers and doors. If necessary, set up a drop cloth in an adjacent room.

2 Unscrew and remove all hinges, knobs, pulls, and attached hardware. Stand drawers upright on the drop cloths. You don't want any edge that you'll be painting to touch the cloth. Place doors on small scraps of wood to raise them off the cloth so you can paint the edges.

3 Use a roller, pad, or brush—whichever you are comfortable with— to paint the drawer faces and doors. Be consistent: A roller will leave a slightly different finish than a brush, and you want all of the surfaces to look alike.

4 Paint the inside surface of the doors first. Wait a day for the paint to dry, then flip the doors. Paint the edges and then the outside faces. If the doors have raised moldings, paint the moldings first, then the inner panels. Paint the perimeter of the moldings last. As you work, check for drips and runs. Smooth these out as soon as you notice them.

5 Begin painting the cabinet frames at their least accessible point. This way you're not apt to disturb fresh paint. Do the inside edges first, then the outer faces. Use either a brush or a roller for the entire job so the finish looks consistent.

6 Wait until the paint is completely dry to reassemble the doors and drawers, and add the hardware. Check the paint manufacturer's instructions for drying time.

Step 5. Start at the inside of the cabinets and work your way out.

painting woodwork

Much like ceilings, painted woodwork that looked OK prior to a fresh coat of wall paint can appear dingy after the walls have been painted. Yes, painting woodwork is time-consuming, but believe me, the finished result is well worth the effort.

TOOLS AND MATERIALS:
- **Sash brush**
- **Painter's tape or painter's shield**
- **Drop cloth**
- **Paint**
- **Damp rags**
- **Roller**

DOUBLE-HUNG WINDOWS

1 Use painter's tape to mask the windowpanes. Start by painting the muntins, if there are any, then work outward. Move the sashes several times while the paint is drying to make sure the sashes do not dry shut.

2 Remove the tape as soon as you finish painting. If you wait until the paint is dry, you could crack and peel the paint.

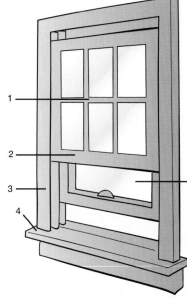

Step 1. On a double-hung window, start painting the inner trim and work your way to the outer trim.

Paint the upper sash first, then the lower sash

CASEMENT WINDOWS

1 Use painter's tape to mask the windowpanes. Open the window slightly and leave it open until the paint is dry.

2 Begin painting the inner woodwork and work outward.

3 Remove the tape as soon as you finish painting so you won't crack or peel the paint.

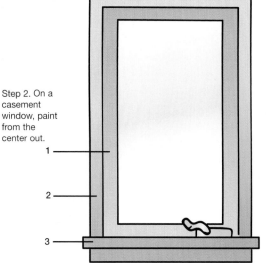

Step 2. On a casement window, paint from the center out.

WYNN TIP:
To save time, skip taping the window glass. Work carefully, but don't worry about getting some paint on the glass. After the paint dries, scrape it off the panes with a razor blade.

FLUSH OR FLAT-PANEL DOORS

1 Choose either a brush or a roller, and use it for the entire surface. Open the door and leave it open until the paint dries.

2 Paint the entire door surface using vertical or horizontal strokes.

TRIM

1 Wait until the wall paint has dried completely and then apply painter's tape to mask off the trim.

2 Apply a stain-killing primer to any woodwork that has been stained to prevent the stain from bleeding through the paint. Allow the primer to dry.

3 Paint the top edge of a baseboard first. Then cut in along the floor. Fill in the remaining area. Follow similar steps for crown molding or chair rail.

4 Immediately wipe away any drips or overlapping paint with a damp rag. They are easiest to remove while wet.

5 Remove the painter's tape as soon as you finish painting. If you wait until the paint is dry, you could crack and peel the paint.

RAISED-PANEL DOORS

1 Paint the raised moldings first and then the panels within the moldings. Keep your brushstrokes consistent across all panels.

2 Next paint the top flat portion, then the middle area between panels, and finally the bottom area below panels.

3 Use a cross-brush technique, particularly with high-gloss paints. Apply paint on the door horizontally, then make vertical finishing strokes.

WYNN TIP:
Use high-gloss paint on woodwork. It dries to the toughest finish, withstanding the dings accidentally inflicted on trim, plus it can be washed and scrubbed to remove most scuff marks.

WYNN TIP:
Always finish painting a door in the same work session you start it. Otherwise you'll leave lap marks.

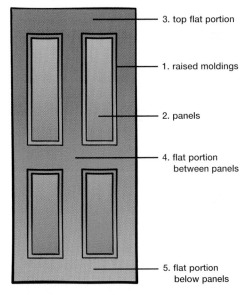

3. top flat portion

1. raised moldings

2. panels

4. flat portion between panels

5. flat portion below panels

Paint a paneled door in the order shown here.

cleaning up after painting

If you're like me, the sooner you can clean up after painting, the better—and the easier it will be to do the final cleanup. This means immediately tackling those small spills and splatters, as well as your paint tools and materials.

TOOLS AND MATERIALS:
- Damp rags
- Bucket with dishwashing detergent and water, or paint solvent
- Razor-blade scraper
- Hammer
- Tight-sealing glass jar
- Cloth
- Wood block

1 Before you finish painting, watch for spills, drips, and splatters. Clean these immediately using a rag, with dishwashing detergent and water for latex paint, or paint solvent for solvent-thinned paint. After you wipe away paint with solvent, clean the area with soap and water.

2 Remove all painter's tape while the paint is still wet. Otherwise the paint will tear and you'll end up with a ragged edge, or if a large area pulls away, you'll have to repaint a section.

3 Use a razor-blade scraper to remove large paint splotches that have already set.

4 Reseal paint cans if you have more than a quarter of the paint left. Place the lid on the can, cover with a cloth to prevent splatters, and place a wood block on top. Tap the block with a hammer, working around the edge of the lid until the entire lid is shut tightly. If you have less than a quarter of the paint left, transfer the paint to a glass jar that seals tightly; the paint will keep better.

5 Store paint cans upside down to prevent a skin from forming. If you store paint cans upright, next time you need the paint, skim off the skin and throw it away rather than trying to mix it into the paint. Otherwise it will make a mess of your next paint job.

6 Follow the steps on pages 92–93 for cleaning and storing brushes and rollers.

Step 4. A tight seal adds to the shelf life of a stored can of paint.

WYNN TIP:

The exception to the "clean right away" rule is scuff marks on freshly painted walls. Wait at least a month before scrubbing the area, or you will remove the paint and create a bigger problem.

replacing a cracked wall tile

A cracked tile not only presents itself as an eyesore, but also could become a hazard. Cracked or chipped tile has very sharp edges that can easily cut. The opening created by the crack also allows water to seep into the structural components of your home, weakening the floor or walls. Before you remove the tile, it's best to determine what type of adhesive was used for the initial installation.

TOOLS AND MATERIALS:
- Hammer
- Grout saw
- Drill
- Carbide-tipped holesaw
- Cold chisel
- Putty knife
- Grout
- Beater block
- Safety glasses
- Margin trowel
- Adhesive
- Replacement tile

Step 3. Cracking the damaged tile allows for easy removal and replacement. Wear appropriate eye protection.

1 If grout is removed first, it will be much easier to remove the cracked tile, and there will be less chance of damaging surrounding tiles. Use a grout saw to loosen the grout around the tile. Then you can use a screwdriver to remove the excess grout.

2 If the tile is already loose, you may be able to simply pry it off with a cold chisel or putty knife. If it still adheres tightly to the wall, use a drill with a carbide-tipped holesaw, and drill several holes over the surface of the tile. This weakens the tile and makes it easier to break off. Be sure to wear protective eyewear.

3 Using a cold chisel and hammer, strike the center of the tile gently. Hold the chisel carefully— you want to avoid coming into contact with, and potentially damaging, the surface underneath.

4 Using a putty knife, gently remove the cracked tile, being careful not to damage the

surrounding tiles. If any surrounding tiles begin to crack, it is an indication that there is greater damage on the surface underneath. Remove as many tiles as needed to repair the surface before continuing.

5 Use a putty knife or margin trowel to scrape away all of the old adhesive. Remove any remaining grout from the joints. Create a smooth, clean surface for the new tile.

6 If possible, use the same adhesive type used on the original installation. Spread a thin coat of the adhesive over the entire back of the replacement tile. Spread another coat on the setting bed. Press the tile into place, giving it a gentle twist.

7 Use a beater block and hammer to set the tile flush. If necessary, hold the tile in place with masking tape. Wait one or two days before grouting, then wait several more days and seal the grout.

Step 6. Spread a thin coat of adhesive over the entire back of the replacement tile.

WYNN TIP:
Unless you saved extra tile from the original installation, you will need to find matching tile. Look on the back of the removed tile for the manufacturer's name. If you can't find it, take the broken tile to a home center or tile store to help find a match. Don't forget to match the grout too.

installing base molding

Finishing touches are a great part of any do-it-yourself home project, giving you that extra sense of satisfaction for improving your home's style. With this project, accent a room with molding.

TOOLS AND MATERIALS:
- **Molding**
- **Tape measure**
- **Miter box and backsaw, or power miter saw**
- **Coping saw**
- **Hammer**
- **Drill**
- **Nail set**
- **Finish nails**
- **Pencil**
- **Wood filler**
- **Sandpaper**

Step 5. A straight cut gives a clean, professional look to any joint.

1 Measure and mark precisely before cutting. Start on a short wall that requires an inside-to-inside piece. Hold a piece of molding in place and use a pencil to mark about $\frac{1}{16}$ inch longer than the space to ensure a tight fit.

2 Use a miter saw to cut a 45-degree angle at the pencil mark. Look down the blade of the miter and position the molding so the blade will cut just to the scrap side of the pencil mark. Grasp the molding firmly with one hand so it will not slide.

3 Set the first piece into position; you may need to arch it slightly. Drill pilot holes within 3 inches of the edges, then drive finish nails as needed.

4 Continue to measure, cut, and install base molding around the room. When you get to an outside corner, butt one end of the molding against the wall and let the other end extend past the corner. Mark even with the corner.

5 Use a miter saw to cut a 45-degree angle at your pencil mark. Follow Steps 4 and 5 to mark and cut another 45-degree-angled piece that will form the other half of the outside corner. Check to see that the mitered ends close neatly before cutting the opposite end to fit.

6 An alternative method for inside corners is to make a coped joint. Follow Steps 1 and 2 to cut one piece at a 90-degree angle. Install the first piece. Mark the second piece for a coped angle cut. Make an inside 45-degree miter cut first. Then use a coping saw to cut away the excess wood along the molding profile. Cut more off the back of the piece than the front. Check for a neat fit.

7 Drive the nails below the surface using a nail set. Fill the holes with wood filler. If staining, use wood filler that closely matches the stain. Allow to dry; then sand and finish. (You may want to stain or prime the pieces before installing; see the opposite page.)

Step 6. Angle the coping saw to cut along the profile.

WYNN TIP:
Installing base molding is easier than you might expect, though it does take some practice. Cut yourself a little slack by first practicing with the miter and coping saws on scrap pieces. Once you've built up confidence, start the actual installation in an area of the room where the molding will be least visible.

getting more out of base molding

Add trimwork where floor meets wall to give a room a finished look.

olding is a great way to finish off a room, but it can be tricky to cut and install. As with anything new, give yourself a chance to practice. Remind yourself it's OK to make some mistakes. Base molding is easier to install than crown molding, and thankfully, it's more common. You need base molding to give a room a finished look, while crown molding acts as a decorative detail.

I must admit, even after years of doing professional carpentry work, I still cringe when a project calls for crown molding. It's tricky to get it right. Get comfortable with cutting and installing base molding first. Move on to crown molding if you like, but only if the design style of the room really calls for it.

Here are a few helpful tips for installing base molding:

- **For accuracy,** hold a piece of molding in place and mark it with a pencil.
- **Start on a short wall.** Most likely you'll only need one strip of molding. Cut each end at a 45-degree angle or use a coped joint to join with the molding on the adjacent walls.
- **Avoid splitting trim ends.** Drill pilot holes through the trim when using nails within 3 inches of the end.
- **Don't use too many nails.** Use only as many nails as necessary to hold the trim flush against the wall.
- **Sand and stain molding** or prime it before installing. Paint molding after it's installed; the paint will cover the joints and nail holes.

2

Section Two: Floors

Carpentry—center stage

When I started my degree work at Penn State University, the floor I dreamed about working on was center stage, and my dream was to perform. Now, as a professional carpenter, when I work on floors, I'm fixing or constructing them. So how did I go from having visions of center stage performances to the life I love, doing carpentry work?

Well, one of the requirements of the Penn State theater program is to take classes in all aspects of theater production. My first semester I took a basic carpentry class, and I was hooked. From the first cut of the blade, I loved it and knew immediately that my dreams had changed. Carpentry gives me the opportunity to be creative, just as someone performing on stage. I especially like being able to see physical evidence of a hard day's work.

Much of the repair work covered in this book is designed to keep your home operating smoothly and safely. You'll have the long-lasting satisfaction of knowing that you handled those repairs yourself. You'll also develop the confidence to tackle more difficult projects and save a lot of money by doing the work yourself.

replacing a broken floor tile

You don't have to live with a cracked or broken floor tile. With a little muscle and patience you can remove the old tile and replace it.

TOOLS AND MATERIALS:
- Safety glasses
- Heavy-duty gloves
- Cold chisel
- Putty knife
- Grout
- Tile adhesive
- Hammer
- Beater block

WYNN TIP:
Apply masking tape to adjacent tiles to protect them from damage.

Step 1. Be sure to wear safety glasses and heavy-duty gloves when removing old tile.

1 If the tile doesn't simply pop out, break its connection to adjacent tiles by sawing through the grout joints. With a hammer, tap the damaged tile to crack it into smaller pieces. Don't hit too hard; you could damage the substrate or shake other tiles loose. Use a cold chisel with the hammer to chip away the pieces. Be sure to wear eye protection.

2 Use a putty knife or margin trowel to scrape away all of the old adhesive. Remove any remaining grout from the joints. Create a smooth, clean surface for the new tile.

3 Use the same adhesive used on the original installation. If you don't know what it was, use an adhesive recommended by an expert at your local home center or tiling store. Spread a thin coat of the adhesive over the entire back of the replacement tile. Spread another coat on the setting bed. Press the tile into place, giving it a gentle twist. Use a beater block and hammer to set the tile flush with the surrounding tile. Wait one or two days before grouting, then wait several more days and seal the grout.

Step 3. Cover as much of the surface with adhesive as possible to ensure a good seal.

WYNN TIP:
Examine the substrate beneath the tile. If damaged, repair it. This may require removing more tiles. Creating a solid base will help avoid future repairs in the same area.

silencing floor squeaks

You've finished watching *Late Night*, and you're creeping down the hall so as not to wake the kids. SQUEAK … that floorboard creaked again and now everyone is awake. Next weekend take a few simple measures to silence those floorboards so everyone can sleep better.

TOOLS AND MATERIALS:

- **Drill and drill bits**
- **Hammer**
- **Nail set**
- **Ringshank nails or finish screws**
- **1¼-inch roundhead screws**
- **Shims**
- **Carpentry glue**
- **Wood putty**
- **Washer**

Step 1. Silence a loose board by driving fasteners at 45-degree angles.

Shims. Shore up a loose subfloor by driving a shim between it and the joist.

SQUEAK FROM ABOVE

1 Drill pilot holes in the loose board at 45-degree angles as shown below.

2 Drive ringshank nails or finish screws into the pilot holes. The fasteners should be long enough to extend through the floorboard and solidly into the subfloor.

3 Sink the fastener heads below the surface and fill with wood putty.

SQUEAK FROM BELOW

Shims

If one subfloor board is loose, dip the tip of a tapered shim into carpentry glue and tap the shim between the joist and the loose subfloor board. Keep tapping the shim until snug.

Cleats

1 If a series of subfloor boards is loose, cut a 2×4 to span the length of the loose boards.

2 Force the 2×4 against the subfloor using a long board as a temporary prop.

3 Nail or screw the 2×4 to the joist. Repeat on the other side of the joist.

Screws

1 If the finished floorboards are loose and causing the squeak, use a 1¼-inch roundhead screw to pull the board tight against the subfloor. Drill pilot holes first, being careful not to drill through the finished floorboards. If you do, fill the hole with wood putty on the finished side.

2 Place a washer over the screw so the screw won't pull through the subfloor. Tighten the screw, pulling the finished board tight.

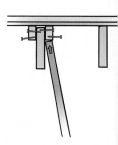

Cleats. Cleats provide additional support to span a length of loose boards.

Screws. A screw through the subfloor draws down a loose board to fit snug.

Bridging between joists

1 Drive new longer nails or screws through the bridging into the joist at an angle.

2 If the squeaks continue, install steel bridging. Push it tight against the subfloor. Drive a nail through the bottom to the inside of the joists.

TIME TO CALL IN A PRO?

If your floor has a noticeable sag, it probably requires an additional support. A jack post anchored on a new concrete pad will fix the problem.

A section of the existing basement floor will need to be broken and a pad poured for the new jack post. After the concrete pad has cured, position an adjustable jack on the pad with beams spanning several joists on top of the jack. Jack up the beam until it is snug against the joist, then raise it slightly higher.

Each week raise the jack a quarter turn until the sag is gone. Trying to eliminate the sag too quickly can cause structural damage.

This process can be accomplished by a do-it-yourselfer, so tackle the job if you choose. But if it seems overwhelming, call in the pros.

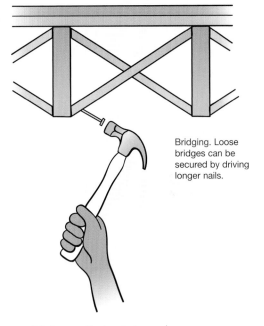

Bridging. Loose bridges can be secured by driving longer nails.

WYNN TIP:

Avoid splitting wood when hammering nails near the end of the bridging. Drill pilot holes to assist with guiding the nails and minimize the chance of them bending while you're driving them.

silencing stair squeaks from below

It's best to make stair repairs from underneath the stairs. The fixes tend to be stronger, more durable, and less visible than those made from above. The problem, of course, is getting underneath, and that may not be possible. If that's the case, check the solutions on the opposite page.

TOOLS AND MATERIALS:
- Drill
- Hammer
- Screwdriver
- Utility knife
- 2×2 hardwood
- Wood screws
- Angle brackets
- Hardwood wedges
- Wood glue

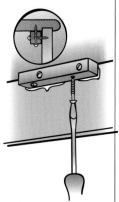

Step 4. Draw down a loose riser or tread by pulling it back with a screw from beneath.

IF A SMALL PORTION OF A TREAD OR RISER IS LOOSE

1 Cut 2×2 oak, birch, or other hardwood approximately 4 inches long.

2 Drill four pilot holes, two in the bottom and two on the side. Space the holes so they don't intersect.

3 Apply wood glue to the back and side of the block (the sides without holes). Press the block firmly into place where a tread and riser need support.

4 Select wood screws that extend through the 2×2 block and into the tread and riser, but not so long they poke the surface of the tread. Drive in the screws.

IF THE ENTIRE TREAD IS LOOSE

1 Position two or three angle brackets across the length of the tread where the tread and riser meet. Use large brackets to support the entire tread.

2 Mark for screws and drill pilot holes. Select wood screws that will not poke through the surface of the tread. Drive the screws to secure the brackets.

IF WEDGES ARE LOOSE

Remove any loose wedges. If the wedges are in good shape, apply wood glue to them and hammer back into place until tight. If the old wedges are damaged, use new hardwood wedges.

Replace old, worn wedges with new ones to repair squeaky stairs.

WYNN TIP:

Install metal brackets to the underside of treads to silence squeaks. Make sure you use screws shorter than the depth of the tread. The screws draw the tread tight to the riser, taking care of that annoying squeak.

silencing stair squeaks from above

Stair squeaks usually result from a loose tread rubbing against a riser or a stringer. Finding the culprit is probably not a problem; you usually know exactly which tread squeaks. If not, rock back and forth on each tread until you find the one that chirps.

TOOLS AND MATERIALS:
- Hammer
- Pry bar
- Drill
- Utility knife or chisel
- Screwdriver bit
- Nail set
- Wood putty
- Nails and screws
- Hardwood wedges
- Glue
- Paint or stain
- Molding
- Sandpaper

Step 2. Silence loose treads by fastening at opposing angles.

IF THE FRONT OF THE TREAD IS LOOSE

1 Drill pilot holes at opposing angles at the front of the loose tread. This obviously leaves small holes, so decide if you'll be more annoyed by the squeak or holes.

2 Drive in ringshank flooring nails or trim-head wood screws. Countersink the fastener heads and fill with wood putty.

IF THE BACK OF THE TREAD IS LOOSE

1 Coat hardwood wedges (not softwood shims) with glue and tap into place with a hammer. Let dry according to the glue manufacturer's instructions.

2 Cut off exposed wedge ends with a utility knife or a chisel, taking care to cut away from yourself.

3 Finish the exposed wood with the same paint or stain as the rest of the stair.

ADD MOLDING

1 Measure the width of the treads. Mark and cut ¾-inch quarter-round molding to length. For a uniform appearance, cut molding for each step, not just the one with the offending squeak.

2 Apply glue to the molding. Position the molding where the riser and tread meet.

3 Drill pilot holes. Then drive finish nails into both the riser and the tread. Use a nail set to sink the nail heads. Repeat for each step.

4 Fill with wood putty. Allow the filler to dry. Sand and finish to blend with the surrounding area.

Step 3. Adding molding provides additional strength to silence treads and risers.

WYNN TIP:
If you've noticed an annoying squeak just as you're getting ready to host guests, squirt powdered graphite into the joints. Wipe away any excess. Be forewarned that this is only a temporary fix. After everyone's left, follow the repair steps on this page for a permanent solution.

tightening rails and balusters

Wobbly handrails and loose balusters present more than an annoyance. They can easily become safety issues, particularly if you have young children or household members who rely heavily on the railing for support. Assess and repair the railing as soon as you notice a problem.

TOOLS AND MATERIALS:
- **Drill**
- **Screwdriver**
- **Hammer**
- **Miter box and saw**
- **T-bevel**
- **Utility knife**
- **Wood putty**
- **Trim-head screws**
- **Finish nails**
- **2×2 hardwood**

IF A SINGLE BALUSTER IS LOOSE

1 Drill a pilot hole at an angle through the baluster into the railing. Countersink a trim-head screw in the hole.

2 Drill another pilot hole at an angle through the baluster into the tread. Countersink a trim-head screw in the hole to secure the bottom of the baluster. Fill the hole with wood putty.

3 Measure the length between two balusters. Cut the piece to length. Next cut an angle at the other end for a snug fit.

4 Continue cutting enough blocking pieces to fit between each pair of balusters.

5 Drill pilot holes through the blocking and into the handrail. Apply wood glue to the holes and drive finish nails or trim-head screws.

Step 5. Blocking between balusters, secured to the handrail, gives stability to a loose handrail.

IF THE ENTIRE HANDRAIL IS LOOSE FROM THE BALUSTERS

1 Use a T-bevel to measure the angle between the handrail and each baluster. Transfer the angle to a power miter saw.

2 Double-check the angle before cutting. Miter cut one end of a piece of 2×2 hardwood to the measured angle.

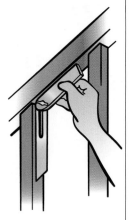

Step 1. Measure the cut angle of a baluster using a T-bevel.

WYNN TIP:
Occasionally the bracket attaching a handrail to the wall becomes loose. Determine whether tightening a screw will secure it to the wall. If not, the supports may be compromised, and they will need to be reattached. Wall-mounted handrail supports must be anchored to studs in the wall. Loose railings can be the result of supports that don't anchor into the studs. If this appears to be the case, remove the support brackets and fill the existing holes. Locate a stud at each end of the handrail and drill pilot holes into the studs. Attach the supports in the new locations.

Plan to fix problem spots

Keeping your home in good repair is important, as a recent incident at my house reminded me.

One of the stair railings in my home was loose. I knew it, but I just didn't take the time to fix it—until it caused a minor accident. My mom was visiting and leaned on the railing. It gave way, and down she went. Fortunately she wasn't hurt. The fall wasn't more than a couple of steps, but it was an embarrassing reminder of how critical it is to fix problems as soon as you notice them.

If you've been lax about fixing small problems, grab a pad of paper and pencil. Tour your home. Jot down all of the problems—big and small. Include the annoying, the unsightly, and especially anything creating potential safety issues. Depending on your schedule and the length of your list, block out a whole day, a weekend, or an hour each day until you have everything crossed off your list.

repairing a floorboard

Hardwood floors are beautiful, and if installed properly and maintained well, they should last the life of your home. Sometimes, though, individual boards become damaged. Avoid the expense of replacing the entire floor by replacing the damaged board.

TOOLS AND MATERIALS:
- Drill with spade bit
- Hammer
- Chisel
- Claw hammer
- Pry bar
- Circular saw
- Rubber mallet
- Steel wool
- Solvent
- Sandpaper
- Wood filler
- Scrap wood
- Adhesive

TO REMOVE SCRATCHES
Using steel wool and a solvent, such as mineral spirits, rub with the grain. Rinse, and refinish with wood finish.

TO FILL IN DEEP CUTS
Sand with the grain and work in wood filler with a brush. Let the filler set overnight. Sand with the grain and refinish with wood finish.

TO REPLACE A DAMAGED FLOORBOARD

1 Using a spade or Forstner bit, bore several holes across the width of the damaged board at the ends and in the middle. Take care to drill only through the flooring board; don't go through the subfloor as well (you will do some damage to the subfloor).

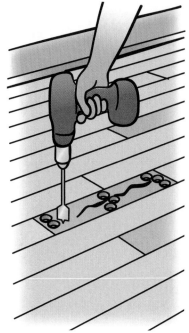

Step 1. Prep a damaged board for removal by boring it.

2 Use a wood chisel to split the board lengthwise between the drilled holes. Tap the chisel with the hammer, driving it into the wood.

3 Slip a flat pry bar into the split. Place a scrap of wood under the bar to protect the good flooring. Pry out the split pieces from the middle and then pry out the rest of the board. Remove any slivers left under the tongue of the adjacent board.

WYNN TIP:
Matching new tongue-and-groove flooring to old can be difficult. If you find the right size and type, the new strips have to be sanded and stained to match the existing floor. The solution is to find existing pieces from elsewhere in the house. Pry out boards from a closet or from under carpeting. Allow for the waste from drilling and cutting. Fill the resulting voids with plywood.

4 Using a claw hammer, pull out all the old nails remaining in the subfloor. Use a scrap of wood to protect the good flooring.

5 Cut the new board to length. The piece should fit snug but not too tight.

6 Prepare the replacement board by turning it over and cutting or chiseling away the shoulder of the groove. Removing this allows you to slip it into place.

Step 6. Remove the lower shoulder of the replacement board's groove so it slips easily into place.

Step 3. Splinter the damaged board and remove all pieces.

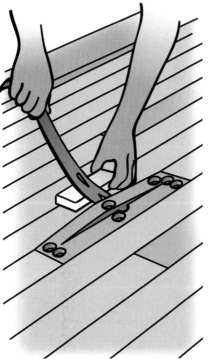

7 Test-fit the replacement piece. Recut it if necessary, or sand it if you are really close.

8 Apply flooring adhesive to the subfloor and the tongue and half-groove of the replacement board. Tap it into place with a rubber mallet. If using a hammer, use a scrap of wood to protect the flooring surface as you tap.

WYNN TIP:
If you have more than one damaged floorboard and you're not certain of the cause, take the time to investigate. If boards have tunnels running through them, termites or carpenter ants are the likely culprits. Call an exterminator. If more than a few boards are cracked, the subflooring may be weak. See pages 106–107.

refinishing a wood floor

A great feature of a hardwood floor is it can be sanded and refinished when it begins to show too much wear. I'll admit, this task is certainly not my first choice of how to spend a weekend—it's tough, messy work. But I think you'll find the result worth it. Choose a day when you can open the doors and windows to let out the dust, and be sure to wear a mask rated to filter fine particles.

TOOLS AND MATERIALS:
- Hammer
- Nail set
- Drum or random-orbital sander
- Disc-type edge sander
- Paint scraper or chisel
- Vacuum
- Tack cloth
- Putty knife
- Paintbrush or wax applicator
- Pry bar
- Sandpaper
- Wood filler
- Polyurethane finish
- Painter's tape

Step 2. Place a board between the molding and pry bar to protect the molding.

1 Remove all accessories and furnishings from the room. Seal off interior entrances to the room and vents with plastic secured by painter's tape. Sanding produces a fine dust that works its way throughout your home.

2 Pry off the baseboard shoe molding—the piece at the very bottom—and the baseboard. If there is no shoe, remove the baseboard. If the molding is in good condition and you plan to reuse it, number the pieces on the back so you can easily reinstall. Otherwise plan to install new molding. See page 102 to install base molding.

3 Use a nail set to drive popped nails below the surface—protruding metal will quickly tear a sanding disc or belt.

4 Plan the sanding pattern. Different situations call for different sanding techniques. Most floors require three

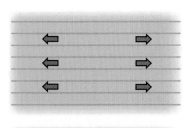

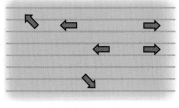

Step 4. Sanding patterns follow the grain unless a diagonal pass is required for cupped or warped boards.

WYNN TIP:
Never sand across the grain with a drum sander. You'll create scratches.

sandpaper grits—rough, then medium, and finally fine—each time sanding with the grain. Be aware that several passes with each grit may be required. Badly cupped or warped old

WYNN TIP:
Using a drum sander requires concentration and smooth movements. Ask for a demonstration and practice session at the rental center before you take the sander home. Always keep the sander moving to prevent it from digging into the floor.

floors may require four passes—two diagonal passes—the first with rough grit and the second with medium grit—then two passes with the grain—the first with medium grit and the last with fine grit. Always overlap with each pass.

5 Make the first cut with rough-grit sandpaper. Use rough grit until bare wood is reached. When you reach the bare wood most of the scratches have disappeared.

6 Vacuum the floor thoroughly after each sanding pass. Assess your progress. If you seem to be getting nowhere sanding with the grain, try one diagonal pass, but never sand directly across the grain.

7 Use medium- and fine-grit sandpaper for the next two cuts. At each stage, expect to use several sheets of sandpaper.

8 Use an edge sander for hard-to-reach areas. Work slowly. Finish with a very fine-grade sandpaper so the circular lines will not be visible. In corners the sander cannot reach, use a sharp paint scraper or chisel, always working with the grain. Don't worry if the corners don't look quite as good as the rest of the floor. Once the furnishings are repositioned, it will not be as noticeable.

9 Vacuum the floor thoroughly to prepare for the finish. Use a tack cloth after the last vacuuming to pick up remaining dust.

10 Fill all holes and gaps between the boards using paste wood filler. Apply it with a putty knife. Remember, always work with the grain. When the filler begins to set, wipe across the grain with an old rag to remove excess. Let the filler dry overnight.

11 Apply two to four coats of polyurethane finish with a brush or a wax applicator, sanding with fine sandpaper between coats. Use a tack cloth to pick up dust between coats. Do not apply wax over a polyurethane finish.

Step 8. Work slowly with an edge sander in hard-to-reach places.

WYNN TIP:
If your floor is free from deep scratches, try a random-orbital sander instead of a drum sander. Its action reduces scratches; you don't have to follow the grain of the wood and are less apt to damage the floor.

repairing vinyl flooring

You probably don't pay too much attention to your floors—until there's a problem. Some damage is repairable and well within the skills of a homeowner. In the case of damaged sheet flooring, you can cut out the offensive spot and install a patch. Take time to carefully match the pattern of the patch to the surrounding area, and once you're finished, you'll hardly notice it.

TOOLS AND MATERIALS:
- Utility knife
- Framing square
- Putty knife
- Adhesive spreader
- Adhesive
- Plywood
- Iron
- Towel
- Pencil
- Scrap plywood
- Floor wax
- Seam-welding product

1 Use a framing square to mark and cut around the damaged area. Cut with a utility knife. If your floor has a distinct pattern with lines or borders, consider cutting a slightly larger area so you can follow the lines. This makes easy work of matching the pattern with the patch.

2 If the entire floor has been laid in adhesive, work a putty knife underneath and peel up the damaged piece. You may need to apply heat with a medium-hot iron to loosen the damaged area. If so, lay a towel on top of the flooring before applying the iron. Some newer types of flooring designed especially for do-it-yourself installation require adhesive only at seams and edges. In this case,

it will be easy to lift out the damaged area.

3 Lay the cutout on a piece of matching material so the pattern lines up precisely. Use a pencil or felt-tipped pen to trace around it. Accuracy is essential for a good fit.

4 Either leave the cutout in place as a template or use a framing square as a guide to cut along the traced lines. Place a scrap of plywood under the patching material to prevent damaging the floor.

5 Clean the underlayment. Remove all of the adhesive. Test-fit the patch. If it is too large, sand the edges. Patches that are too small will have to be tossed and a new patch made.

6 If the area around the patch is not set in adhesive, lift up the edges and apply adhesive around the perimeter. Apply adhesive to the patch with a

Step 1. Cut along the pattern. It will be easier to match.

WYNN TIP:
Though you don't want to clutter up your house by saving everything, it is a good idea to save some leftover materials from most any home improvement project—excess flooring, paint, wallpaper, bricks, siding. Designate a small storage area to keep all of the items together so when you need patching material for a repair, you'll know where to find it.

serrated spreader or a brush. Align one edge, matching the pattern of the existing flooring, and lower the new section into place. Wipe off adhesive that has oozed out from the edges.

7 Weight down the patch evenly with a piece of plywood that completely covers the patch and some of the surrounding area. Set heavy books or bricks on top of the plywood and leave the weight for at least 24 hours.

SCRATCHES

Fill shallow scratches with floor wax or acrylic finish. The scratches often seem to disappear. For deeper cuts, compress the edges of the torn flooring by dragging a worn coin along—not across—the cuts.

TEARS

1 Lift the edges of the tear and scrape away any old adhesive. Work until you remove all of the existing adhesive.

2 Apply fresh adhesive and press the edges down so they stick. For the repair to lie flat, you may need to sand one edge.

3 Place a weight on the repaired area for 24 hours.

BLISTERS

Make a clean cut through the center of the blister. Alternating edges, press down on one edge of the cut and work adhesive underneath the other edge. Apply weight to the area for 24 hours.

HOLES

Fixing small holes actually requires the most specialized materials. Check with the flooring manufacturer for a special seam-welding product that dissolves the vinyl, then sets up again to complete the repair.

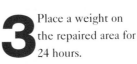
Step 5. Clean the underlayment to eliminate bumps and debris.

Amy Wynn Pastor

From: Ayoungfan@anyplace.usa
Sent: Tuesday, October 2, 2003 4:12PM
To: Amy Wynn Pastor
Subject: Halloween Costume

One of my most exciting moments as a TV carpenter came via an e-mail. The mother of a four-year-old sent an e-mail to tell me about her daughter's choice for her Halloween costume. The girl wanted to be a Powerpuff Girl. Her mom was working on making her costume when the girl burst into the room. "Stop, Mom," she said. "I know what I really want to be for Halloween. I want to be Amy Wynn the Carpenter." It meant so much to me that this little girl thought it was cool to be a female carpenter. I just hope it helped her realize that she can be anything she puts her mind to be.

wynn insight

repairing carpet

Wall-to-wall pile carpeting or machine-made area rugs can be repaired with relative ease. Handmade or Oriental rugs, however, require special care and should be taken to a professional.

TOOLS AND MATERIALS:
- Hammer
- Putty knife
- Utility knife
- Double-sided tape
- Seam cement
- Nails
- Vacuum
- Seam tape
- Clean can lid
- Iron
- Towel
- Board
- Heavy book or brick
- Instant glue
- Coin

Step 1. Tacking a template over damaged carpet ensures an even cut.

PATCH DAMAGED CARPET

1 Partially nail a clean can lid or other template over the damaged area. Leave the heads of the nails projecting so they can be easily removed later.

2 Using the lid as a guide, cut through the carpet with a sharp utility knife.

3 Repeat Steps 1 and 2 on a piece of scrap carpet to make a matching patch.

4 Remove and vacuum up loose fibers. Slip double-sided tape halfway under the cutout edges of the old carpet. Apply a thin ribbon of seam cement to the edge of the carpet patch.

5 Press the patch into place. Weight the patch down overnight with a board. Place a heavy object such as a book or a brick on the board for additional pressure. This will ensure a good seal.

SECURE A LOOSE CARPET EDGE

Press it back into place with a putty knife. Tap it with a hammer to secure it to the tack strip along the perimeter of the room.

REPAIR A TEAR OR SLICE

Pull back the carpet to reveal the underside. Apply seam tape. Lay down a towel and heat the area with a warm iron.

LIFT AN INDENTATION AFTER YOU MOVE FURNITURE

Lay a damp towel over the area. Press with a heated iron for a few seconds. Lift up the towel and rub the indentation with the edge of a coin. Repeat if necessary.

PATCH A SMALL HOLE

Cut a replacement section of pile. Attach it to the padding or flooring using instant glue.

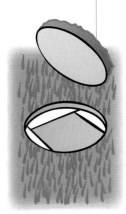

Step 4. Double-sided tape holds the patch, giving the seam cement a chance to dry.

WYNN TIP:
Burned spots in shag or dense carpets can be fixed provided the burn is not too deep. Use a razor blade to carefully shave off the melted ends of the carpet. Remove as little of the area as possible until you're satisfied with the look.

patching resilient tile

Since each resilient tile covers only a small area, it's easier to remove and replace an entire tile if one becomes damaged. When you install new resilient tile, order a few extra to keep on hand for this purpose.

TOOLS AND MATERIALS:
- **Putty knife**
- **Straightedge**
- **Utility knife**
- **Sanding block**
- **Clothes iron**
- **Adhesive applicator**
- **Towel**
- **Cloth**
- **Adhesive**
- **Tile mastic**
- **Floor wax**
- **Mild detergent**
- **Plywood piece**
- **Weight**

STAYING SAFE

Some older resilient floor tiles contain asbestos, a health hazard. Tiles containing asbestos were used in many building products until the 1970s. Asbestos materials that are in good shape and are undisturbed do not cause problems, so leave them alone. If, however, your floor is damaged, a pro will need to either properly repair or remove the material. If you suspect your resilient floor tiles are more than 20 years old, call in a pro to evaluate the material before tackling this repair job.

PATCH A DAMAGED TILE

1 Lay a towel on top and soften the tile with a medium-hot iron. Take care that the iron doesn't overlap onto adjacent tiles.

2 While the tile is hot, slip a putty knife under a corner and pry it up. Make sure not to pry against the surrounding tiles.

3 Use a putty knife or a paint scraper to remove all the adhesive from the underlayment. If it does not come up, try heating the area with a heat gun or hair dryer. You may need to sand away the last remnants of adhesive. Take particular care to remove adhesive from the perimeter of the patch.

4 Be sure the new tile will fit and lie flat. If the tile is slightly large and you have to force it in, use a sanding block, plane, or utility knife to shave one or two sides until it fits properly.

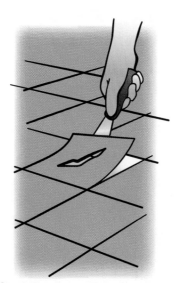
Step 2. Warming the tile releases the adhesive grip, making replacement easy.

5 Apply adhesive to the underlayment with an applicator, a notched trowel, or a brush. Check the adhesive manufacturer's instructions before purchasing it to make sure it will work for your project. With some types of adhesive, you must wait until the adhesive has dried to a tacky feel before setting the tile. With other types, the tile should be set while the adhesive is wet.

6 Protect the new tile's surface with a cloth. Use the iron to soften the tile and make it more flexible.

7 Set—do not slide—the new tile into position. Wipe away any squeezed-out adhesive using a cloth dampened with water or mineral spirits, depending on the type of adhesive.

8 Weight down the patch evenly with a piece of plywood that completely covers the patch and some of the surrounding area. Set heavy books or bricks on top of the plywood and leave the weight on for at least 24 hours.

SECURE A LIFTED TILE

Surface-printed tiles are often made to be self-sticking. Be aware that self-sticking adhesive may not be very strong. Use tile mastic to enhance sticking power when replacing damaged tiles. Mastic also works well to secure an existing tile that has lifted.

FILL SCRATCHES

Fill shallow scratches with floor wax or acrylic finish. That may hide them.

REMOVE STAINS AND MINOR BURNS

Commercial tile has flecks of color that run completely through the tile, making it fairly easy to remove surface problems. Rub stains with a mild detergent solution. If that doesn't work, try a white appliance wax. As a last resort, scour stains with very fine steel wool and a household cleanser. Scouring will also remove minor burns.

Step 5. Adhesives vary, so read the instructions before using them.

WYNN TIP:
Wax on older floors tends to yellow in exposed areas over time. Installing a patch from a hidden area will stand out because of this. Discolored wax can be removed with a commercial-strength wax remover. Clean the floor to a uniform color before repairing, and the patch should blend with the surrounding floor.

solving basement water problems

Basement leaks not only make life miserable, they can also weaken the foundation of your home. Before attempting to fix the leak, you need to determine what is causing the problem. Check the chart on the opposite page.

TOOLS AND MATERIALS:
- Cold chisel
- Hammer
- Brush
- Protective gear
- Bucket
- Cleaning materials
- Garden hose
- Downspout extensions
- Cement mix
- Cement-based sealer

IF THE WALLS LEAK ONLY DURING HEAVY RAINS

1 Add extensions to your gutter downspouts to direct rainwater away from the basement walls.

2 Check the slope of your yard. If the slope is toward the basement, it rainwater will flow toward your home. Build up the area next to the exterior walls to correct the slope so that water will run away from the foundation.

FOR SLOW SEEPAGE OR DAMP WALLS

1 Clean away dirt, grease, and dust from the wall with spray cleaner to prepare the surface for a sealer.

2 If there are any large cracks or holes, follow the steps for plugging cracks and holes that follow before proceeding to Step 3.

3 Wet the wall thoroughly with a fine mist from a garden hose or sprayer.

4 Thoroughly mix the liquid and powder components of a cement-based sealer. Apply the sealer with a stiff brush.

Step 4. Make sure to completely cover the surface with sealer.

5 As you brush, be sure to fill in all the pores in the wall. Go over cracks several times to fill them.

FILL LARGE CRACKS AND HOLES

1 Put on protective eye and ear wear. Also wear heavy work gloves. Enlarge the hole or crack with a cold chisel and hammer. Undercut to make a "key" so that the plug won't come loose. Make the hole at least ½ inch deep. Remove all fragments of concrete.

2 In a bucket, add water to the dry hydraulic cement mix until it has a puttylike consistency. Then work it by hand. For a hole, roll it into the shape of a plug. Roll a long snake shape for a crack.

3 Squeeze the cement into the opening. Keep pushing and pushing to make sure it fills every tiny crevice. Any water leaking through the wall at the time of the repair should stop running. Hold the cement in place for several minutes to allow the patch to set.

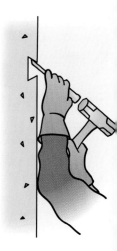
Step 1. Wear safety gear, including eye protection, when chipping away concrete.

Step 3. Force in enough cement to completely fill the crack and stop water from seeping in.

wet basement solutions

WYNN TIP:
You can remedy many wet basement problems by addressing the source of the problem—which may be outside. Water from downspouts, for example, may be seeping into the ground near the foundation. Install extensions that will carry the water away from the house. Also make sure the ground slopes away from the foundation, not toward it.

PROBLEM	SYMPTOMS	TEST	POSSIBLE CAUSES	SOLUTIONS
Condensation	Damp walls, dripping pipes, rusty hardware, mildew	Tape a mirror in the dampest spot. If the mirror is foggy or beaded with water 24 hours later, suspect condensation.	Excess humidity	Install a dehumidifier to draw the humidity out of the air in damp basements.
Seepage	Dampness on a section of a wall or floor	Tape a mirror to the wall. If moisture condenses behind it, suspect seepage.	Water forcing through pores in foundation or expansion joint; leaky window well; poor drainage outside	Improve exterior drainage. If the problem is minor, apply an interior sealer. If major, waterproof the outside of the foundation.
Leaks	Localized wetness that seems to be trickling from wall	Run a garden hose outside near the suspected leak.	Cracks; poor drainage outside	Plug any cracks or holes. Improve exterior drainage to minimize future leaks. For widespread leakage, waterproof the foundation.
Subterranean water	Thin, barely noticeable film of water on basement floor	Lay down plastic sheeting on the basement floor. Leave it for two days. If concrete underneath becomes damp, suspect subterranean water.	Water from below being forced up under high pressure	Install a sump pump. Installing drainage tile around the perimeter of the foundation may help, but only if water drains to a low spot or a storm sewer.

3

Section Three: Doors and Windows

An open and shut case

Windows and doors are a major investment. Certainly it makes sense to maintain them on a seasonal basis, rather than deal with the costly expense of replacing them. I recommend that you schedule a day on your planner, PDA, or calendar for window maintenance. I know, your schedule is already packed, and thanks to my advice in this book, you've already added several home repair and maintenance projects. Finding a bit more time for door and window maintenance and repair might be a squeeze, but it's worth it. Stick to your commitment, and your doors and windows will last beyond their normal life span, which will save you a good bit of money. Not a bad deal, right?

wynn insight

replacing a screen

Installing screening requires patience, but it's not difficult. The process is similar to how an artist stretches a canvas. Fasten the screening at one end of the frame, pull the material taut, then secure it at the sides and the opposite end.

TOOLS AND MATERIALS:
- Shears or scissors
- Utility knife
- Staple gun
- Saw
- Spline roller
- Splining
- Nails
- Hammer
- Tape measure
- Screening

WYNN TIP:
With wood frames, pry screen moldings loose with a putty knife. Work from the center to the ends, applying leverage near the nails. Should you accidentally break the molding, just replace it.

Wood frames. The wedges provide the tension while you staple so you don't need an extra set of hands.

WORKING WITH WOOD FRAMES

1 With shears, cut the screening a few inches wider and at least 1 foot longer than the frame.

2 Position the screening so it completely covers the frame. Staple the top edge of the screen to the frame.

3 Nail a strip of scrap wood to your workbench. Place bottom edge of frame beside the scrap. Roll the screen over the scrap, and nail another strip on top of the first.

4 Rip-cut two wedges and insert them between the cleats and frame as shown below. Tap the wedges until the screening is tight. Staple the screening to the bottom edge of the frame, then to the sides.

5 Trim the excess and refit the screen moldings.

WORKING WITH ALUMINUM FRAMES

1 Remove the old screen by prying out the spline (the thin vinyl cord fitted in the groove). You may need to buy new splining.

2 Square up the frame, lay new screening over it, and cut it the same size as the outside of the frame.

3 Bend the screening edges and force them into the channel with the convex wheel of the spline roller.

4 Force the tubular spline into the channel with the concave wheel of the spline roller, tightening the screening.

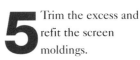
spline

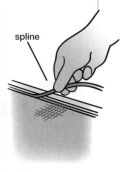
Aluminum frames. The spline is typically one continuous rope and should pull out easily.

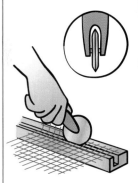
Step 3. A spline roller quickly seats the spline into an aluminum frame.

WYNN TIP:
Standard aluminum screen is less expensive but is subject to staining; silver-gray or charcoal aluminum is easier to maintain. Fiberglass won't stain, but its filaments are thicker, which reduces visibility.

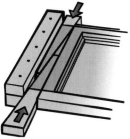
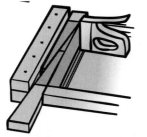

replacing a broken windowpane

Broken windowpanes just seem to haunt some people, whether the result of a foul ball during a backyard baseball game or catching a 2×4 in the workshop door. Single-pane glass can be removed and replaced with new in about 30 minutes to an hour. If the glass happens to be double- or triple-pane, contact a professional rather than tackle the job yourself.

TOOLS AND MATERIALS:
- **Putty knife**
- **Scraper**
- **Caulking gun**
- **Paintbrush**
- **Heat gun**
- **Tape measure**
- **Glass pane**
- **Heavy gloves**
- **Safety glasses**
- **Glazier's points**
- **Caulk or glazing compound**
- **Linseed oil**
- **Turpentine**

1 Put on your safety gear, including heavy gloves, long-sleeve clothing, and safety glasses.

2 Carefully pull out all the pieces of the broken pane. Place them in a sturdy trash receptacle.

3 Use a putty knife or old chisel to remove all old glazing compound from the frame. If glazing remains, soften it with a heat gun, then remove. Make sure the frame is clear of all old glazing.

4 Pull out all the old glazier's points. These are small metal triangles that help hold the pane in place.

5 Use a scraper to roughen the groove in the sash so the new glazing compound will adhere properly.

6 Measure the sash at several points, since many aren't perfectly square. Subtract ⅛ inch from each dimension to determine the glass size. Take the measurements to a hardware store or glass retailer and have the glass cut.

7 Use a paintbrush to apply linseed oil, turpentine, or oil-based paint to the groove. This prevents the wood from drawing oil from the glazing compound and decreasing its holding power.

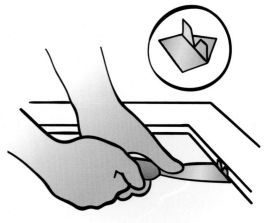

Step 4, 10. Glazier's points hold the glass securely in place.

8 Apply a ⅛-inch-thick bead of caulk or glazing compound to the groove around the entire perimeter. This helps seal and cushion the glass.

9 Line up one edge of the pane in the sash and lower it into place. Press gently with your palm around the edges to seal the pane into the glazing compound.

10 Gently press glazier's points into the sash every 12 inches around the perimeter of the pane. Don't press too hard or you may break the glass. You can use a putty knife to push in the points.

11 Apply glazing compound between the wood and glass around the perimeter of the pane.

12 Working in only one direction, draw a putty knife along the glazing compound. If the compound sticks to the knife, wet the knife with turpentine. If small ridges appear, lightly run your finger in the opposite direction to smooth the compound.

13 Let the compound dry for about a week. Once thoroughly dry, you can paint it.

Step 12. Work slowly when beveling the compound.

WYNN TIP:
Be careful! Always wear heavy gloves, long clothing, and protective eyewear when handling broken glass.

WYNN TIP:
If you have a double-hung window with a tension spring— a flat metal strap that attaches to a spring-loaded drum unit in the sash—finding a replacement may be difficult. A friction sash is made of vinyl or aluminum; it grabs the sash tightly enough that it does not slide down when raised.

replacing a sash cord

Old double-hung windows use sash weights and cords to assist in opening and closing the windows (see page 131). Each sash is connected to two weights that run through channels in each side of the window. A sash cord or chain is secured to the sash and runs through a pulley near the top of the jamb. Depending on the specific problem, you can repair the sash cord or replace it.

TOOLS AND MATERIALS:
- Putty knife
- Utility knife
- Screwdriver or drill
- Hammer
- Pry bar
- Nail or screw
- Sash chain

IF THE CORD HAS COME OUT OF ITS GROOVE

Simply force the cord back into position.

IF THE CORD HAS BECOME DETACHED

Reattach the cord with a short screw.

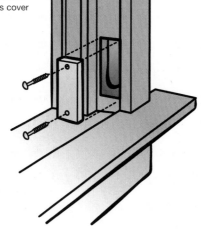

Step 5. The weights will be hidden behind either an access cover or the jamb.

IF THE CORD IS BROKEN

1 Usually you need to remove only one inside stop. Cut through the paint using a utility knife.

2 Using a putty knife, pry carefully at several points to loosen the stop. Remove the stop with a flat pry bar.

3 Lift the sash and swing it clear from the frame. One or both cords may still be connected. Take care that a cord does not come loose and suddenly fly upward.

4 Hang on to the cord and pull it out of the sash; you may need to pry out a nail or unscrew a screw. Be careful never to let go of the cord. Pull it out and slip a nail through the knot so that the cord cannot slip through the pulley.

5 There will most likely be an access cover at the base of the jamb; unscrew the fasteners holding the cover in place. Gently pry it out to reveal the weights.

WYNN TIP:
Replace broken cords with chains. A sash chain will last longer and will look better.

Step 7. Replacing sash chains is tedious work but worth the effort.

If there is no access cover, you may have to pry off the jamb.

6 Untie or cut the cord off of each weight and pull the weight out. Cut new cords or chains longer than they need to be.

7 Feed the new sash cords over the pulleys. You'll need a lot of patience! Even though it's tedious, replace the cords on both sides.

8 Once a new cord is visible through its access hole, tie a knot in the other end so it cannot slip

WYNN TIP:
Even if only one sash cord is broken, replace the cord on the other side of the sash as well. Otherwise it is likely to break soon and you'll have to repeat the whole process.

through the pulley. Tie the cord to the weight and tug to make sure the knot is secure. Slip the weight back in place.

9 Weights should hang 3 inches above the channel bottoms when the lower sash is raised fully. Once you have determined the correct length, knot the other end of the cord and fit it into the groove. Secure the cord with a short screw—don't drive the screw into the windowpane.

10 To replace the cords on an upper sash, you have to remove the lower sash, then one of the parting stops. Use the same techniques as for the lower sash.

11 When you replace stops, partially drive in longer nails. Raise and lower the sash to check the stop positioning; it should be fairly tight yet allow for smooth operation. Once you have the stop positioned correctly, finish driving the nails.

Step 8. Secure the weight to the new sash cord.

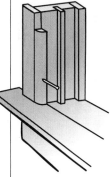

Step 11. Driving longer nails than the originals provides better gripping power.

freeing a stuck sash

When a double-hung window binds or refuses to open, don't force it. Yes, you're probably strong enough to do it, but you may damage the window. Instead, look around the sash. Chances are you will find that paint has sealed the sash shut or a stop molding has warped. The steps shown here will enable you to gently pry and free the sash, preventing damage.

TOOLS AND MATERIALS:
- **Sash knife or utility knife**
- **Flat pry bar**
- **Hammer**
- **Wood block**
- **Chisel**
- **Sandpaper**
- **Candle**
- **Nails**

1 Use a sash knife to break all paint seals. A sash knife is designed specifically for this purpose. If you don't have a sash knife, run a sharp utility knife several times between the sash and stop. Be sure to cut through the paint at every point.

2 Pry from the outside edges with a pry bar. Place a protective block of wood between the pry bar and the trim to protect it. Take your time, using gentle to moderate pressure at several points. Alternating sides, work inward from the edges until the sash pops free.

3 If a sash is binding between its stops—the vertical tracks along the sides of the windowpane—try separating the stops. Tap along their length with a hammer and wooden block that fits tightly between the stops. If the binding is severe, you may need to pry the stop off and nail it in a new position.

4 Once you get the window moving, scrape or chisel any built-up paint off the edges of the sash or between the stops.

5 Lightly sand the jambs; then lubricate with a candle or with paraffin, paste wax, or bar soap.

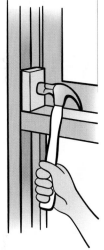

Step 3. Carefully tap a wooden block between tracks to loosen sashes.

WYNN TIP:
If the sash is painted shut, don't force it open. A little patience goes a long way. To open it, carefully push a 4- or 6-inch wide putty knife blade into the joint.

parting stop

blind stop

side jamb

sash weight pulleys

casing

light (windowpane)

lower sash weight

inside stop

top sash

rope to sash weight

bottom sash

stool

upper sash weight

sill

Anatomy of a double-hung window

apron

fixing spring lifts

In newer double-hung windows, spring lifts concealed in tubing assist in raising the sash. These can be adjusted or replaced if they are not working properly. Before bothering to adjust or replace the spring lift, however, check to make sure the window is not painted shut. If so, that's a much easier fix (see page 131).

TOOLS AND MATERIALS:
- Screwdriver or drill
- Utility knife
- Putty knife
- Replacement twist rod/tube unit

Adjust. A stubborn window or one that raises too easily can be fixed by adjusting the spring.

TO ADJUST THE SPRING LIFT

Grip the tube before you remove the screw holding it in place, or the spring will unwind in a hurry.

If the window sails up too easily, hold the screw and let the spring turn a couple of revolutions counterclockwise. If the window is hard to raise, tighten the spring by turning it clockwise. Adjust the lifts on both sides.

TO REPLACE A SPRING LIFT

1 Score the paint between the inside stop and the casing with a utility knife. Pry with a putty knife to remove the inside stop on one side of the sash.

2 Remove the screw that secures the spring lift tube, letting the spring unwind in a counterclockwise direction, then pull out the sash.

3 Remove and replace the twist rod/tube unit. Reinstall the sash. Adjust the tube according to the steps at left.

WYNN TIP:
Since you're working on your windows anyway, now is a good time to assess their safety. Do your windows lock? If not, see page 24. Also consider emergency evacuation: Can everyone open the windows quickly in case of fire? See pages 20–21 for more safety tips.

Step 1. Remove the inside stop using a utility or putty knife.

Step 3. Twist the tube to replace it.

fixing a casement window

Casements, like most windows, need a bit of basic maintenance to keep them operating smoothly. Clean off rust with steel wool and lubricate with graphite or paraffin wax; never use oil, as it attracts dust. Follow the steps below for repairs.

TOOLS AND MATERIALS:
- **Hammer**
- **Screwdriver**
- **Wire brush**
- **Graphite**
- **Towel**

sliding shoe

sill   metal channel

Step 2.
Apply lubricant to the track of a sill-mounted sliding shoe.

WYNN TIP:
If the removable cranks on your casement windows have a habit of disappearing thanks to inquisitive little helpers, contact the window supplier. It should have replacements available.

IF THE SASH IS DIFFICULT TO CLOSE

1 Clean the sliding arm mechanism with a wire brush to remove dirt, grease, and paint buildup. If the window is operated with a sill-mounted sliding shoe, unscrew the channel. Clean the channel and the sill.

2 Lubricate the mechanism with graphite or silicone. Graphite can be messy, so place a towel below where you are working.

3 Remove the handle from the crank. Lubricate the crank with graphite. Reattach the handle.

4 Check to see if the sash operates smoothly. If not, disconnect the slide arm from the sash, and then unscrew the operator from the frame.

5 If the gears are crusty, soak the mechanism in a solvent until a wire brush can remove the buildup. Then apply a multipurpose lubricant to the gears and reattach the operator and slide arm.

IF LATCH SCREWS ARE LOOSE

1 Use a screwdriver to tighten loose screws. If they won't tighten, remove the screws.

2 Tap slivers of wood into the screw holes. Drive the screws again.

IF THE LATCH WON'T PULL THE SASH SNUG

Remove the latch. Add a cardboard shim. Replace the latch above the shim.

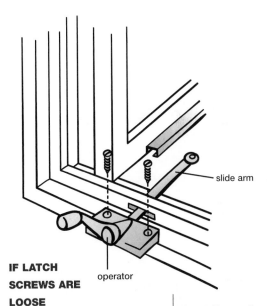

slide arm

operator

Step 4. Remove the operator to get at the gears inside.

repairing a sliding window

Tracks for sliding windows notoriously collect dust and grit, which make it tough to open and close. Routine maintenance will help you avoid costly repairs. Follow these steps to keep sliders in good shape.

TOOLS AND MATERIALS:
- **Hammer**
- **Screwdriver**
- **Large pliers**
- **Vacuum**
- **Silicone lubricant**
- **Wood block**

WYNN TIP:
Newer sliding windows typically have rollers for smooth opening and closing. If the rollers are defective, first check the manufacturer's and installer's warranties. Replacement may be covered.

1 Keep tracks clean with regular vacuuming. Scrub them with water and a mild detergent when grime starts to build up. Scrape away any paint that finds its way into the tracks.

2 To improve performance, spray the tracks with a silicone lubricant.

3 If despite these measures a slider jams, binds, or jumps loose, check if something is lodged in the track. If all seems clear, lift out the sash by partially opening the window, then lifting it up and pulling its lower edge toward you. The second sash may be fixed in place; you may need to remove hold-down hardware before it can be slid over and removed.

4 Check the grooved track edges. Clean and lubricate these too, if needed.

IF THE TRACK IS BENT

1 Cut a wood block to fit snugly in the channel. With a hammer, carefully tap the track against the wood block until it is back in shape.

2 If tapping with a hammer doesn't work, place a piece of metal on either side of the track and squeeze with a large pair of pliers.

IF THE LATCH WON'T CLOSE

1 Remove it. Clean with a brush and vacuum. Spray the latch with silicone lubricant. Check the strike where the latch attaches. Clean away any obstructions.

2 If the latch is broken, remove it. Take it to a home center or hardware store and purchase a replacement.

Step 1. Repair a bent track by inserting a wood block and tapping the track into shape.

fixing strike problems

Minor adjustments will solve most door problems. If a door won't latch or it rattles, the strike plate on the doorjamb probably doesn't align with the latch. Or, if you see scratches on the strikeplate, the latch is hitting the plate and missing the hole. You can fix these problems by repositioning the strikeplate.

TOOLS AND MATERIALS:
- **Screwdriver**
- **File**
- **Chisel**
- **Pencil**
- **Cardboard**

REPOSITION THE STRIKE

1 If the strikeplate is off only ⅛ inch or so, remove the strikeplate and enlarge its opening with a file. You may need to chisel away some wood when reinstalling.

2 For bigger shifts, relocate the strike. Use a pencil to mark where the strike should be. Use a chisel to extend the mortise. Reinstall the strike.

Step 1. Hold the strikeplate firmly in place with a bench clamp while you work on it.

SHIM THE STRIKE

1 If the strike is too far away to engage the latch, first check if the hinges need to be shimmed out (see page 137).

2 If the hinges fit properly, shim out the strike with thick pieces of cardboard.

Step 2. Score the end of the mortise with a knife, then use a chisel to extend it.

WYNN TIP:
A door that does not fit snug against its stop molding probably rattles. To silence it, move the strikeplate or reposition the stop.

fixing a door latch

Sticking latches can be repaired easily with little effort. Most of the time, applying a lubricant fixes the problem. If lubricating a latch does not free it, remove the unit and take it to a locksmith, who may be able to repair it, or buy and install a replacement handle (see pages 140–141).

TOOLS AND MATERIALS:
- Screwdriver
- Powdered graphite

LUBRICATE A LATCH

Turn the handle to retract the latch bolt, and then puff powdered graphite into the latchworks. Turn the handle repeatedly to work the bolt back and forth, and apply more graphite if needed. If this does not solve the problem, you may need a new latch.

FIX A THUMB-OPERATED LATCH

Lubricate a thumb-operated latch lever by puffing graphite powder into the lock body. Move the latch up and down to work in the graphite. Wipe away any excess.

WYNN TIP:
When using powdered graphite to lubricate a lock, place newspaper under the area to protect flooring.

WYNN TIP:
A painted latch may eventually stick. Remove all paint by carefully scraping with a chisel or by using a wire-brush attachment on a drill.

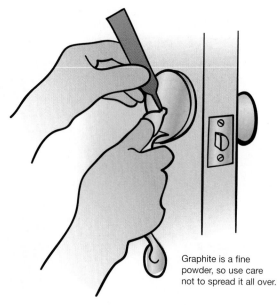

Graphite is a fine powder, so use care not to spread it all over.

what if...

you have a stuck door?

OK, so the door is stuck. Personally I'm not a fan of throwing my weight at the door, forcing it open or closed. A sore shoulder and hip don't have a place in home improvement. Instead, grab your basic tool kit. Here are some quick fixes.

Identifying problems

First you need to identify what's causing the door to stick. If a door sticks or refuses to fit into its frame, open the door and pull up on the handle, then let go. If any of the hinges are loose, the screws need to be tightened.

Next, close the door as far as it will go without forcing it, and examine the perimeter. Look for an uneven gap along the hinge jamb; this means the hinges need attention. Check for layers of paint that have built up—either on the door or the jamb. If the door looks too big for its frame—or out of square with it—mark the tight spots, then sand or plane those spots.

Door and frame problems

Hinge problems

Open the door and place a wedge under it to support its weight. Remove the screws and plug the holes with glue-coated wood splinters, dowels, or golf tees. Drive new longer screws into each plug. Make sure to drive the screws straight so their heads are flat; angled screw heads can cause the door to bind.

If a hinge is recessed into the casing rather than flush with the surface, remove the screws, insert a cardboard shim, and reattach the hinge.

Oversize door or a door out of square with frame

If it's possible, leave the door in place to plane or sand the spots you marked. Use both hands to operate a plane. To avoid chipping the veneer, first bevel it. Turn the plane and cut a bevel downward toward the bottom of your work. Then plane along the length of the door edge.

To trim the bottom or other places you can't reach with the door in place, shim the door so it is stable. Use a nail set to hammer out the hinge pins, bottom first. If the hinge is rusty and the pin is stuck, squirt it with penetrating oil and try again. Once the door is removed, brace the door before planing or sanding the high spots.

repairing screens and storms

Inspect all of your screen and storm doors and windows at the first hint of nice spring weather, and make repairs right away. That way you'll have the task out of the way once the weather is really nice. And you'll increase the energy-efficiency and appearance of your home.

TOOLS AND MATERIALS:
- Needle-nose pliers
- Drill
- Shears
- Screwdriver
- Mending plates
- Screws

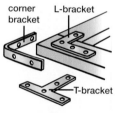

A variety of plates are available for mending corner joints.

corner bracket   L-bracket   T-bracket

WYNN TIP:
Doors that slam or flap whenever there's a wind wear out quickly. Fix the problem and extend the life of your door by adjusting or replacing the screen/storm door closer. A closer should shut the door slowly but completely. Replacement closers are inexpensive and easy to install.

STRENGTHEN A WOODEN FRAME

1 Reinforce corner joints using mending plates. Position a plate over a corner joint. Drill pilot holes.

2 Drive screws to fasten the plate. When possible, install plates on both sides of the frame. Offset them so the screws don't run into each other.

PATCH A METAL SCREEN

Mend a small puncture with a dab of superglue.

1 To fix a hole in a metal screen, cut a patch and unravel a few strands of wire.

2 Fit the patch over the hole, and bend the strands toward the hole. Repairing fiberglass screening is difficult; you're better off replacing the entire screen.

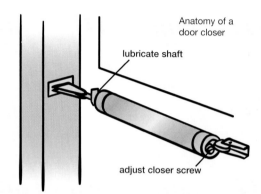

Anatomy of a door closer

lubricate shaft

adjust closer screw

MAINTAIN A CLOSER

1 Every autumn, clean away grime and buildup. Then lubricate door closers by wiping the shafts with oil.

2 Check the adjustment for proper operation. Once a closer starts to fail, replace it.

WYNN TIP:

The parts on an aluminum storm/screen tend to be fragile and will need replacing if they break. To find replacements that fit, look for the manufacturer's name on the frame, or take broken parts to the home center or hardware store.

WYNN TIP:
Wood storm or screen frames that have been painted many times need to be sanded or planed, then repainted.

repairing bifold doors

Bifold doors make great space savers for closets in small rooms. They are lightweight, have slats for circulation, and, when open, allow you to scan all your clothing at a glance. Unfortunately they usually don't tolerate rough handling and occasionally pop out of their tracks.

TOOLS AND MATERIALS:
- **Open-end wrench**
- **Screwdriver**
- **Drill**
- **Hammer**
- **Scrap wood**

STRAIGHTEN A BENT TRACK

1 Place a strip of straight scrap wood inside or behind the track.

2 Tap the track or wood strip with a hammer until the track is straight.

ADJUST TRACK HARDWARE

Ideally, when a bifold door is closed, it should be aligned with the jamb the full length of the door. However, if the opening is out of square, you may need to make a few adjustments so the door fits.

1 Using an open-end wrench, adjust the top assembly guide out or in as necessary.

2 If the door is still out of alignment, check for an adjustable pin and slot at the bottom of the door. Loosen the nut to slide the slot as needed. Other models only require lifting up the door, moving it over slightly, and setting the bottom pin in a different part of the slot.

Step 2. The adjustment pin allows you to align the door vertically without having to remove and reinstall the entire bracket.

Step 1. An open-end wrench allows you to easily reach the adjusting bolt between the door and the track.

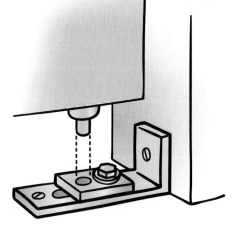

WYNN TIP:
Working with a bifold door is not complicated, but it is awkward to handle alone. Have a helper hold the door while you make repairs.

installing a handle and lock

If you've just moved into a new place or your old doorknob has seen better days, it's time to install a new handle and latch. Door handles now come in a variety of styles, so spend a little time browsing the aisles of a home improvement center or hardware store before you make your choice.

TOOLS AND MATERIALS:
- **Drill with holesaw and bits (see lockset instructions)**
- **Utility knife**
- **Tape measure**
- **Awl**
- **Screwdriver**
- **Chisel**
- **Pencil**
- **Handle set**

Step 1. A template allows you to accurately mark the location of the hole for the handle.

1 The handle set will come with a paper or cardboard template. Tape it or hold it against the door. If a strike already exists in the jamb, align the template with it so you won't have to cut a new mortise for the strike.

2 With an awl or the point of a spade bit, mark for the two holes by piercing through the template.

3 Use a holesaw to drill the larger hole through the face of the door first. To avoid splintering the veneer, drill just far enough that the

pilot bit of the holesaw pokes through. Then drill from the other side.

4 Use a spade bit to drill through the edge of the door, taking care to hold the bit parallel to the surface of the door. Some types of locksets require that you continue drilling into the rear of the large hole approximately ½ inch. Check the manufacturer's instructions before you start drilling.

5 Insert the latch through the smaller hole. Temporarily screw it centered in the door and mark for its mortise with a sharp pencil or a knife. Cut and chisel a mortise (see page 135). Depending on the type of bolt, this mortise may need to be deeper near the center than at the edges.

WYNN TIP:
Use drill bits sizes recommended by the manufacturer of the handle set.

WYNN TIP:
The basic process for installing a door handle is the same for an interior or exterior door. For security purposes, however, make sure you select only a quality exterior handle and lockset for all exterior doors. I also recommend that you install deadbolts on all exterior doors (see pages 26–27).

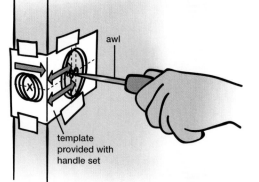

awl

template provided with handle set

6 Install the latch by setting it in the mortise, drilling pilot holes, and driving the screws provided. Then install the lockset or handles according to the manufacturer's directions. Tighten all screws.

7 Test the mechanisms from both sides of the door to make sure they operate smoothly; you may need to clean out or widen your holes.

8 Mark the jamb for the correct location of the strike. The latch or bolt should be vertically centered in the strike opening. Horizontally, make sure the latch will enter the door while holding it fairly tight against the doorstop.

9 Mortise the jamb, drill pilot holes, and install the strike with the screws provided.

WYNN TIP:

When buying a door handle, you have a number of choices. Here are some helpful hints as you make your selection:

- Decide the type of knob you prefer: round, thumb-latch, or lever. Lever handles are easier to operate for the elderly and disabled.
- Install a keyed lock on an exterior door.
- Exterior door handles are exposed to inclement weather. Purchase a quality one that will last.
- When privacy is a concern for an interior door, consider installing a privacy lock that can be opened in emergencies using a flat key or small round screwdriver.

Step 6. Install both sides of the handle at the same time to align them properly.

installing storm or screen windows

Storm windows used to be seasonal. New combination storm/screen windows, however, install permanently. The mounting allows for a seal that creates a dead-air space that insulates to conserve energy. Powder-coat paint technology offers windows in a variety of colors that don't require sanding and repainting.

TOOLS AND MATERIALS:
- Drill
- Screwdriver
- Caulking gun
- Caulk
- Screen or storm window
- Pencil

WYNN TIP:
Consider replacing an old screen with a solar screen. The woven mesh can block up to 90 percent of the hot rays of the sun. Made of strong, durable vinyl-coated polyester fabric, it is an excellent alternative for porch windows.

1 A storm/screen unit has a flange that fits over the window casing. This allows some leeway, so the unit does not have to fit precisely. Check the casing for square and take into account any out-of-square. Measure the width between the inside edges of the side casings and measure the height between the top casing and the sill.

2 Place the combination unit on the sill. Center it between the side casings. The units should be installed square, even if the opening is not square.

3 Check for square by sliding a sash nearly all the way up. It should align with the frame. Sashes should glide smoothly. Any binding means the frame is not straight. Trace the outline of the unit with a pencil.

4 Scrape and clean away any debris that could inhibit a tight seal between the combination window and the casing.

5 Using a caulking gun, run a bead of latex or silicone caulk around the casings, about 1 inch inside the pencil lines. Also run a bead along the sill.

6 Align the frame with the pencil line, press the frame into the caulk, and drive several screws. Test that the sashes operate smoothly and make adjustments if needed. Drive a screw into every available hole. If screws are difficult to drive, or if you are within 2 inches of the end of a piece of casing, drill a pilot hole before driving the screw.

7 Caulk around the outside of the frame where it meets the top and side casings. Also caulk the bottom where it meets the sill.

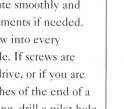

top casing

side casing

caulk

Step 5. To ensure a tight seal, run a bead of caulking around the window before installing the storm/screen window.

what if...

you're planning to buy new storm or screen windows?

Combination windows and doors pay for themselves with energy savings, but beware of shoddy products. Poorly made or poorly fitted units can leak air, are difficult to operate, and eventually turn into eyesores. It's worth the extra expense to buy units that are made of thicker-gauge aluminum with an anodized or powdered coating.

What to look for

- Examine the pins and sliding clips to ensure they are strong and make sure replacement parts are available. Consider buying some replacement parts up front; they may be difficult to find later.
- Better units have warranties against defects. Choose a company that has been around for a while; a fly-by-night outfit may not be there when you need a part or service.
- Check the corners of the frames. Lapped joints are stronger and tighter than mitered joints. If you can see light through the joints, you can be sure that they'll admit air.
- Combinations come in double- or triple-track designs. With double-track units, you must seasonally remove and replace the bottom sash (either storm or screen). Triple-track units have tracks for the top and bottom storm sashes and the screen sash and are self-storing—you don't have to remove the storm or screen sash you are not using. The deeper the tracks are, the higher a unit's insulation value will be.

installing a storm door

Storm doors protect your entry door investment. But that doesn't mean you have to hide your beautiful entry behind an eyesore. Storm doors are available in a variety of styles and colors.

TOOLS AND MATERIALS:
- Hacksaw
- Drill
- Screwdriver or screwdriver bit
- Caulking gun
- Level
- Tape measure
- Storm door
- Wood scrap
- Caulk

WYNN TIP:

Consider installing a combination storm door that features an interchangeable glass panel for winter and a screen panel for summer. Some have both upper and lower interchangeable panels. These maximize solar gain during the winter and allow ventilation during the summer. Others have solid lower panels, which are more practical if you have children and/or pets that constantly push against the lower unit.

1 Unpack all the parts and remove the storm and screen panels from the door. Position the drip cap in the center of the top molding with the fuzzy gasket pointing out. Drill pilot holes and attach the drip cap with two screws. This is only a temporary attachment, so you don't have to drive the screws tight.

2 Make sure you know which side of the hinge flange is up. Measure the opening height on the hinge side, from the bottom of the drip cap to the door sill.

3 Set the hinge flange on a scrap of wood and cut the flange to the measured length, minus ⅛ inch.

4 Apply a bead of caulk to the back of the hinge flange. Have a helper hold the door in position while you work. Align the hinge flange according to the manufacturer's directions. At the top screw hole, drill a pilot hole and drive a screw.

5 Check that the hinge flange is plumb. If it is not, loosen the top screw to reposition the flange. Drill pilot holes and drive screws to attach the door.

6 Remove the drip cap. Apply a bead of latex or silicone caulk to its back and reinstall it so the gap between the top of the door and the cap is even. Drill pilot holes and drive screws to secure

Step 1. Temporarily attach the drip cap to the top molding.

WYNN TIP:
Though I appreciate a good bargain, don't be cheap when it comes to doors that must handle a lot of traffic. Only high-quality doors will withstand children running in and out, and adults carrying grocery bags in both arms.

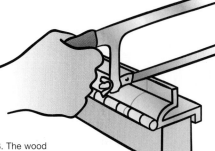

Step 3. The wood scrap provides support so you can cut the flange evenly.

the drip cap.

7 Install the storm or screen panels in the door. Check that the door swings freely. Measure, cut, caulk, and install the latching flange so that the gap between the door and the flange is even.

8 Peel off any protective film from the bottom of the door and the sweep. Slide the rubber gasket onto the bottom of the sweep. Slip the sweep onto the bottom of

the door. Slowly close the door and adjust the position of the sweep so it seals at the sill without binding. Drive screws to secure the sweep.

9 Assemble and install the latch as instructed by the manufacturer. If the latch does not close easily and latch snugly, loosen the screws and adjust the latching pin.

10 Install and adjust the pneumatic door closer. Hold the closer in place and drill holes in the door (some units will have predrilled holes). Fasten the closer to the door and mark for the bracket that attaches to the stop. Drill holes and fasten the bracket in place.

WYNN TIP: Purchasing a storm/screen door with an attractive metal grate provides both curb appeal and security, allowing you the option to leave the main door open and let in cool summer breezes.

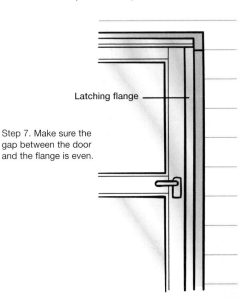

Latching flange

Step 7. Make sure the gap between the door and the flange is even.

Step 8. The sweep serves as a protective seal for the door to minimize drafts.

wiring basics

Electricity deserves your respect, but you can make basic repairs and upgrades yourself and avoid the expense of hiring a professional.

many homeowners who quickly develop the confidence to build bookcases, replace faucets, and install deadbolt locks shy away from even the most basic electrical repair for fear of injury or burning down the house. Yes, electricity does deserve respect. You need to be focused and careful when you work. But you can complete basic electrical repairs and be safe while doing it.

The most critical steps are shutting off the power—either to an individual circuit or to the whole house—double-checking the power is off before you start working and taking measures to ensure the power stays off while you work. If you do this every time and follow the steps and helpful tips I share in this chapter, you can avoid the expense of calling an electrician for most minor repairs and upgrades.

Electrical safety

Maintaining a sound electrical system is one important aspect of maintaining a safe home, so I've also included a home wiring safety check in this chapter. It guides you through a simple inspection for identifying common problems, such as frayed cords, overloaded receptacles, and bulbs too big for their fixtures. I recommend conducting this inspection as soon as possible and then setting up an annual check to catch new problems that develop.

wiring toolbox

You don't need many specialized tools to complete most home wiring repairs. If you purchase any tools specifically for wiring projects, select those with insulating rubber grips, if possible. They help protect against shock. Also, avoid purchasing tools with metal extending through their handles, even if it's covered in plastic.

MULTILEVEL TESTER
This flexible tester works for standard 120- and 240-volt circuits as well as low-voltage wiring such as door chimes and thermostats.

TWO-PART CIRCUIT FINDER
Easily determine which devices are on which circuit breakers.

CONTINUITY TESTER
Use this to determine if a device or fixture wiring is damaged.

RECEPTACLE ANALYZER
Just plug it into a receptacle and it will test for voltage, grounding, and polarization. Buy a good-quality tester to ensure accuracy.

NEON VOLTAGE TESTER
This is the simplest type of voltage tester, which lets you know if power is present in a cable or device.

SIDE-CUTTING PLIERS
Snip wires in tight places and cut sheathing from cable.

LINEMAN'S PLIERS
Two flat surfaces grab wires firmly and make it easy to neatly twist wires together for a solid electrical splice. You can also use these pliers to cut wires.

FUSE PULLER
This is a must if your house has cartridge fuses.

COMBINATION STRIPPER OR ADJUSTABLE STRIPPER
Buy one with a self-opening spring; without this spring, stripping is much more laborious.

NEEDLE-NOSE PLIERS
Use to bend wires into the loops required when connecting to terminals.

SCREWDRIVERS
Designed for use on electrical projects, with insulating rubber grips that protect against shock. Buy sizes #1 and #2 of both slot and phillips types.

ROTARY SCREWDRIVER
This is a great tool to have when you need to quickly drive or remove the little screws that anchor devices and coverplates.

changing lightbulbs

Forget all the old jokes: It takes only one do-it-yourselfer to change a lightbulb. But what do you do if the bulb breaks off in the socket while you are removing it? Or if the bulb is shattered through some sort of mishap? Here are a couple of tricks for removing what's left of the bulb.

TOOLS AND MATERIALS:
- Ladder
- Broom handle
- Potato
- Lightbulb

WYNN TIP:
To avoid the cold, industrial light from standard fluorescent tubes, choose a tube labeled "full spectrum" or "daylight." These deliver illumination similar to the sun.

1 If a light fixture or lamp suddenly stops working, you probably need to change the bulb. First try screwing it in; it may be loose. If a bulb flickers when screwed in tight, the light fixture may have a loose wire connection (see pages 166–168). Shut off the lamp or fixture, unscrew the bulb, hold it next to your ear, and jiggle it. A burned-out bulb usually makes a tinkling sound.

2 If a bulb is broken, shut off the power to the circuit. Depending on how much of the glass envelope remains, you may be able to grip the bulb by inserting a broom handle or other piece of wood into the center.

3 If a broomstick does not do the job, try jabbing the broken shards with a potato. After unscrewing, throw away the potato and the bulb base.

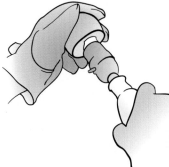

Step 3. Before using the potato, put on a pair of gloves to protect yourself from any stray glass shards, and cover the area below where you are working.

WYNN TIP:
Check the label on the lamp or light fixture for wattage limitations. Avoid installing a bulb with a wattage rating greater than the fixture rating. It will overheat. The heat is not enough to immediately start a fire, but it could damage the wire insulation or socket, creating problems later. If more illumination is desired, consider a screw-in fluorescent or a halogen bulb, each of which delivers more light for less wattage. Or install a new fixture.

WYNN TIP:
Incandescent bulbs labeled "long life" will more than pay for themselves. However, they are not energy efficient. Consider purchasing fluorescents designed for regular sockets. They last longer and use less energy. Most take a few seconds to become bright. If that is a problem, consider a halogen bulb, which is nearly as energy efficient and lights up immediately.

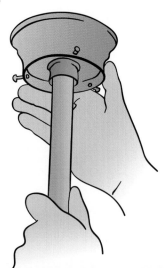

Step 2. Take care to remove the glass fragments from the end of the broom handle before using it for cleaning.

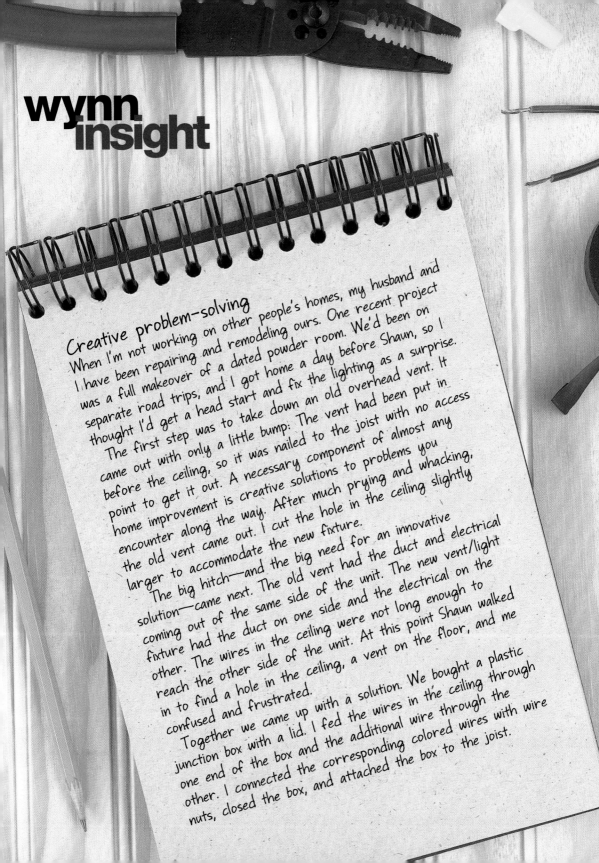

wynn insight

Creative problem-solving

When I'm not working on other people's homes, my husband and I have been repairing and remodeling ours. One recent project was a full makeover of a dated powder room. We'd been on separate road trips, and I got home a day before Shaun, so I thought I'd get a head start and fix the lighting as a surprise.

The first step was to take down an old overhead vent. It came out with only a little bump: The vent had been put in before the ceiling, so it was nailed to the joist with no access point to get it out. A necessary component of almost any home improvement is creative solutions to problems you encounter along the way. After much prying and whacking, the old vent came out. I cut the hole in the ceiling slightly larger to accommodate the new fixture.

The big hitch—and the big need for an innovative solution—came next. The old vent had the duct and electrical coming out of the same side of the unit. The new vent/light fixture had the duct on one side and the electrical on the other. The wires in the ceiling were not long enough to reach the other side of the unit. At this point Shaun walked in to find a hole in the ceiling, a vent on the floor, and me confused and frustrated.

Together we came up with a solution. We bought a plastic junction box with a lid. I fed the wires in the ceiling through one end of the box and the additional wire through the other. I connected the corresponding colored wires with wire nuts, closed the box, and attached the box to the joist.

turning off and testing for power

Before starting any electrical repair project, shut off the power and test to make sure it is off. This basic rule is simple and vital. You'll notice that the first step in almost every project in this chapter is to turn off the power. Don't skip it!

TOOLS:
• Voltage tester

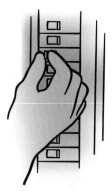

After you identify which circuit you want to turn off, switch the toggle to the "Off" position.

PRACTICE ELECTRICAL SAFETY

• Act as if the power is on even when you know it is off.
• Wear gym shoes or other shoes with rubber soles.
• Use tools made specifically for electrical work. These typically have generous rubber grips so you never need to touch metal.
• Remove jewelry and watches.
• If you are working in the basement, stand on a wooden platform rather than on concrete.
• Use a nonconducting ladder—fiberglass is a good choice—rather than metal.

SHUT OFF POWER TO A SINGLE CIRCUIT

In most cases it is sufficient to shut off power only to the circuit you're working on. To do this, flip a breaker or remove a fuse. If your service panel is well-indexed, you can easily find the circuit. Be aware, however, that the label may be incorrect, so always test for power after turning it off.

SHUT OFF POWER TO ALL CIRCUITS

For major projects, or if you are unsure which breaker or fuse controls the wiring you will work on, shut off power to the entire house. In most cases, the main breaker or fuse is located at the top of the panel. Be aware that even after you have shut off the main breaker, the wires entering the box from outside the house are still live.

WYNN TIP:

Remove potential distractions when working on wiring. Don't allow children or pets in the area where you are working. Turn off the radio or TV so you can focus only on the repair you're making.

SEE THAT THE POWER STAYS OFF

To ensure that nobody restores power while you work, tape a note to the box. For greater security, lock the panel; most service panels have a place for a padlock.

TEST FOR POWER

Use a voltage tester to double-check the power is off before starting any repairs. Insert the probes of the voltage tester into the slots. You can also use a receptacle analyzer or a multitester. (In a pinch, you can test for power by plugging in a reliable lamp or radio.) To test a switch's wiring, a ceiling fixture, or a junction box for power, remove the cover and touch the probes to the bare ends of a white wire and a colored wire.

WYNN TIP:

A voltage tester is an essential part of your personal safety equipment. So give it the attention it deserves. Retire old, dated equipment that may malfunction or might not be up to current standards. Doing so might just save your life.

WYNN TIP:

A shock from a standard 120-volt circuit will jolt you, but probably not seriously harm you if you are working in a dry area wearing rubber-soled shoes. However, it can seriously injure you if you have a heart condition or are standing on a wet surface.

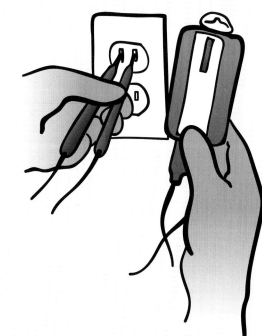

Voltage testers provide a quick way to ensure that there is no power in the circuit.

home wiring safety check

Conduct a safety inspection to identify and correct potentially dangerous situations.

aintaining a home that's free from electrical problems is critical to your family's safety. If you know what to look for, you can spot most electrical problems by doing a basic home check. Repeat this wiring safety check each year.

If you discover a problem, shut off the power to the circuit, test to make sure the electricity is off, and correct the problem before turning on the power.

If you spot a potential wiring problem that you do not understand, call a professional electrician for an evaluation. Never work on wiring you do not understand.

OUTSIDE YOUR HOME
Check the point of attachment.

- Power enters your home through a weatherhead or an underground cable. Conduct a visual inspection, but do not touch anything. Make sure the wires are firmly secured and the insulation is in good condition.
- Overhead wires should be high enough to avoid contact with trees, outdoor structures, cars, and people.
- If you see anything that might be a problem, call your electric utility company for an inspection. Do *not* attempt to make any repairs where power enters your home.

Inspect outdoor connections.

- From the point of entry, cables or conduits travel down your home's siding until they enter a meter. The meter may be inside or outside. From the meter, the wires run to the service panel.
- All conduits and cables should be solidly fastened to the house. Check visually that all outdoor attachments are watertight.

- Contact the utility company if you find any potential problems. Again, do not attempt to make any repairs where power enters your home.

INSIDE YOUR HOME
Look for missing knockouts.

Any exposed hole in an electrical box poses a serious danger. Children or even adults can easily poke a finger in and get a painful shock. Buy a knockout filler and anchor it firmly to fill the hole.

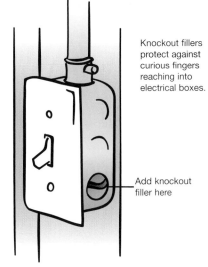

Knockout fillers protect against curious fingers reaching into electrical boxes.

Add knockout filler here

Replace cracked or missing coverplates.

Check for hairline cracks as well as major damage. If a coverplate is even slightly damaged, replace it. Purchase a replacement cover before removing the existing coverplate. Unscrew the screw to remove the old plate. Replace it immediately with the new cover.

Test GFCI receptacles.

Ground fault circuit interrupter (GFCI) receptacles normally don't wear out. On the few occasions one does, it will supply power but not protection. Test GFCIs every month. When you push the test button, the power should shut off. If it does not, replace the device.

Check cord insulation for damage.

- Conduct a visual inspection of each cord in your home. Insulation can become brittle and crack easily,

especially if subjected to high heat. Cords are also easy to nick.
- Make a temporary repair with electrical tape. Remember, this is only a short-term fix. To be safe, replace the entire cord. Also replace any cracked or wobbly plugs (see pages 164–165).

Look for missing cable clamps.

Cable clamps secure electrical cables to receptacle or switch boxes. They protect the wire connections from being pulled apart, help protect the insulation from nicks, and seal the boxes' holes. An unclamped cable is dangerous.

1. Purchase cable clamps made for the type and size of cable and box you have.
2. Turn off the power. Test for power.
3. Disconnect the wire connections.
4. Attach the clamp to the cable and then to the box by tightening the locknut.
5. Reattach the wires.
6. Turn on the power.

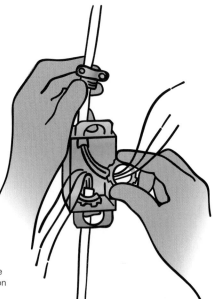

The clamp holds the cable securely in place, minimizing the potential for insulation cracks and shorts.

Inspect for loose cable.

- Wherever cable is exposed (typically in a basement, garage, or attic), it should be fastened tightly with straps or staples specifically made for attaching wiring. Unsecured cables are susceptible to damage.
- Do not use cables as clotheslines or to otherwise support loads.

Identify overloaded receptacles.

Plugging too many cords into a receptacle poses the risk of overloading a circuit. An arrangement like this also makes it easy to accidentally pull out a plug and create a tripping hazard. Move some of the load to other circuits.

Check for proper wattage.

It's tempting to install a 100-watt bulb in a fixture rated for only 60 watts, but doing so will cause the fixture to overheat. The extra heat may melt insulation or cause it to become brittle and may start a fire. Check the wattage rating of the fixture. Replace too-powerful bulbs with those of proper wattage. If you need more light, replace the fixture with one that has a higher wattage rating.

Cover bare bulbs in closets.

A lightbulb, even a low-wattage one, gets hot. Code requires closet fixtures to have protective globes. If you don't have a globe, keep clothing and flammables a minimum of one foot away from the bulb until you can install a new, safer fixture.

Inspect receptacles for incorrect wiring.

- Whenever you open a box, inspect the wiring. The wire ends should be attached firmly to terminal screws, and the insulation should be free of nicks.
- On a receptacle, the white wire goes to the neutral (silver) terminal, and the black wire connects to the hot (brass) terminal screw.
- If you see any problems, rewire the box or call an electrician.

Check for crowded boxes.

If a box contains so many wires that they have to be crammed in, overheating or shorts could result. If possible, install an extension ring to enlarge the box. Otherwise replace the box with a larger one.

Inspect for loose ceiling fixtures.

- A heavy ceiling fixture, such as a chandelier or ceiling fan, should be attached to a fan-rated box, which is stronger than a normal ceiling box (see pages 174–175).
- If the fixture has come loose from the box, try to reattach it.
- If the box itself is loose, you may be able to secure it by driving screws into an abutting joist. Otherwise remove the fixture and install a new fan-rated box.

Wires are color-coded so you can easily identify the neutral and hot wires for proper connection.

Check the service panel.

1. Open the service panel and inspect the wiring. Do not reach into the panel.

2. A 14-gauge wire should be connected to a 15-amp breaker or fuse, and a 12-gauge wire should be connected to a 20-amp breaker. If the amperage of a breaker or fuse is too high for the wire, the wiring could dangerously overheat before the breaker trips or the fuse blows.

POTENTIAL PROBLEMS WITH OLDER HOMES

Older homes present unique electrical problems. Electrical codes have changed over the years—for good reason. This does not mean you need to have your home rewired, but you do need to be able to identify and correct problems.

An older home may have an inadequate and unsafe electrical service. The wiring can be confusing as well. If you are unsure about your home's wiring, have a professional check it out.

Some older systems have only two wires—rather than three—entering the house from the utility company. This arrangement does not have the capacity for the 240-volt circuits needed for ranges, clothes dryers, and other appliances.

3. Replace any improper fuse with one of the correct amperage. If a breaker is incorrect, call an electrician to check and replace it.

Check for unsafe wire routing.

With the service panel open, inspect the wire routing. Wires should run neatly around the perimeter inside the box. If wires are bunched together or close to electrical connections, shut off the main breaker or fuse and gently move the wires to the side. If you see charring or melted insulation, or if the wiring is badly disorganized, call an electrician for an evaluation.

Check an old service entrance.

• Conduct a visual inspection of the service where power enters your home. A point of attachment may lack a watertight entrance head. Make sure the porcelain insulator is not cracked.

• Chances are, the utility company will install a better attachment if you call them. Do *not* attempt any repairs to the service entrance yourself.

Check the inside of your home for the following safety risks:

60-AMP FUSE BOX

Open the service panel and inspect the inside. A house built in the 1950s or before may have only 60-amp service and a fuse box that contains only four fuses. This small number of circuits limits how many fixtures and appliances you can safely run.

DAMAGED INSULATION

- Old, brittle wire insulation can easily crack, and the resulting exposed wire poses a danger.
- If the problem occurs in only a few spots, shut off the power. Wrap the wire with electrical tape as a temporary fix only.
- Purchase special shrink-wrap sleeves made for protecting old wires and install them over the exposed areas.
- If you notice extensive cracked wire insulation, call an electrician.

DARKENED INSULATION

In some older homes, cloth wire insulation has darkened to the point where you cannot tell a white (neutral) wire from a black (hot) wire. Sometimes this leads to incorrect wiring. If a switch is wired using the neutral wire rather than the hot wire, the switch will turn off the light, but power will still be present in the fixture's box. To be safe, flip the switch off and use a voltage detector to check for power in the fixture box. Replace the wire, switch, or both, if necessary.

KNOB-AND-TUBE WIRING

With this type of wiring, appliances usually are not grounded. To upgrade, you need to have an electrician rewire your home. However, this type of wiring is generally safe if it is correctly installed and protected from damage or contact.

OLD CEILING BOXES

Look for old ceiling boxes. An old home with plaster ceilings may have pancake ceiling boxes. Wires often run through a center pipe, which may have once been a gas line. A box like this is usually not strong enough to hold a heavy fixture such as a ceiling fan. To attach a modern light fixture or ceiling fan, you may need to buy special hardware or replace the box (see pages 174–175).

home wiring **safety check** *continued*

UNGROUNDED RECEPTACLES

Check all the receptacles in your home. If a receptacle has only two slots and no ground hole, it is not grounded. You can have an electrician update your electrical system so that it is grounded. Otherwise, if you need to replace a receptacle, only install a two-prong ungrounded receptacle and do not plug in any appliance that has a three-prong plug. *Never* break off the third prong of a three-prong plug to use it in a two-prong receptacle.

WYNN TIP:

Most electricians do not recommend using a grounding adapter in a two-slot receptacle. If you insist on installing an adapter, follow these suggestions: Use an adapter only if it is firmly attached to the mounting screw and the mounting screw is grounded. Test the adapter with a receptacle analyzer to ensure it is grounded. If it is not, remove the adapter and use only devices with two-prong plugs.

NONPOLARIZED RECEPTACLES

A receptacle with two slots the same length is not polarized. Polarized plugs reduce shock hazards in electrical devices. Almost all devices, from hair dryers to stereos, have polarized plugs that will fit into a nonpolarized receptacle. Replace it with a polarized receptacle. Connect the neutral wire (white) to the silver terminal and the hot (black) wire to the brass one.

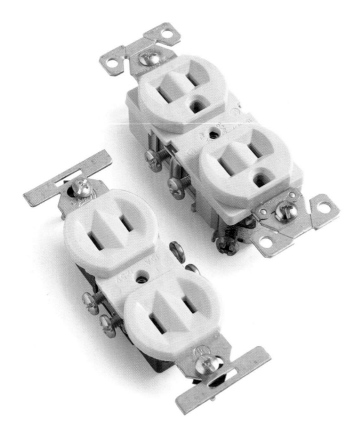

what if...

you don't know what each electrical circuit in the service panel controls?

TOOLS AND MATERIALS:
• Paper
• Pencil

WYNN TIP:
If you must work alone, plug in a radio turned to peak volume to find the general area covered by the circuit. The radio will go silent when you switch off the power to that particular circuit.

When you open the door to your service panel, if you don't find a detailed list of what each circuit breaker controls it's time to make a circuit map. The resulting list will make it easier to turn off the correct circuit for repairs or improvements.

Take special precautions while working in a service panel. Don't remove the coverplates. Keep the door shut and locked when you are not working so children can't get into the panel.

MAP THE CIRCUITS

Begin by making a map of each floor in your home. Include every receptacle, switch, appliance, and fixture. Remember that most 240-volt receptacles will have their own circuits. You may have to make more than one drawing per floor for a large house.

In the service panel, mark each circuit breaker or fuse with a number. Turn on all the appliances and lights on one floor. Plug a lamp into every

receptacle. Turn off one circuit. Send a helper around the house with the map to write the circuit number next to each outlet that went dead. Continue this process until you've accounted for every receptacle, switch, appliance, and fixture in your home.

Based on the maps, create a detailed list of what each circuit controls. Tape the completed list to the inside of the service panel door. File the detailed map somewhere you can find it easily.

WYNN TIP:
Remember, even if you have shut off the main power breaker or switch, there is still power entering the service panel.

— MAIN LEVEL CIRCUITS —
CIRCUIT - AREA
1 - LIVINGROOM
2 - LIVINGROOM
3 - DININGROOM
4 - KITCHEN EAST WALL
5 - KITCHEN NORTH WALL
6 - KITCHEN -APPLIANCES
7 - KITCHEN STOVE · 240
8 - BATHROOM 1
9 - BEDROOM 1
10 - MASTERBATH
11 - MASTER BEDROOM
12 - BEDROOM 2
13 - DEN
14 - LAUNDRY ROOM · 240
15 - GARAGE 1
16 - GARAGE 2
16 - MUDROOM

troubleshooting circuit breakers

A circuit breaker protects you from electrical hazards. When the breaker is in the "on" position, current flows through a set of contacts. A bimetal strip under tension holds the contacts together, allowing the current to flow. When the circuit experiences a short or overload, the bimetal strip heats up and bends, breaking the contact. Power to the circuit will remain off until you reset the breaker. It's important to determine the cause for a tripped breaker so you can fix it.

**TOOLS AND
MATERIALS:**
- **Electrical tape**
- **Neon tester**
- **Continuity
  tester**

CHECK CONNECTIONS IN BOXES

Short circuits can occur in electrical boxes. A wire might have pulled loose from the switch and shorted out against the box. Reattach the wire (see page 178).

INSPECT WIRING

Frayed or nicked insulation will expose wire and could cause a short. Wrap damaged insulation with electrical tape.

WATCH FOR OVERHEATED FIXTURES

The heat from lightbulbs can melt insulation. Never use bulbs with higher wattage than the fixture's rating.

IDENTIFY OVERLOADED CIRCUITS

The problem may be an overload. If you have several big energy users on one circuit (see pages 157–158), unplug or turn off one of them.

TESTING THE CIRCUIT

To find out whether the problem has been corrected, reset the breaker. It will shut itself off again if there's still a problem. If the circuit breaker keeps tripping even though it isn't overloaded, suspect a short. Recheck everything on the circuit for a defective plug, cord, or socket.

Tripped position: off to reset, press in and release

Tripped position: center to reset, flip off, then on

Tripped position: off to reset, flip to on

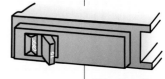

Tripped position: red flag showing, switch in center to reset, flip off, then on

WYNN TIP:

If after resetting a circuit breaker you still have no electricity, try turning off the main breaker and all the circuit breakers in the panel. Turn the main breaker back on and reset each individual breaker.

troubleshooting fuses

Fuses predate circuit breakers and serve the same purpose: shutting down a circuit when there is a short or overload. A fuse, however, can't be reset because when too much current in the circuit produces heat, a strip of metal in the fuse melts. When this happens, you must first eliminate the short or overload. Then you'll need to replace the blown fuse.

TOOLS AND MATERIALS:
- **Fuse puller**
- **Continuity tester**
- **Replacement fuses**
- **Flashlight**

WYNN TIP:
Never touch the ends of a cartridge fuse with your bare hands. It could fatally shock you.

normal unblown fuse

shorted fuse

overloaded fuse

IDENTIFYING A BLOWN FUSE

Use a flashlight to examine the fuse window. A short circuit usually explodes the strip, blackening the fuse window. An overload usually melts it, leaving the window clear.

REMOVING CARTRIDGE FUSES

1 For safety, use a plastic fuse puller to firmly grab the fuse and pull it out.

2 The ends of a cartridge fuse get very hot, which makes sense when you consider that heat melts the strip to open the circuit. Don't touch the ends immediately after you've pulled the fuse.

TESTING CARTRIDGE FUSES

1 Sometimes identifying a blown cartridge fuse is difficult. Remove the suspected fuse using a fuse puller.

2 Check it with a continuity tester. Clamp or hold the clip on one end and touch the probe to the other. The bulb will light if it is not blown.

3 Replace the fuse or insert a new one using a fuse puller. Push the fuse into one clamp, then the other.

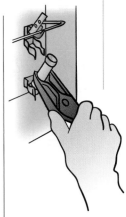

A fuse puller allows you to safely remove the fuse without coming into contact with the leads.

WYNN TIP:
The design of tamperproof fuses makes it impossible to install a fuse with a higher amperage rating than the circuit is designed for. Time-delay fuses help prevent fuses from blowing because of the surge when a large energy user, such as a washing machine, starts up. Only a sustained overload will blow this fuse.

replacing a round-cord plug

Plugs and cords take a lot of abuse. We step on them, bump up against them, and yank them. It's no wonder that faulty plugs present the most common shock and fire hazard in the home. Regularly inspect for loose connections, damaged insulation, and bent prongs. Replacing a faulty plug is quick, and it'll make your home safer.

TOOLS AND MATERIALS:
- Wire stripper
- Screwdriver
- Needle-nose pliers
- Replacement plug

WYNN TIP:
Some plug designs have clamps that grip the cord where it enters the base. You do not need to tie an Underwriter's knot for these types of plugs.

Step 3. An Underwriter's knot keeps tension off the lead connections so there is good contact.

REPLACING A ROUND-CORD PLUG

1 Clip off the old plug. Slide the cord through the body of the replacement plug.

2 Use a combination stripper to strip off 3 inches of outer insulation and about ½ inch of wire insulation.

3 Tie an Underwriter's knot (see below left). Pull the cord back so the knot fits tight to the plug. Twist the wire strands tight with your fingers.

4 Use needle-nose pliers to shape clockwise hooks to wrap around the screws.

5 Hook the wires on the screw shanks. Attach the black wire to the brass screw. Tighten the connections. Tuck in any stray strands. Make sure all wires and strands are neatly inside the plug. Slip on the cardboard cover.

REPLACING GROUNDED ROUND-CORD PLUGS

1 Snip off the old plug and slip the plug shell onto the cord.

2 Strip about ½ inch of insulation from the ends of all three wires. Twist the strands tight. Use needle-nose pliers to form hooks.

3 Connect the black and white wires to brass-colored terminals. Attach the green wire to the silver-colored terminal.

4 Tuck in any loose strands as you tighten the terminal screws. Push all the wires in place and tighten the cord clamp. Slip on the cardboard cover.

Step 4. Don't leave any wire strands sticking out as you tighten the terminal screws.

WYNN TIP:
Flat-cord plugs work for lamps, radios, and other low-amperage devices. Newer lamp and extension-cord plugs are polarized, with one blade wider than the other. Round-cord plugs accommodate thick wire and are used for higher-current appliances, such as irons. Standard grounded plugs have a third, round prong for grounding; the two flat prongs are polarized.

replacing a flat-cord plug

Replacing a worn or faulty plug probably isn't at the top of your to-do list, but it should be. To avoid damaging plugs in the first place, always disconnect a plug from a receptacle by grasping the plug and pulling straight out. Yanking on the cord may loosen the connections, and forcing the plug out at an angle may bend the prongs. If a plug does become damaged, replacing it is quick and easy.

TOOLS AND MATERIALS:
- Scissors
- Needle-nose pliers
- Wire strippers
- Replacement plug

Step 3. Hook the leads around the terminals in a clockwise direction.

WYNN TIP:
Never remove the grounding prong from an appliance plug. That prong may protect you from a shock.

REPLACING FLAT-CORD PLUGS

1 Remove the old plug by cutting the cord. Slide the new shell over the cord.

2 Peel apart the wires and strip away ½ inch of insulation.

3 Twist the strands of each wire tight with your fingers. Use needle-nose pliers to form hooks on the ends of the wires so they will wrap clockwise around the screws.

4 Hook the wires on the screw shank and tighten to secure the connection. The hooks will draw inward as you tighten the screws. Tuck in any loose strands.

5 Pull the shell of the plug over the core until it snaps into place.

ATTACHING QUICK-CONNECT PLUGS

1 Snip off the old plug and pry up the lever on top of the new plug. Insert the zip cord into the hole.

2 Close the lever. This pierces the wire and holds it in place. Push the lever firmly down until it is seated in the plug.

Step 1. Insert the end into the plug. No stripping is necessary.

WYNN TIP:
Keep a couple of quick-connect plugs in your toolbox so you'll never be tempted to put off replacing a damaged plug.

rewiring a lamp

If you enjoy treasure hunting for antiques and flea-market finds, you may have discovered what you thought was a perfect lamp, only to find out it doesn't work. Don't toss your find on the trash pile; rewire it.

TOOLS AND MATERIALS:
- Wire strippers
- Needle-nose pliers
- Screwdriver
- Replacement cord and socket
- String or tape

WYNN TIP:
Even if your lamp works but the cord insulation is cracked near the socket, replace the cord to avoid fire and shock hazards.

REPLACING THE CORD

1 Unplug the lamp and take it to a place where you have plenty of room to work. Disconnect the old cord from the lamp socket and snip off the plug.

2 Tie the new cord to the old one with a piece of string or some tape. The trick is to make the connection thin enough that it slides through the center rod of the lamp.

3 Pull the new cord through as you pull out the old one. Untie the old cord and discard it. Separate the two wires of the new cord about 3½ inches.

4 Tie an Underwriter's knot (see page 164) at the top of the cord, leaving about 2½ inches of each wire to work with beyond the knot.

5 Strip ½ inch of insulation from the end of each wire and twist the strands tight.

6 Use needle-nose pliers to form the ends of the wires into hooks and wrap them clockwise around the terminal screws.

7 Tighten the terminal screws, tucking in any loose strands.

8 Reassemble the socket and install the harp. Attach a new plug if necessary (see pages 164–165). Now put in a bulb, attach the shade, and plug in your lamp.

WYNN TIP:
When a lamp doesn't work and you know the bulb, cord, and plug are OK, the problem is most likely in the socket.

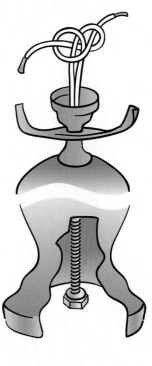

Step 4. An Underwriter's knot prevents the electrical connections from being pulled loose and creating a potential shock hazard.

REPLACING THE LAMP SOCKET

1 Unplug the cord and take the lamp to a workspace with plenty of room to lay out the lamp parts. Remove the harp.

2 Examine the socket shell and find the word "press." Push hard at that point so the unit pulls apart. Remove the cord from the socket.

3 Slip the new socket base onto the cord and tie an Underwriter's knot (see page 164).

4 Strip about ½ inch of insulation from the wires and twist the strands tight.

5 Form the ends into hooks with needle-nose pliers and wrap the wires clockwise around the shafts of the screws. Tighten the screws.

6 Reassemble the cardboard insulation and the outer shell. Attach the new socket to the lamp. Put harp, bulb, and shade back in place.

Step 5. Wrap the wire hook securely around the terminal screw.

WYNN TIP:
Most lamps have felt bases that must be removed before you repair the lamp. Pare off the felt with a utility knife. After the repair, reapply the felt with white glue.

WYNN TIP:
Never work on a lamp or appliance while it is plugged in.

WYNN TIP:
A cracked or nicked wire may not look dangerous, yet damaged cords can cause fires and are potentially painful sources of electrical shock. If you see a damaged cord and need to continue to use the lamp, wrap the damaged area with electrical tape. Doing so is at best a temporary solution. Replace the cord as soon as possible.

checking light fixtures

Problems occur in light fixtures for several reasons. The socket might be damaged, heat damage may occur from overrated bulbs, or connections may be faulty. If the fixture refuses to light, the wall switch may be the problem (see pages 170–171).

TOOLS AND MATERIALS:
- **Screwdriver or steel wool**
- **Electrical tape**

Step 2. Remove the fixture and inspect for bare wires, loose connections, heat-cracked wire insulation, and peeling drywall paper. These are signs you may need to repair the fixture

Peeling paper

Heat-cracked wire insulation

CHECK THE BULB

1 Switch off the fixture and remove the cover. A label on the fixture tells you the maximum bulb wattage allowed. Don't install higher-wattage bulbs or your fixture will overheat, burn up bulbs quickly, and become dangerous.

2 Look for heat-cracked wire insulation and drywall paper peeling near the fixture. These are signs your fixture is overheating. If the bulb wattage is OK, check the wiring.

INSPECT THE SOCKET

1 Shut off the circuit that supplies power to the fixture. Remove the globe and inspect the socket. If cracked, or if wires are scorched or melted, replace the socket or the entire fixture. If it's OK, remove the bulb.

2 Check the contact at the socket base. Scrape corrosion from the contact with a flat screwdriver or steel wool, and pry up on it. Turn on the power and retry the light.

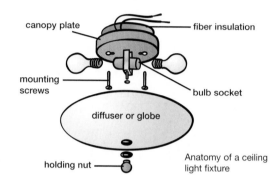

canopy plate

fiber insulation

mounting screws

bulb socket

diffuser or globe

holding nut

Anatomy of a ceiling light fixture

CHECK THE WIRING

1 If the problem remains, shut off the circuit again. Remove the mounting screws and drop the fixture from its outlet box. Look for loose connections and for nicked insulation. Check again for peeling drywall paper and heat-cracked wire insulation.

2 Cut back or replace bare wires. As a temporary fix, wrap bare spots with electrical tape.

WYNN TIP:

Even though it will make it a bit more difficult to install a new light fixture, leave the fiber insulation in the canopy plate. It provides extra protection against shorts.

installing a GFCI receptacle

A faulty power tool or appliance can give you a serious shock even when the grounding wire is properly connected. Ground fault circuit interrupters (GFCI) protect you from electrical shock in areas where you may come into contact with water. This makes it a good idea to install GFCI protection in areas such as kitchens, bathrooms, and outdoors.

TOOLS AND MATERIALS:
- **Screwdriver**
- **Lineman's pliers**
- **Wire stripper**
- **Wire caps**
- **Electrical tape**
- **GFCI receptacle**
- **Wire connectors**

WYNN TIP:
A GFCI receptacle is bulkier than a standard receptacle, so it may be a tight fit in a box. If gently pushing the wires back doesn't help the GFCI fit, don't force it. You might break the case or loosen the wire connections. Instead install a box extender.

1 To replace an existing receptacle with a GFCI receptacle, turn off the power and remove the old receptacle. Check to make sure the GFCI receptacle will fit in the old box. If not, the box will need to be replaced.

2 Attach the GFCI receptacle connecting multiple wires with wire connectors. First twist the wires firmly together. Do not depend on a connector to do the joining. Twist the wire connector on, turning it by hand until it tightens firmly. As a final precaution, wrap the connector clockwise with electrical tape, overlapping the wires.

3 Incoming power goes to the LINE terminals. LOAD lines carry power from the GFCI to other receptacles on the circuit. So if

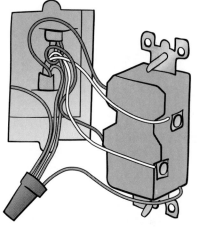

you install a GFCI as the first receptacle of a circuit, the entire circuit will be protected.

4 If you are installing a GFCI at the end of a line, cap the load leads with wire connectors, or buy a version that protects only one receptacle.

You may need a larger electrical box, since GFCI receptacles are larger than standard receptacles.

WYNN TIP:
There are three types of GFCIs: plug-ins, receptacles, and breakers. To install a portable plug-in unit, simply insert its blades into a receptacle and plug in the appliance. A GFCI receptacle replaces a conventional receptacle and, properly placed, can protect other receptacles on the same circuit. Install a GFCI breaker into a service panel to protect a circuit.

testing and replacing switches

Switches get a lot of use. We flip, pull, and tug on them thousands of times, so it's no wonder they wear out. Fortunately, switches are easy to test and easy to replace.

TOOLS AND MATERIALS:
- **Neon tester**
- **Continuity tester**
- **Screwdriver**
- **Electrical tape**

WYNN TIP:
Work safely! Until you test for power, hold only the top and bottom metal flanges of the switch when pulling it out of a box—even if you believe the power to the circuit is off. Do not touch the terminal screws or allow the screws to touch the edge of the box. The switch may be on a different circuit than you thought.

Step 2. Touch the probes to the switch terminals. Be careful not to touch the screws with your fingers.

TEST A SWITCH WITH A NEON TESTER

1 Shut off power to the switch at the circuit breaker or fuse box. Use a screwdriver to remove the coverplate and the screws holding the switch. Pull the switch out from the box so you can work on it.

2 Turn the switch to the "off" position and restore power to the circuit. Touch the probes of a neon tester to the switch's screw terminals. If the tester glows, the box has power.

3 Flip the switch on. Touch the probes to the terminals again. If the tester glows this time, the switch is blown and must be replaced.

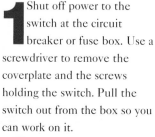

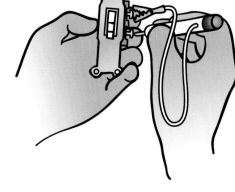

Step 2. Secure the tester clip to one terminal and touch the other with the probe.

TEST A SWITCH WITH A CONTINUITY TESTER

1 Shut off the circuit leading to the switch. Pull the switch out of the box so you can work on it. Use a screwdriver to disconnect all wires.

2 Fasten the tester clip to one of the terminals and touch the probe to the other. If the switch is working, the tester will glow when the switch is in the "on" position and not glow when the switch is off.

WYNN TIP:
Never use a continuity tester on live wires. Always shut off power and disconnect wires before testing. The continuity tester uses a battery that generates a small current to test for the flow of electricity from one point to another. It is not made to handle household current.

TEST A THREE-WAY SWITCH

1 To check a three-way switch, shut off the power to the circuit at the service box. Attach the clip to the common terminal (usually labeled on the switch body). Touch the probe to one of the other screws.

2 Flip the switch. If it's OK, the tester will light when touching one of the two terminals.

3 Flip the switch to the other position. The tester should light when the remaining terminal is touched.

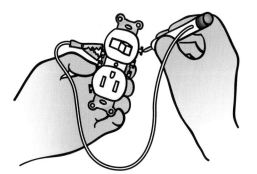

Step 1. Attach the clip to one of the switch terminals and touch the probe to the other switch terminal.

TEST A SWITCH THAT HAS A RECEPTACLE

1 To test a device that has both a switch and a receptacle, begin by shutting off power. Attach the continuity tester clip to one of the switch terminals.

2 Touch the probe to the top terminal on the other side. If the switch is working, the tester will glow when the switch is on and not glow when it is off.

REPLACE A SWITCH

1 Shut off power to the switch at the service panel. If a switch is damaged, remove the screws holding the switch to the box and gently pull out the device. Test to make sure the power to the circuit is off.

2 Loosen the screw terminals and disconnect the wires. Inspect the wires in the box. Wrap any damaged insulation with electrical tape.

3 Attach the wires to the terminals of the new switch. Wrap electrical tape around the body of the switch so the terminals are covered.

4 Carefully tuck the wires and switch back into the box. Connect the switch to the box by tightening the mounting screws. Don't force anything; switches crack easily.

5 Restore the power to the circuit and test the switch.

WYNN TIP:
Looking to create a little mood lighting? Consider a dimmer switch. Installation is easy—similar to installing a normal toggle switch (see page 173).

replacing a fixture-mounted switch

Small switches that mount on fixtures are operated by pulling a chain, flipping, or twisting a knob. These switches are not long-lived, so if a light fixture does not work and the bulb is not blown, the switch is likely to blame.

TOOLS AND MATERIALS:
- **Neon tester**
- **Screwdriver**
- **Electrical tape**
- **Replacement switch**

TEST THE SWITCH

1 Shut off power to the fixture at the wall switch or unplug the cord from the wall receptacle before you begin.

2 Remove the connectors holding the switch leads. Leave the bare wires twisted together, and arrange them so the connections are not in danger of touching each other or anything else.

3 Restore power to the fixture and carefully touch a neon tester to the connections. If the switch is turned on and the tester lights, this indicates the switch is bad and needs replacing.

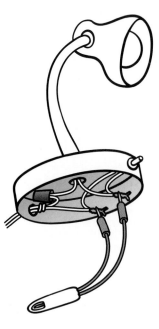

Step 3. Touch the probes against the wires to determine if you need to replace the switch.

WYNN TIP:

Some fixtures have an integrated switch. In such cases, you'll have to replace the entire fixture. Lamp pull chains cannot be repaired. Buy a new pull-chain socket and replace the old one.

REPLACE A FIXTURE-MOUNTED SWITCH

1 Shut off power at the wall switch or unplug the cord from the wall receptacle.

2 Remove the fixture and disconnect the wires. Release the pull-chain switch by loosening the terminal screws and two screws in the base of the socket. Install a replacement switch of the same type and size.

installing a dimmer switch

Dimmer switches allow you to set the mood, giving you greater control over the atmosphere of a room. Softer light gives a feeling of coziness. Brighter light is more active as well as being more suitable for reading.

WYNN TIP:
Use caution when working with electricity. It's OK to call an electrician if you're unsure or uncomfortable with any job.

1 Always shut off the power before removing or installing a switch. Locate the circuit breaker or fuse for the circuit and switch it to the "Off" position. Don't take for granted that you have turned the power off. Double-check the circuit by flipping the light switch to the "On" position. If the light remains off, you have selected the correct circuit. Still work as if power is live.

2 Remove the old switchplate and switch using a screwdriver. Pull the switch out of the box and disconnect the wires. If you have enough wire to work with, cut off the bare wire just below where the insulation begins, then strip off ⅜ inch of insulation. The new wire will give a better connection.

3 Use a pair of pliers to connect the black wire from the dimmer switch to the electrical black wire by twisting in a clockwise direction. Twist a wire connector over the wires until tight, making sure no bare wires are exposed. Repeat for the neutral and ground wires.

4 Gently bend and push the wires into the electric box and seat the switch into place. Connect the switch to the box and install the new switchplate. Turn on the power and test your work.

WYNN TIP:
Most dimmers are larger than conventional switches, so you may have to rearrange wires in the box before it fits. Don't force a dimmer because the case might crack.

Step 3. Twisting the wires together, then fastening with a wire cap creates a solid electrical connection that is safe.

WYNN TIP:
Dimmer switches not only give you control over the usage of light in a room but helps you save money. Operating a bulb at less than its full intensity helps extend the life of the bulb and saves on energy usage.

installing a ceiling fan

Few electrical fixtures affect the comfort of a room like a ceiling fan. And you don't have to sacrifice style for comfort. You can choose from fans in a wide variety of colors and styles. Best of all, ceiling fans have become easier to install—practically everything you need comes right in the box. Forget the wire strippers, pliers, and drill, provided you have an electrical box that will support the weight.

TOOLS AND MATERIALS:
- **Ceiling fan**
- **Neon tester**
- **Screwdriver**
- **Safety glasses**
- **Dust mask**
- **Wire nuts**

1 Turn off the power to the fixture at the service panel. Close and lock the panel door so power isn't accidentally restored. Place a note on the panel so others will know not to restore power until you are finished. Test the wires with a neon tester to ensure the power is off (see pages 170–171).

Step 3. Fasten the mounting bracket securely to the electrical box.

2 Wear eye protection. It's also a good idea to wear a dust mask if you need to cut into the ceiling. Dismantle and properly dispose of the old ceiling fixture. Inspect the existing fixture box to make sure it is metal and mounted properly to hold the ceiling fan. Check the manufacturer's instructions for specifications.

3 Remove the mounting bracket from the fan canopy. Fasten the mounting bracket to the ceiling electrical box using mounting screws. Some fan manufacturers use a J-hook to hold the weight of the fan assembly, leaving hands free for wiring installation. If your model includes a J-hook, install the mounting bracket with the J-hook toward the floor. (You can make a temporary hook from coat hanger wire if needed.)

4 Carefully lift the fan assembly. Hang the fan on the hook and feed

WYNN TIP:
Never mount a ceiling fan to a plastic electrical box. Mount only to a metal box securely attached to a joist or the building structure. Fans heavier than 35 pounds will need to be secured to a brace between ceiling joists. One option is to install an expandable metal ceiling fan hanger bar.

the electrical wires through the center hole of the mounting bracket.

5 Follow the manufacturer's instructions to connect the wires. Typically you'll work as follows: Connect the ground wire of the electrical box to the fan-assembly wire marked "ground." Use a wire nut to connect the white neutral wire in the electrical box to the fan assembly's white neutral wire.

6 Fasten the black wire in the electrical box to the black wire of the fan assembly using a wire nut. If your fan assembly includes a light fixture, you will need to connect the black wire in the electrical box to the black-and-blue wire of the fan assembly.

7 Spread the wires apart so that the green and white wires are on one side of the box, and the black and blue wires are on the other side.

8 Push the wire nuts up into the electrical box. Secure the ceiling canopy to the mounting plate per the manufacturer's instructions.

9 Install the fan blades, shades, and lightbulbs. Restore the power to the circuit and test your newly installed ceiling fan.

Step 6. Connect similar color wires using wire caps to secure and protect the electrical connection. Be sure to look at the wiring diagram included with the fan.

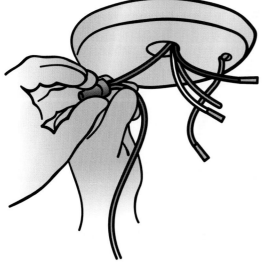

WYNN TIP:

For safety, fan blades must be at least 7 feet above the floor and 24 inches from any obstruction. For best air circulation, select a fan with larger blades for a large room.

testing and replacing receptacles

It's tough to know if receptacles have been damaged. Small cracks develop into a short. Older receptacles may not hold plugs firmly in place. Fortunately, receptacles are inexpensive and easy to replace. Don't hesitate to replace one for any reason, even if it is just paint-glopped or doesn't look good with a new wall color.

TOOLS AND MATERIALS:
- Neon tester
- Receptacle analyzer
- Needle-nose pliers
- Screwdriver
- Electrical tape
- Receptacle

TEST FOR A FAULTY RECEPTACLE OR SEE IF A RECEPTACLE IS LIVE

1 With the power to the circuit on, insert one probe of a neon tester into each slot of the receptacle. Do not touch the metal probes; only touch the insulated wires of the tester.

2 If the tester glows, the receptacle is working. Test both plugs of a duplex receptacle.

TEST FOR POWER TO THE BOX

1 If the receptacle is not live, check its power source. Shut off power to the outlet at the service panel.

2 Remove the coverplate, disconnect the screws holding the receptacle to the box, and pull the receptacle out.

3 Restore power and touch one probe of the neon tester to a brass screw terminal and the other to a silver-colored terminal. The tester light will glow if power is coming to the receptacle. If the tester indicates no power, there's a problem with the cable or the current. Call an electrician.

TEST FOR GROUNDING AND POLARIZATION

1 Do not turn off the power. Insert one prong of a neon tester into the receptacle's short (hot) slot and the other into the grounding hole.

2 If the tester glows, the receptacle is grounded and the slots are polarized.

3 If the tester doesn't glow, put one probe in the grounding hole, the other in the long slot. If the tester glows, hot and neutral wires are reversed. If this is the case, turn off the power and switch the hot and neutral wires, following steps 4–7 in "Replace a Receptacle," page 178.

4 If the tester doesn't glow in either place, the device isn't grounded.

WYNN TIP: Replace receptacles that will not securely hold a plug. The exposed plug leads pose a shock hazard to fingers young and old alike.

TEST A TWO-SLOT RECEPTACLE FOR GROUNDING

1 With the power on, insert one probe of a neon tester into the short (hot) slot and touch the other probe to the coverplate screw. The screw head must be clean and paint-free. If it's not, remove the coverplate and insert one probe in the short slot and touch the other to the metal box.

2 If the neon tester glows, the box is grounded, and you can install a grounded three-hole receptacle (see page 178).

3 If the tester doesn't glow, insert one prong into the long (neutral) slot and touch the other to the coverplate screw or the box. If the tester glows, the box is grounded, but the receptacle is not correctly polarized; the hot and neutral wires are reversed. If this is the case, turn off the power and switch the hot and neutral wires, following steps 4–7 for "Replace a Receptacle," page 178.

4 If the tester doesn't glow in either position, the box is not grounded. Do not install a three-hole receptacle.

USE A RECEPTACLE ANALYZER

1 With this handy device, you can perform a series of tests almost instantly, without having to dismantle anything.

2 Leave the power on, but unplug all equipment and flip all switches to "off" on the circuit of the receptacle you will be testing. Insert the analyzer into the receptacle. A combination of glowing lights will tell you what is happening with your receptacle.

ground not connected

neutral wire not connected

hot wire not connected

hot and ground wires switched

hot and neutral wires switched

receptacle wired correctly

A receptacle analyzer is a quick and easy way to troubleshoot a receptacle without having to tear into it.

testing and replacing receptacles *continued*

REPLACE A RECEPTACLE

1 Turn off power at the service panel and test the receptacle to make sure the power is off.

2 Remove the coverplate, disconnect the screws holding the receptacle to the box, and pull out the receptacle.

3 Note which wires are attached to which terminals. If necessary, make notations on pieces of tape and wrap them on the wires. Loosen the terminal screws and disconnect the wires.

4 Inspect the wires in the box, and wrap electrical tape around any damaged insulation.

5 Attach the wires to the new receptacle, positioning each wire so it hooks clockwise on the terminal screw. Firmly tighten the terminal screws.

6 Wrap the body of the receptacle with electrical tape so that all the terminals are covered.

7 Carefully tuck the wires and the receptacle into the box and connect the receptacle to the box by tightening the mounting screws. Don't force the receptacle into place— it may crack.

Step 5. Hooking the wires clockwise around the terminals draws them tight as you tighten the terminals.

WYNN TIP:
If a receptacle produces sparks, makes noise, or has a burning smell, shut off the power and replace it with a new receptacle. If this does not take care of the problem, call a professional electrician.

Step 6. Wrap electrical tape around the body to hold connections.

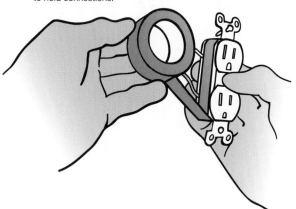

installing a programmable thermostat

A programmable thermostat reduces energy costs. It automatically adjusts the temperature in your home during sleeping and waking hours. You can also set it to automatically change settings when you're away. Before you purchase one, write down the brand names and model numbers of your old thermostat and heating and air-conditioning units to assure you buy a thermostat compatible with your system.

TOOLS AND MATERIALS:
- **Screwdriver**
- **Thermostat**
- **Level**

Step 1. Label the wires if they are not color-coded as you remove them from the old thermostat.

1 Remove the housing from the old thermostat. As you remove wires from the old thermostat, label them if they aren't color-coded.

2 Remove the old thermostat and tuck the old wires safely to the side. Be careful that they don't fall back into the wall.

3 Pull the wires through the new wall plate and mount the plate securely to the wall. Check that it is level and adjust as necessary.

4 Push excess wire back into the wall and hook up the wires clockwise around the terminals according to the manufacturer's instructions.

5 Attach the body to the coverplate. Set the clock and program the unit according to the manufacturer's instructions.

WYNN TIP:
To prevent wires from slipping into the wall before you can attach the new thermostat, fold a piece of tape around each wire with the ends of the tape sticking out to the side.

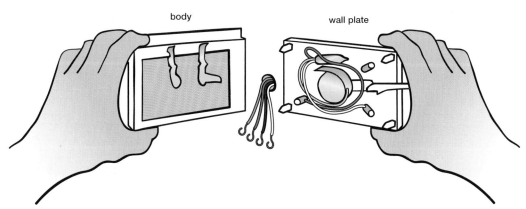

body

wall plate

plumbing basics

Keeping your home plumbing running is a snap once you understand the basics, know how to perform routine maintenance, and have clear instructions for common repairs.

ome plumbing seems pretty simple when everything is working properly. You turn the faucet on, and water flows. You turn the faucet off, and water stops. The showerhead delivers a soothing, cleansing, warm stream of water. Toilets flush waste out of your home. Garbage disposals whisk away leftover food.

But when the sink is clogged, the toilet is overflowing, or only cold water dribbles out of the showerhead, your home plumbing system might seem frustrating and complex. In this chapter, I provide you with the straightforward information you need to address these problems. I also offer lots of maintenance tips and suggestions to help you avoid most problems in the first place.

Upgrade projects

With instructions in this chapter, you can replace a toilet seat—or install a brand new toilet—to better suit the style of your bathroom. You can replace a showerhead with one that will make your bath more of a spalike retreat, and add a convenient hand shower. You can replace a faucet, or install a new sink in a kitchen or bath.

You still may find yourself calling a plumber for major projects—you'll see on page 214 when I had to make that call myself. But armed with patience, willpower, and the right know-how, you'll no longer be daunted when your home plumbing system doesn't function as you'd like. You'll make the repair to get it working right.

plumbing toolbox

GROOVE-JOINT PLIERS
Purchase a high-quality pair that adjusts to grab almost any diameter pipe. You may want to get a couple of sizes.

HACKSAW
Cut metal pipe with this tool. Hacksaw blades dull quickly, so purchase extra blades.

ADJUSTABLE WRENCH
It snugly fits the nuts on faucets and other fixtures. Locking versions are available to ensure the opening stays to size.

NEEDLE-NOSE PLIERS
These are ideal for delicate tasks such as removing faucet O-rings and clips.

DRAIN AUGER OR SNAKE
A hand-cranked version will clear clogs that won't plunge away. Choose a 25-foot length to reach most home clogs.

PLUNGER
Select a plunger with a flange extension, which makes it easier to get a good seal in a toilet bowl. You can also use this type for bathtubs and sinks.

BLOW BAG
When plunging or augering don't clear a clog, hook this up to a garden hose, insert it into the drainpipe, and turn on the water. The bag seals the pipe and uses water pressure to move the clog.

FLASHLIGHT
You'll need it to peer into wall cavities and under sinks. Keep spare batteries on hand.

CLOSET OR TOILET AUGER
Safely remove objects stuck in toilets without damaging the porcelain bowl.

plumbing toolbox

ADJUSTABLE PIPE WRENCH
It's essential for working with threaded iron pipe. Look for a sturdy wrench that tightens firmly to size.

SPUD WRENCH
This tool is handy for installing or removing the large nuts that secure the basket strainers of kitchen sinks and toilet tanks.

SEAT WRENCH
This tool is specially designed to get at a damaged faucet seat.

BASIN WRENCH
You'll want this tool when you work on faucets and sinks to reach into small spaces to install or remove nuts you can't reach with pliers.

unclogging a toilet

Don't continue to flush a toilet when it clogs or you'll soon regret it—you may flood the bathroom floor. Remove water from the toilet until the bowl is about half full. This will be enough water to create a tight seal around a plunger.

TOOLS AND MATERIALS:
- **Plunger**
- **Bucket**
- **Closet auger**

WYNN TIP:
Never use a chemical drain cleaner to unclog a toilet. It won't work. You'll then need to plunge or auger through chemicals that could burn your skin or eyes.

USING A PLUNGER

You can clear a clogged toilet with an ordinary plunger, but a molded-cup plunger generates stronger agitation to dislodge clogs.

1 If there is no water in the bowl, pour some into it. The water helps seal the plunger head. Work the plunger up and down vigorously a dozen or so strokes. Quickly remove the plunger.

2 If the water disappears, you're done plunging! Before using the toilet, pour a couple of buckets of water into the bowl so it empties several times.

3 If plunging didn't work the first time, try several more times. If it still doesn't work, try augering.

USING A CLOSET AUGER

Don't use just any auger to clear a toilet; it could scratch or crack the bowl. A closet auger is a specialized tool with a long handle and a plastic cover at the bend to protect your toilet.

1 Retract the auger spring all the way into the handle. The spring should barely be visible in the plastic protective cover.

2 Insert the auger into the bowl outlet. Crank the handle. When you feel a resistance or blockage, pull back slightly. Wiggle the handle and try again. Keep at it until the blockage is dislodged.

WYNN TIP:
A closet auger grabs and dislodges most blockages. However it does not work well on objects such as toys. If you are unable to clear the blockage, you may have to remove the toilet to get the toy out.

Step 2. The design of the closet auger allows it to navigate turns while protecting the porcelain.

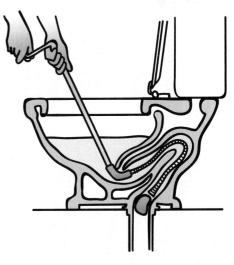

WYNN TIP:
Act fast when a toilet begins to overflow. Remove the tank lid. Pull the float up and push the flapper down into its seat (see page 206). This will stop the toilet from filling.

opening a clogged sink drain

Clearing a sink drain requires only a few basic tools. Addressing it yourself saves the expense of hiring a plumber. Just acknowledge your limitations and don't be too aggressive. You don't want to damage the drainpipe by applying too much force.

TOOLS AND MATERIALS:
- Plunger
- Auger
- Screwdriver
- Pipe wrenches
- Bucket
- Rags
- Tape

WYNN TIP:
The best auger is a coiled cable that wraps inside a housing. The housing should have a handle and a crank on it for spinning the cable inside the drain.

OPENING A CLOGGED SINK

Once a clog has formed, preventive measures will not work. It's time to get out the plunger.

1 Partially fill the sink with enough water to cover the plunger head. If you have an overflow opening, stuff a wet rag into the opening. This will focus the plunging pressure on the clog.

2 Plunge up and down vigorously, keeping the plunger sealed against the bottom of the sink.

3 If water isn't swishing back and forth, or if it doesn't feel that you are getting enough resistance, air may be escaping through the second drain or overflow opening. Have a helper hold the wet rag firmly in place.

4 Once you have broken the clog loose, run hot water through the drain to flush out the debris.

UNCLOGGING A DOUBLE SINK

1 Cover the drain on one side of a double sink with a rag or plug. Have a helper hold the rag in place while plunging the other side. Make sure there is water in the side being plunged to form a seal.

2 Once the clog releases, run hot water through the drain to flush out remaining sludge.

WYNN TIP:

Avoid reaching for chemical products to clear a blockage. They can help slow-running pipes, but when a blockage occurs they create a safety hazard. The caustic chemicals will pool in the standing water, and when you work on the drainpipe you can come into contact with them.

CLEARING STUBBORN CLOGS

If the plunger just doesn't seem to work, it is time to try a drain auger. You can go through the drain or you can remove the trap as described below. Use your judgment based on where you believe the clog is located.

1 Place a bucket under the trap to catch water in the drainpipe.

2 Remove the trap using a pipe wrench. Wrap tape around the jaws of the wrench to prevent the teeth of the tool from marring the surface.

3 Remove the slip nuts and washers holding the trap in place. You need direct access into the horizontal stretch of pipe.

4 Carefully feed the auger cable into the drain or horizontal pipe. When you feel resistance, you're probably up against the clog.

5 Pull an extra 18 inches of cable out of the housing, tighten the setscrew securing the cable, and turn the crank on the auger by applying moderate force.

6 As the free cable works its way into the pipe, loosen the setscrew and pull out another 18 inches. Continue until the cable has reached the larger vertical drainpipe or you have extended the full length of the auger.

7 Pull the cable out, cleaning it and feeding it back into the housing. Reassemble the trap. Run hot water through the drain to flush out any remaining sludge. If water backs up, there may still be some loose debris in the line left behind by the auger. Try plunging to get rid of residual debris. Flush with hot water.

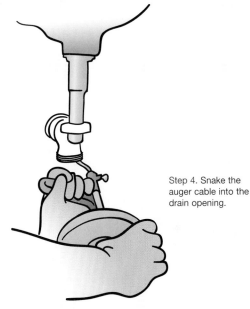

Step 4. Snake the auger cable into the drain opening.

WYNN TIP:
The bathroom sink can use a good flushing every couple of months to clear hair and grease buildup. Boil some water in a teapot and pour it down the sink. Boiled water is hotter than tap water and will dissolve the sludge coating the walls of your drainpipes.

WYNN TIP:
Wrap electrical or masking tape around the jaws of your wrench or pliers to protect the chrome nuts.

unclogging a tub drain

To unclog a tub drain, reach for a plunger and auger. They are safer than dumping chemicals down the drain. If you have poured chemicals into the drain, run hot water into the drain or tub for several minutes to remove or dilute the chemicals before plunging.

TOOLS AND MATERIALS:
- Plunger
- Auger
- Screwdriver
- Old rag

PLUNGE FIRST

1 If your tub has a pop-up stopper, remove it before plunging. Wiggle it to free the linkage assembly—the mechanism that connects the trap lever with the stopper mechanism.

2 Plug the overflow hole with an old rag. Fill the tub with an inch or so of water. This will help the plunger seal.

3 Plunge vigorously. If the tub is still clogged, move on to augering.

AUGER THROUGH THE DRAIN

1 Unscrew or pry up the strainer, if your tub has one.

2 Insert the auger. Going through the drain will only allow you to reach as far as the tee where the drain joins the larger pipe. Clogs farther down will have to be addressed through the overflow tube. Be careful that you don't chip or damage the tub surface with the auger.

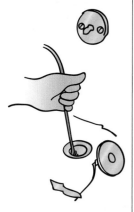

Step 2. The tub surface is more fragile than you may think, so use care when augering.

3 Fish the auger down the drain until you feel resistance. Try to push through another foot or so. Set the setscrew. Turn the crank. Don't use too much force.

4 Retrieve the cable and turn on the water to flush out any remaining debris.

AUGER THROUGH THE OVERFLOW

1 Unscrew the overflow plate and remove the pop-up or lever. Pull out the assembly.

2 Feed the auger into the overflow tube. Continue fishing out enough length to extend down into the trap or beyond.

3 If you reach the end of your auger and the blockage still remains, remove the auger. Locate a clean-out plug on the drain line and try augering there.

WYNN TIP:
Sluggish drains may not need plunging or augering. Carefully pour boiling water down the drain. Hot water works well dissolving the grease and soap buildup that binds most clogs. Be patient. It may take a couple of gallons.

Step 2. Augering through the overflow tube may be easier than through the drain.

unclogging a shower drain

Shower drains eventually become clogged with soap and hair. Fixing a sluggish drain before it becomes clogged can be as simple as filling the base with an inch of water and vigorously plunging. If plunging doesn't do the trick, you don't always need a plumber. Try using an auger or garden hose to clear the clog.

TOOLS AND MATERIALS:
- Auger
- Garden hose attached to a spout
- Rags
- Blow bag

USING AN AUGER

1 Remove the strainer. Push the auger end down the drain and through the trap. Push and pull several times to remove a soap clog.

2 If the auger won't advance farther into the drain because of a blockage, try pulling out the auger. If you're lucky, the blockage will come with it. Otherwise, use the auger to push the clog into a larger drainpipe downstream.

3 Flush the drain with water for a few minutes.

USING A HOSE

If an auger doesn't seem to do the trick, try forcing out the blockage with a hose.

1 Remove the strainer. Feed the hose down the drain as far as it will travel.

2 Pack rags tightly around the hose at the drain opening. Hold the rags firmly in place and be prepared to get a little wet.

3 Have a helper turn the water fully on and off a few times.

Step 2. You may be surprised at the amount of back pressure from a hose, so hold the hose and rags firmly in place.

WYNN TIP:
The garden hose can be effective for clearing clogs; putting a blow bag on the end adds greater force. Blow bags are available at most home centers.

cleaning out a fixture trap

Traps hold water so sewer gases don't enter your home. Occasionally the traps become clogged with soap and hair, in turn clogging your sink. Traps can also save the day if you accidentally drop jewelry down the drain—don't run any water down the drain or the jewelry may travel farther down the drainpipe. In either case, you'll need to dismantle the trap to clean it out.

TOOLS AND MATERIALS:
- **Groove-joint pliers**
- **Teflon tape or pipe joint compound**
- **Washers**
- **Dishpan or bucket**
- **Wire brush**

1 Turn off the supply valves. Place a small bucket or dishpan beneath the trap to catch the water that will spill out as you remove the trap.

2 Loosen both slip nuts. Once they're loose, unscrew by hand. Slide the slip nuts back out of the way.

3 Remove the flexible washer on each end of the trap. Dump out the water that sits in the trap.

4 Remove any sludge lodged in the trap by using a wire brush or running a piece of cloth through it. Rinse the trap and washers.

5 Replace washers showing signs of wear. Wrap the trap threads with plumber's tape or brush with joint compound.

6 Place the washers on both ends of the trap and position. Hand-tighten the slip nuts to hold in place. Finish tightening the nuts using an adjustable wrench. Don't overtighten or they'll crack.

7 Turn on the water. Test for leaks by filling the bowl then removing the plug.

Step 2. Use groove-joint pliers to loosen the slip nuts.

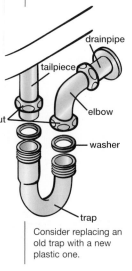

drainpipe

tailpiece

slip nut

elbow

washer

trap

Consider replacing an old trap with a new plastic one.

WYNN TIP:
When working on drainpipes, don't just turn off the faucet. Take the extra precaution of turning off the supply valves. If you have to step away from your project, this will prevent someone else from trying to use the sink and creating a mess.

replacing a sink strainer

If you find you have a slight leak at the tailpiece under the sink, you most likely have a poor seal around the sink strainer. Replacing a sink strainer isn't difficult, if you have the proper equipment.

TOOLS AND MATERIALS:
- **Adjustable wrench and hammer (and possibly a spud wrench)**
- **Putty knife**
- **Plumber's putty**
- **Pipe joint compound or plumber's tape**
- **Replacement parts**

1 Turn off the water supply just in case you have to step away from the project for any length of time.

2 Loosen the slip nut beneath the strainer body using an adjustable wrench. Also loosen the slip nut above the trap bend. Finish unscrewing the slip nuts by hand.

3 Remove the tailpiece. Remove the locknut with a spud wrench. If you don't have a spud wrench, place a screwdriver against a rib of the locknut. Gently tap the screwdriver with a hammer until the locknut loosens.

4 Unscrew and remove the locknut and rubber gasket. Lift out the strainer body.

5 Scrape away the old putty with a putty knife. Clean the opening thoroughly. If putty residue remains, soak a scouring pad in paint thinner to remove the rest.

6 Place a rope of new putty around the lip of the opening.

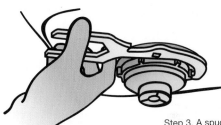

Step 3. A spud wrench is specially designed to fit the large locknut of a sink drain.

strainer basket

strainer body

rubber gasket

fiber washer

locknut

slip nut

tailpiece

Anatomy of a sink strainer

7 Press the strainer seating into the putty.

8 Install the rubber gasket, then assemble the sink strainer. Fasten under the sink with the locknut.

9 Tighten the locknut using the spud wrench. Reinstall the tailpiece. Turn on the water to test your work.

Step 6. When tightened, the strainer will seat against the putty, forming a strong seal.

WYNN TIP:
The locknut can be difficult to remove, mainly because it is hard to get to it. Purchase a spud wrench, which is specially designed to fit on locknuts. It'll make the job easier.

adjusting drain assemblies

I find it annoying when I fill up a sink or tub only to look down and find the basin empty. A slow-draining tub or sink is also frustrating. Adjusting the drain assembly can correct either problem.

TOOLS AND MATERIALS:
- **Screwdriver**
- **Pliers**

WYNN TIP:
A bent rod will not allow a pop-up drain assembly to properly seat. Replace pivot rods that appear bent or damaged.

ADJUSTING A BATHROOM POP-UP DRAIN

1 If you've cleaned out the strainer or stopper and the problem persists, pull and check the stopper seal. If it's damaged, replace any rubber parts, or replace the stopper itself.

2 Under the bathroom sink, examine the pivot rod. When the stopper is closed, it should slant slightly up from the pivot to the clevis. If it doesn't, loosen the setscrew, raise or lower the clevis on the lift rod, and retighten the setscrew.

ADJUSTING A STOPPER

1 Mark the hole the rod is in so you don't forget. Squeeze the spring clip and pull the pivot rod out of the clevis.

2 Reinsert the rod into the next higher or lower hole. If water drips from the pivot, try tightening its cap.

3 If water still slowly seeps out of the bowl, replace the seal inside.

Anatomy of a sink pop-up drain

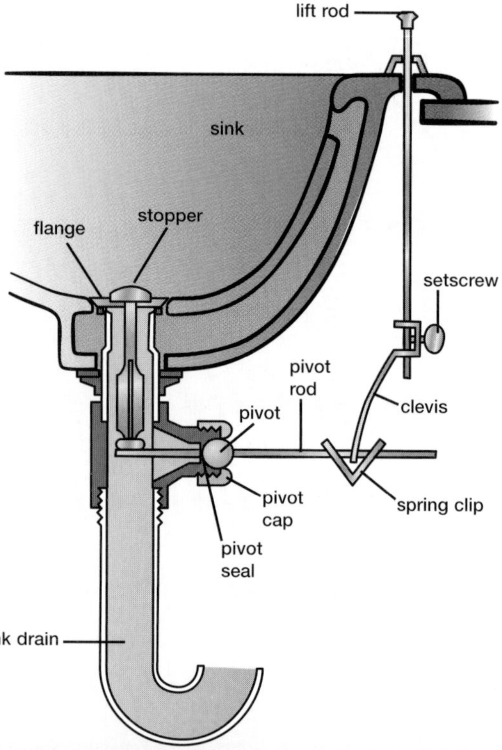

WYNN TIP:
Pull up the strainer or stopper periodically to clean away soap or other gunk that may keep it from seating properly.

lift rod

sink

flange

stopper

setscrew

pivot rod

pivot

clevis

spring clip

pivot cap

pivot seal

sink drain

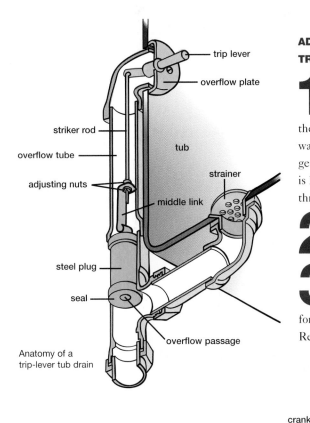

trip lever

overflow plate

striker rod

overflow tube

adjusting nuts

middle link

tub

strainer

steel plug

seal

overflow passage

Anatomy of a
trip-lever tub drain

ADJUSTING A TRIP-LEVER DRAIN

1 A trip lever lifts and lowers a seal plug at the base of the overflow tube. When the seal plug drops into its seat, water from the tub drain can't get past. But because the plug is hollow, water can still flow through the overflow tube.

2 Unscrew the overflow plate. Pull out the trip-lever assembly.

3 Loosen the adjusting nuts. Check the seal on the bottom of the plug for wear. Replace if it's worn. Reassemble.

ADJUSTING A TUB POP-UP

1 Unscrew the overflow plate. Fish out the entire drain assembly.

2 Loosen the adjusting nuts. If the stopper doesn't seat tightly, move the middle link higher on the striker rod. If the tub is slow to drain, lower the link. Reassemble.

overflow plate

crank

lever

Anatomy of a tub
pop-up drain

striker rod

stopper

adjusting
nuts

middle link

striker spring

rocker arm

tub drain

assessing noisy pipes

Do your pipes rattle, chatter, hiss, or moan? Those sounds can be annoying, especially if you're a light sleeper. For most fixes, you don't need to call in a professional. You can determine the cause and remedy the situation.

TOOLS AND MATERIALS:
- Foam pipe insulation
- Sound-insulating pipe hangers

Step 3. If a pipe vibrates, there should be enough room to wedge insulation behind it.

VIBRATING PIPES

1 Vibrating pipes bang into the house frame because of sudden changes in water pressure. To find out what's causing the vibrating, start by checking appliances such as clothes washers and dishwashers, which require periodic demands for water at high pressure. Even a sudden demand or stop in the water flow—such as turning a faucet on or off—can cause the vibration.

2 Once you determine the cause, have a helper turn on the faucet or appliance while you track down the offending pipe.

3 Insert pieces of foam pipe insulation between the pipe and the stud or joist.

TICKING PIPES

1 Hot water pipes that cool and suddenly reheat can produce a hissing sound. Locate the noisy pipe.

2 Install insulators for pipe—available at home centers—around the pipe. The insulation allows the pipe to hold heat then cool down more slowly, thus dampening the noise.

PIPES THAT CHATTER OR MOAN

1 Water pressure that is set too high can produce chattering or moaning.

2 Pay attention to whether the problem is a one-time occurrence or if it happens repeatedly. If the problem is persistent, call a professional to check the pressure.

WYNN TIP:
Pipes aren't always to blame for annoying noises. If when you barely open a faucet, you hear a rattle, it's probably a defective seat washer.

WYNN TIP:
Vibrating pipes may be attached or held in place with pipe hangers. Instead of cushioning the pipe with foam insulation, purchase and install sound-insulating pipe hangers.

what if...

you need to shut off the water supply to your home?

Be ready to shut off the main water supply quickly. You never know when you'll experience the misfortune of a burst water pipe or faulty pipe connection. Every family member who is capable should know where the main water valve shutoff is located and how to operate it.

Location, location

Where you'll find your main water valve shutoff depends on the part of the country in which you live. Look for where the water service enters your home. This may be in the basement or on the first floor. Water supplied by a municipality or private utility will have a meter installed at this point. You should find either one or two valves—one on either side of the meter. Operate the valves by opening and closing them. If you need a special tool to operate the shutoff valves, keep the tool handy.

In areas with a temperate climate, the shutoff valve may be located outside your home. The valve, with the meter, will typically be in a shallow box buried in the ground. Locate it, and keep grass and debris cleared so you can access the valve if necessary.

If you don't have a shutoff valve inside your home, I recommend you have a professional plumber install one.

WYNN TIP:
Never block the path to the main water shutoff valve with boxes or other items because you may need to get to it in an emergency.

Whether you have a ball-type (above) or gate valve (right), it is important to have one installed inside your home in case of emergencies. That way you can quickly turn off the water supply.

fixing pipe leaks

Pinhole leaks do minimal damage if caught early. However, they can cause a great amount of damage over time, so do a repair as soon as you notice the problem. Here are some quick temporary fixes to stop the leak until you can do a complete repair.

TOOLS AND MATERIALS:
- Screwdriver
- Putty knife
- Electrical tape
- Automotive hose clamp
- Rubber
- Pipe clamp and gasket
- Plumber's epoxy
- Cleanout plug

WYNN TIP:
A drip does not a leak make. If a pipe drips along its length, you might be seeing condensation from humid air, rather than a leak. You can fix this quickly by wrapping the pipe with insulation.

QUICK FIX WITH TAPE
Grab a roll of electrical tape. Start about 6 inches to one side of the leak, and wrap the tape over the pipe, continuing 6 inches past the leak. Continue wrapping the pipe tightly with several layers of tape.

Remember, this is an extremely temporary fix. It should give you enough time to run to the local home center to purchase a pipe clamp and rubber gasket for a permanent repair.

QUICK FIX WITH A CLAMP
This temporary fix creates a slightly better leak stopper than the tape.

Cut a piece of rubber that fits around the pipe. Wrap it over the leak. Open an automotive hose clamp and place it over the rubber. Tighten, making sure the clamp directly covers the hole.

Clamp. Cut the rubber to fit completely around the pipe, but don't overlap it.

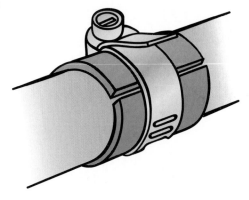

WYNN TIP:
Although wastewater lines are less likely to leak than supply pipes, they occasionally do leak. When wastewater begins to seep out, you'll want to fix it in a hurry. The wastewater not only smells, it presents a biohazard. Always wear appropriate safety protection when working with wastewater.

INSTALLING A PIPE CLAMP AND GASKET

1 A pipe clamp seals cracks and pinhole leaks and should last for several years. Position the gasket so it is centered over the leak. Place the two halves of the clamp around the gasket and tighten by hand. Be careful not to move the gasket while you work.

2 Using a wrench, draw the nuts down on the clamp, evenly working from one to another until tight.

clamp

rubber gasket

nut

Step 1. Hand-tighten each screw on the clamp until all are snug, then finish tightening with a wrench.

FIXING A LEAKY FITTING

1 Don't clamp a fitting leak. You won't get a good seal and may further damage the fitting. Use plumber's epoxy to stop the leak. Remember, this is only a semi-permanent fix.

2 You don't need to shut off the water when using plumber's epoxy unless the leak sprays all over and is a nuisance.

3 The epoxy comes in two parts. Cut equal portions of each part of the putty. Knead the two pieces together. Once they turn a uniform color, you're ready to stop the leak.

WYNN TIP:
Older homes may have galvanized pipes, which tend to rust from the inside out. Be prepared. If one leak appears, others may follow as the pipes deteriorate. Purchase a supply of pipe clamps rather than run back and forth to the home center. Remember to buy different sizes to fit all of the lines.

4 Pack the epoxy into the leak by pushing it with your thumb. Keep packing and pushing until the leak stops.

SEALING A LEAKY CLEANOUT

1 First warn everyone in the house not to use any fixtures. Wear proper clothing and take precautions against splashes by wearing gloves and safety goggles. Remove the plug—it may unscrew or just pull out.

2 Replace with a new plug. Or reseal screw-in plugs with a new application of plumber's tape to the threads. If the plug has an O-ring, replace it.

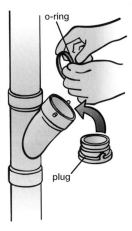

o-ring

plug

Step 2. Replace with a new cleanout plug rather than fix the old plug. New plugs are inexpensive.

sealing a leaking baseplate

If you find water in the cabinet below the sink, it could be from three places: the supply lines, the drain, or the faucet baseplate. The problem may be solved by simply tightening the supply lines (see page 201). If the leak comes from the drain, see page 192–193. If neither of those is the cause, you may have a leaky baseplate that allows splashed water to seep through mounting holes.

TOOLS AND MATERIALS:
- **Putty knife**
- **Groove-joint pliers or basin wrench**
- **Plumber's putty**
- **Gasket**

SEALING PUTTY-SEALED BASEPLATES

1 If putty forms the seal around the baseplate, you may not have to remove the faucet. Use pliers or a basin wrench to loosen the mounting nuts so you have about a ½-inch clearance between the baseplate and the sink.

2 Scrape away old putty using a plastic putty knife so you don't scratch the surface.

Step 1. First try to loosen the mounting nuts with pliers. If you can't reach them, try a basin wrench.

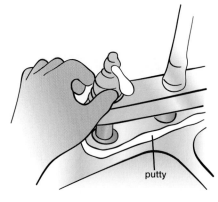

putty

3 Make a rope of plumber's putty. It should be about ¼ inch in diameter. While holding the baseplate, press the rope evenly on the bottom of the baseplate.

4 Seat the faucet against the sink. Tighten the mounting nuts. Turn the faucet on and check for leaks.

Step 3. Press the putty onto the sink or bottom of the baseplate to create an even seal.

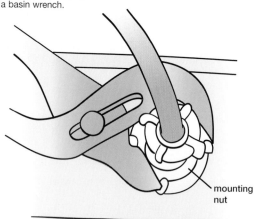

mounting nut

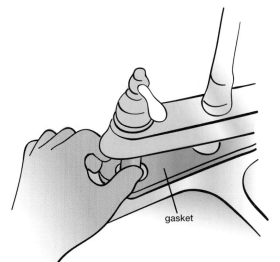

gasket

Step 3. Position the gasket so it fits beneath the baseplate for a good seal.

WYNN TIP:
Many of the plumbers I know say putty lasts longer than gaskets. You may want to discard the gasket and seal with putty instead, but check the manufacturer's warranty before you do.

REPLACING A BASEPLATE GASKET

1 Turn off the water supply to the faucet at the stop valves or main supply valve.

2 Use a basin wrench or pliers to disconnect the mounting nuts. Lift off the faucet. Don't try to repair an old gasket. Throw it out.

3 Purchase a new gasket from your local home center. Set it in position and seat the faucet over it.

4 Connect the mounting nuts and turn the water on to check for leaks.

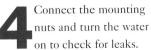

WYNN TIP:
Not all leaks occur because of cracked or damaged baseplate seals. The baseplate may have worked itself loose over time. Try tightening the mounting nuts with a basin wrench to solve the problem.

Here's the beef

Plumbing emergencies always seem to occur at the worst possible times. I was preparing to serve my first holiday dinner to my entire family. Naturally I was a bit nervous. Our traditional family holiday dinner is beef brisket. I made a practice brisket a couple of days before the event. The trial run went well, and I was feeling confident. The day of the dinner, my mom was helping me clean up the kitchen before the rest of the family arrived. She pulled the remaining old brisket out of the refrigerator and shoved it into the garbage disposal. Gooey meat-infused liquid started oozing up into the sink and out from the cabinet below. A bad scene anytime, but a disaster with dinner just hours away.

The problem turned out to be easy to fix, once I calmed down. After unplugging the disposal, I disassembled the P-trap under the sink, fished out what was left of the brisket, replaced the disposal, and reattached the pipes. Everything was cleaned up before I had a houseful of family giving advice. If it hadn't made such a funny after-dinner story, no one would have known—except you and my mom, of course.

stopping a leak in flexible supply line

Supply lines bring water to fixtures. If one leaks, it isn't difficult to fix. Just be aware of the three basic types of flexible supply lines: plain or chrome-plated copper tubing, flexible plastic, and braided metal. Of the three, braided lines are the easiest to install because they are flexible and attach with threaded fittings.

TOOLS AND MATERIALS:

- **Basin wrench or groove-joint pliers**
- **Adjustable wrenches**
- **Plumber's tape**
- **Joint compound**
- **Supply line**

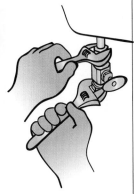

Step 1. Stabilizing one wrench allows you to turn the other without damaging the pipe.

FIX A SUPPLY-VALVE LEAK

1 Often, fixing a leak at a supply valve requires little more than tightening the nut. Don't tighten too much, though, or you may crack the nut or strip the threads. Use two adjustable wrenches. Don't use pipe wrenches. Hold one side of the supply line with one of the wrenches while tightening the nut with a ¼ turn of the other wrench.

2 If the valve still leaks, turn off the water supply and unscrew the offending nut.

3 Wrap the threads or ferrules with plumber's tape or joint compound. Reconnect and test.

INSTALL A NEW LINE

1 If the leak persists, don't bother messing with the old line anymore. Shut off the water.

2 Remove the old supply line using two adjustable wrenches.

3 Purchase a new flexible line. Wrap plumber's tape or joint compound around the threads or ferrules.

4 Connect the new line. Make sure both ends are tight. Turn on the water and test the line for leaks.

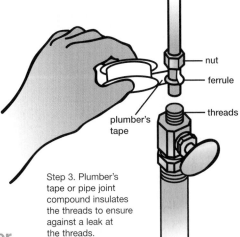

Step 3. Plumber's tape or pipe joint compound insulates the threads to ensure against a leak at the threads.

— nut

— ferrule

— threads

plumber's tape

WYNN TIP:

When purchasing a new line, make sure it is long enough. Measure twice, or take the old one with you to the home center.

fixing a sprayer, diverter, and aerator

Sink sprayers are handy for kitchen cleanup, when they work properly. Before you can fix a problem, you need to determine the cause. Sprayers can be obstructed at the connections, gaskets, or nozzle.

TOOLS AND MATERIALS:
- **Groove-joint pliers or wrench**
- **Old toothbrush**
- **Paper clip, awl, or nail**
- **Vinegar**
- **Bucket**
- **Masking tape**

DIAGNOSE THE PROBLEM

1 If no water comes out of the sprayer, the problem is likely a faulty diverter valve in the base of the faucet. You can replace either the rubber seal or the diverter. Remove the diverter and take it to your supplier to be sure you get the correct replacement.

2 If your faucet (or sprayer) has low water pressure, check the aerator, the screen on the end of the spout (and some sprayer heads). Aerators may develop leaks if their seals are worn or clogged.

CLEAN THE AERATOR

Over time, the buildup of minerals in water will restrict the flow of water.

1 Remove the aerator from the faucet or sprayer by unscrewing it. If you see large deposits of minerals in the aerator holes, use a small nail, paper clip, or awl to remove them.

2 Soak it overnight in vinegar. Clean with an old toothbrush and reassemble.

REPLACE A WORN SPRAYER

1 Turn off the water supply to the sink either at the stop valve beneath the sink or at the main water shutoff valve.

2 Remove the sprayer hose from the faucet sprayer nipple, located beneath the sink. Have a bucket ready because you will need to drain any water remaining in the hose.

3 Use pliers or a wrench to remove the sprayer mounting nut. Lift out the entire sprayer assembly.

4 Inspect for worn parts. If parts are worn, it's best to replace the entire sprayer. Home centers sell a variety of sprayers to fit your existing faucet.

5 Install the sprayer following the manufacturer's instructions.

6 Turn the water back on and test the sprayer. If it does not work, check the diverter valve on the faucet; it may need attention.

WYNN TIP:
Low or no water pressure may not be the fault of the sprayer. Check the hose for kinks.

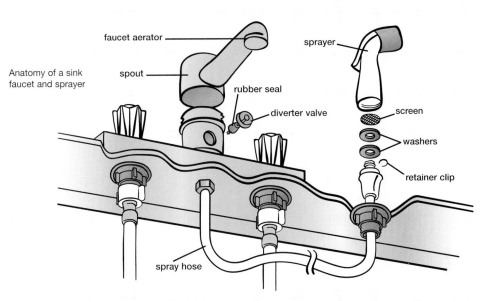

Anatomy of a sink faucet and sprayer

faucet aerator

spout

rubber seal

diverter valve

sprayer

screen

washers

retainer clip

spray hose

Anatomy of an aerator

housing

rubber washer

plastic washer

screen

threaded retainer

Step 3. Scrub the parts with an old toothbrush.

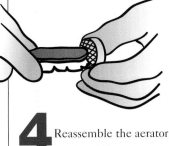

CLEANING A FAUCET AERATOR

1 Unscrew the aerator from the faucet. You may need to use a pair of pliers to remove a stubborn aerator.

2 Disassemble the aerator and inspect it. If it's heavily clogged or punctured, buy a new one.

3 Scrub all the parts with a brush to remove loose debris. Soak overnight in vinegar. Brush and rinse the following day.

4 Reassemble the aerator and install it on the faucet.

CLEANING A DIVERTER VALVE

1 To locate the diverter valve on a typical one-handled faucet, you'll need to remove the faucet spout with pliers. Wrap the teeth of the pliers with masking tape so they don't damage the spout surface. The valve should be located in the front, facing toward you.

2 Remove the diverter. Inspect it for signs of mineral buildup or excessive wear. If it's worn, take it to your local home center and buy a replacement.

3 If the valve has mineral buildup, soak it overnight in vinegar. Clean it with an old toothbrush.

4 Reinstall and assemble the faucet. Turn on the water supply.

maintaining a garbage disposal

Garbage disposals make life easier when cleaning up after meals. But if you abuse them, they can become jammed. If you hear a clanking sound, or if the disposal stops, shut it off. Remove the object that has caused the problem by following the steps described here.

TOOLS AND MATERIALS:
- Allen wrench or disposal turning tool
- Flashlight
- Broom handle

WYNN TIP:
Don't use chemicals of any type to attempt to clear a blocked drain line. You'll be in danger of getting splattered with the stuff when you work to clear the line.

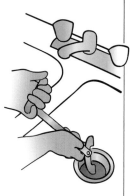

Step 2. Your disposal may have come with a turning tool. If not, an allen wrench will turn it from under the motor.

REMOVING STUCK OBJECTS

If a fork, bottle cap, or other solid object drops down through the splash guard, it can cause the disposal to jam.

1 Turn off the power. Remove the splashguard and peer down the disposal with a flashlight. If you can reach the object, remove it.

2 If you can't free the object, rotate the grinder. Your disposal may come with a tool like the one shown at left that fits into the opening of the disposal. If not, you can purchase one. Or your unit may have an allen wrench. Place the allen wrench into the bottom of the disposal and turn the disposal back and forth. This should free the grinder.

3 Remove any obstructions. Replace the splash guard. Turn on the cold water and test the disposal.

RESETTING AN OVERLOADED DISPOSAL

If your disposal motor shuts off during operation, its overload protector has sensed overheating and has broken the electrical connection.

1 Wait a few minutes for the unit to cool. Push the red reset button on the bottom of the disposal.

2 If that doesn't work, check to see that you have power to the unit by inspecting the cord and the fuse or circuit breaker.

Step 1. Resetting will solve most overworked disposal problems.

WYNN TIP:
Always run cold water before you turn on your disposal. Gradually feed in food waste. Never stick a spatula or any silverware past the splashguard. With the cold water continuing to flow, run the disposal for a few seconds after the food has been ground.

fixing a sweating toilet tank

Porcelain and humidity don't mix. You know this if you live in a humid climate and have an older-style porcelain toilet. They get cold, clammy, and sweaty—creating a mess, not to mention an unsightly appearance. With mastic, polystyrene foam board, and a little time, you can reduce the condensation.

TOOLS AND MATERIALS:
- Tape measure
- Straightedge
- Scissors
- Utility knife
- Mastic
- Polystyrene foam board
- Pencil
- Sponge
- Bucket
- Towel
- Paper

1 Spread all materials on the floor near the sweaty tank, leaving enough room to work. Find the shutoff valve to the toilet, typically below the tank and behind the bowl. Turn the valve to the "off" position. If there is no stop valve, you'll need to shut the water off at the main shutoff. (Now would be a good time to install a stop valve for future repairs. See page 219). Remove all the water from the tank. Use a sponge and bucket to begin; use a towel to dry.

2 Place a piece of paper over the inside of one of the tank walls. The paper should be large enough to completely cover one side. Mark the paper where it meets the edges of the wall. Remove the paper and redraw the lines with a straightedge. Cut along the lines to create the template. Repeat this process for the

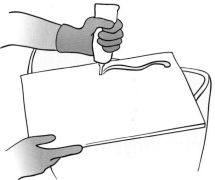

Step 3. Apply a generous amount of mastic to the back of the polystyrene.

other tank walls. Using the templates, cut out pieces of polystyrene foam. Secure the templates to the foam so you get a precise cut. You want to create a tight fit so water will not seep behind the foam pieces.

3 Apply a bead of waterproof mastic to one side of a foam piece. Press the panel into place against the wall of the tank. Repeat with remaining foam panels. Let the mastic dry overnight before refilling the tank.

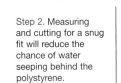

Step 2. Measuring and cutting for a snug fit will reduce the chance of water seeping behind the polystyrene.

WYNN TIP: Working with mastic can be messy, and it can pose a health hazard due to fumes or mishandling. Read the manufacturer's instructions carefully. Work in a well-ventilated area and always wear gloves and safety glasses.

fixing toilet tank run-on

Problems common with toilets occur in their tanks where most of the mechanical action happens. Diagnosis is simple and is based on observation of what is happening under the tank lid. Don't be afraid of the water in the tank; it's clean. However, if you're working in the bowl, definitely wear gloves, protective eyewear, and long sleeves.

TOOLS AND MATERIALS:
- **Screwdriver**
- **Groove-joint pliers**
- **Abrasive pad**
- **Vinegar**
- **Rag**

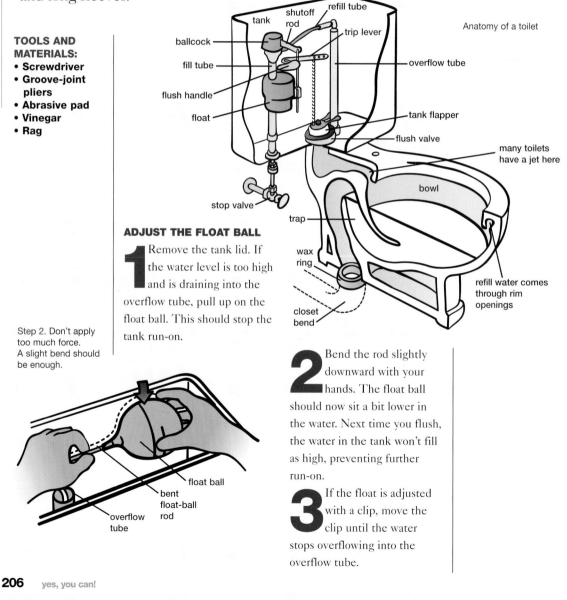

Anatomy of a toilet

Labels: refill tube · shutoff rod · tank · trip lever · ballcock · overflow tube · fill tube · flush handle · float · tank flapper · flush valve · many toilets have a jet here · bowl · stop valve · trap · wax ring · closet bend · refill water comes through rim openings

ADJUST THE FLOAT BALL

1 Remove the tank lid. If the water level is too high and is draining into the overflow tube, pull up on the float ball. This should stop the tank run-on.

Step 2. Don't apply too much force. A slight bend should be enough.

Labels: float ball · bent float-ball rod · overflow tube

2 Bend the rod slightly downward with your hands. The float ball should now sit a bit lower in the water. Next time you flush, the water in the tank won't fill as high, preventing further run-on.

3 If the float is adjusted with a clip, move the clip until the water stops overflowing into the overflow tube.

Step 2. Even new valves need to seat properly to work, so make sure the opening is clean.

flush valve seat

flapper

flush valve seat

IF WATER TRICKLES INTO THE BOWL

1 The cause is most likely a leaky flush valve or flush valve seat. Shut off the water to the tank.

2 Inspect the flapper or ball drop. If worn, it will not seal the bottom of the tank, allowing water to trickle into the bowl. If the flapper is not worn, inspect the flush valve seat. It may just need cleaning with an abrasive pad. Flexible seats can be pried out, cleaned, and replaced. Metal seats should always be replaced.

3 Pry out the flap or ball valve. Take it to a home center. Replace it with one that matches.

REPAIR A DIAPHRAGM BALLCOCK

1 Turn off the water to the toilet. Flush the toilet to remove water in the tank.

2 Unscrew the four screws on top of the ballcock. Lift off the ballcock. Inspect it for deposits, and clean it either by soaking it overnight in vinegar or wiping it with a rag.

3 Any worn parts should be replaced, including the plunger. If the whole unit looks worn, replace the entire ballcock.

4 Reassemble. Turn on the water supply.

Step 3. A new diaphragm ballcock is inexpensive, so don't spend too much time repairing one.

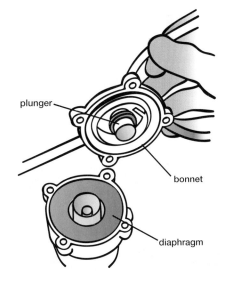

plunger

bonnet

diaphragm

fixing toilet tank run-on *continued*

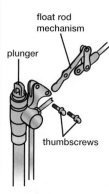

float rod
mechanism

plunger

thumbscrews

Step 3. The
thumbscrews make
removing the float rod
easy work.

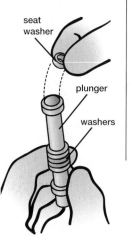

seat
washer

plunger

washers

Step 4. Remove and
replace all of the
washers.

REPAIRING PLUNGER BALLCOCKS

1 Shut off the water and flush the toilet until most of the water is removed.

2 Plunger ballcocks are the oldest style of ballcock. You can try cleaning them, but a number of the internal parts might be worn. I recommend replacing a plunger ballcock with a diaphragm or float-cup ballcock. If you prefer, follow the steps below to fix it.

3 Remove the thumbscrews holding the float rod in place. Lift up and out. Set the rod aside.

4 Pull up on the plunger to remove it. Remove and replace all of the washers.

5 Reassemble. Turn the water back on and test your work.

REPAIRING FLOAT-CUP BALLCOCKS

1 Shut off the water at the supply valve. Flush the toilet to remove all the water in the tank.

2 Pry off the cap. Take off the bonnet by lifting up the lever on the float rod while pushing down on the mechanism and twisting firmly counterclockwise at the same time.

3 Clean out any buildup or debris. Replace the seal if it looks worn. Reassemble. Turn on the water and test to make sure it works.

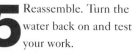

cup

shutoff lever

seal fits
under lever
mechanism

Step 2. A seal that
sits under the lever
mechanism will need
to be removed.

WYNN TIP:

Did you know that a leaky toilet tank can significantly add to your water bill? It makes economic sense to replace old, worn tank equipment with new. Replacement parts are plentiful and inexpensive.

replacing a toilet seat

You've just redecorated your bathroom and that avocado green toilet seat just doesn't work with the new decor. Or you're tired of an old, dingy, cracked seat, but the rest of the toilet is fine. Ditch the seat and replace it with one more your style.

TOOLS AND MATERIALS:
- **Wrench**
- **Screwdriver**
- **Old toothbrush**
- **New seat**

OUT WITH THE OLD

1 Lower the seat and cover. Pry up the lids that cover the toilet seat bolts.

2 Hold the nut from below so it doesn't turn with a wrench. Unscrew the bolts. Lift the old seat off.

IN WITH THE NEW

1 Clean out the area around the mounting holes using an old toothbrush or abrasive pad. Be careful not to damage the surface.

2 Align the new seat over the holes. Insert the new bolts. Thread nuts over the bolts.

3 Tighten the bolts. Be careful not to overtighten. Tighten just enough to hold the seat firmly in place.

Step 2. Use a wrench to hold the nut in place while you unscrew the bolt from the other side.

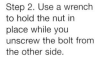

WYNN TIP:

Toilet seats aren't immune to fads and fashion. For example, there was a time when cushioned seats were all the rage. Because seats are easy to replace, you can coordinate colors, make a statement, or just go for comfort.

Don't be afraid to ask

I've mentioned several times that one of my goals for this book is to help you develop the confidence to start a project, because I'm convinced once you start, you'll find a way to finish. But it's also important to know that you can and should ask for help when you need it. Even if you have this book propped open next to you as you're working and you're following every step, you may run into an unexpected problem that I couldn't cover in these pages. Maybe a solution will come to you. If not, and the problem seems daunting, go to where the experts are and ask questions. I've generally gotten great advice and assistance when I've asked questions of other experts.

Many home improvement centers and hardware stores make it a practice to hire former electricians, plumbers, and other home contractors. When asked detailed questions about home projects, these folks can deliver a wealth of information. Rely on that friendliness and knowledge. I bet you'll learn a solution and realize the problem wasn't that daunting after all.

If you do hire a professional, watch what he or she does and ask questions. Remember, it's your house. Everything the pros know, they had to learn. By watching someone else take care of a problem and understanding the process, you can try to tackle the problem on your own next time.

resealing a tub

Silicone sealants fill the gap between the bathtub and wall, preventing water from damaging walls, floors, and ceilings. Unfortunately, the silicone doesn't last forever. When pieces tear, wear away, or pull loose, reseal the gap quickly—it doesn't take many showers for water to damage wallboard, framing, and flooring. And those problems are more costly to repair than a tube of sealant.

**TOOLS AND
MATERIALS:**
- **Putty knife**
- **Mild abrasive
  pad**
- **Caulking gun**
- **Silicone sealant**
- **Rag**
- **Scissors**

WYNN TIP:
You don't have to wait until gaps show in the seal to replace it. Being proactive will prevent even minimal water damage.

1 Using a putty knife, start peeling back as much of the existing sealant as possible. You may wish to use a plastic putty knife to guard against gouging or chipping the tub.

2 Clean any remaining putty with a mild abrasive pad and rag. It's important to have the surface as clean as possible for a strong, lasting seal.

3 Load a caulking gun with a silicone cylinder rated for bathtubs. If you have any questions about which type of silicone to purchase, ask your local home center representative for advice. You can purchase a tube of silicone if you don't have a caulking gun, but you won't get the same coverage.

4 Cut the tip of the cartridge to allow for a ¼-inch bead.

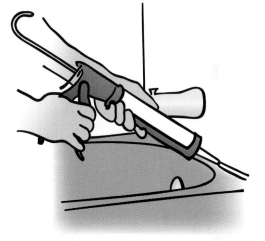

5 Squeeze the trigger of the caulking gun with uniform pressure while you lay a continuous rope of silicone along the joint between the tub and wall.

6 Wash your hands, then press your thumb or finger along the bead of sealant to spread it evenly for a professional-looking seal.

Step 5. Apply a uniform amount of pressure on the trigger to create a continuous bead.

repairing tub and shower controls

Tub and shower controls work much the same way as sink faucets. The important difference is there may be a diverter valve. But repair is a snap if you follow the directions and pay attention to what you're doing.

TOOLS AND MATERIALS:
• Screwdriver
• Pliers
• Wrenches
• Stem wrench
• Washers

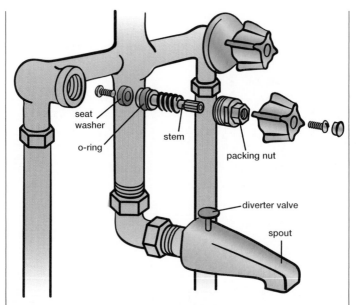

Anatomy of a two-handle control

REPAIRING A TWO-HANDLE CONTROL

The handles on this type of control contain stems with washers. Washers press against a seat to turn off the flow of water.

1 Shut off the water. Pop off the handle cover and remove the screw beneath it. Slide off the handle.

2 Using a special stem wrench or a deep socket wrench, remove the stem. If you still aren't able to remove the stem, you may have to chip away at the surrounding tiles to get at it.

3 Remove the screw holding the washer in place. Take off the washer. Clean away any residual debris out of the seat. Replace the washer.

4 Reassemble. Turn on the water and test for leaks.

WYNN TIP:
If a diverter valve on the spout does not work properly, don't mess with it. Just replace the spout.

REPAIRING A THREE-HANDLE CONTROL

The difference between a two-handle control and a three-handle control is a central handle that operates a diverter valve. Diverters send water up to a shower or down to the spout.

1 Shut off the water at a supply valve. Pop off the handle cover. Remove the screw beneath it. Slide off the handle.

2 Using a special stem wrench or a deep socket wrench, remove the stem. Unfortunately, if the stem won't come off, you may have to chip away at the tiles to get at it.

3 Remove the screw holding the washer in place. Take off the washer. Some diverters have O-rings; just remove them. Clean away any residual debris out of the seat.

4 Replace the washer or O-rings. If you wish, you can replace the whole stem with a new one.

5 Reassemble. Turn on the water and test for leaks.

WYNN TIP:
When working on faucet controls, cover the interior of the tub with a drop cloth or a couple of towels. Not only do you not want to lose parts down the drain, but you would be surprised how easily a dropped tool can damage the tub surface.

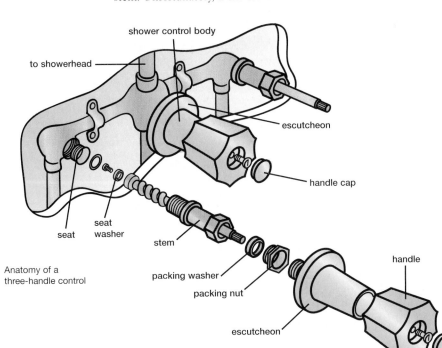

shower control body

to showerhead

escutcheon

handle cap

seat

seat washer

stem

packing washer

packing nut

escutcheon

handle

Anatomy of a three-handle control

wynn insight

Be thankful for a pro

I firmly believe if you keep trying, you can handle almost any home repair or improvement project yourself. There are, however, times when it makes sense to call in the pros. Here's one of those times:

Our home seems to be prone to plumbing problems during holiday events (see page 200). This time, my husband, Shaun, and I faced an overflowing sink downstairs, 10 minutes before my family was supposed to arrive for Thanksgiving dinner. Because the overflow was at the lowest drain in the house, it meant we could not use any other fixtures in the house—no kitchen sink, no bathrooms! Not a good thing anytime, but particularly bad when a large family is supposed to spend the day enjoying holiday cheer.

After a quick assessment, we discovered the clog was in the main drain line. Shaun tried to clear it with the snake we have at home. No luck. By this time my father-in-law had arrived. He went home, brought back a bigger snake, and worked on the clog for at least 30 minutes. Nothing. So we found a plumber (who was willing to work on the holiday!). He wasn't able to fix the problem in time for dinner, but my house guests were able to shower the next morning.

cleaning a showerhead

Does your showerhead seem to spray everywhere except where you want it to, or does it spray unevenly? Take it apart and clean it or replace it.

TOOLS AND MATERIALS:
- **Wrench**
- **Pin or thin wire**
- **Old toothbrush**
- **Vinegar**
- **Rag**

1 Remove the showerhead. This is a simple matter of unscrewing the nut at the shower arm. Take care not to mar the finish of the showerhead or arm. Use a wrench rather than pliers.

2 Showerheads often spray unevenly because the tiny holes have gotten clogged with mineral deposits. Use an old toothbrush to clean the head. Then run a sharp blast of water backward through the showerhead.

3 For a thorough cleaning, take the head apart, use a pin to poke out any mineral buildup or debris, and brush away all deposits. Then soak the parts in vinegar overnight to dissolve remaining mineral deposits. Reassemble and reinstall the showerhead.

WYNN TIP:
As an added precaution when removing a fixture, cushion the wrench with a rag as you work.

WYNN TIP:
If the showerhead leaks at the arm or doesn't stay in position, tighten the retainer or collar nut. If that doesn't work, replace the O-ring—or replace the showerhead.

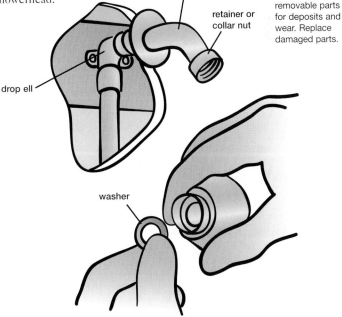

shower arm

retainer or collar nut

drop ell

washer

Step 3. Inspect washers and removable parts for deposits and wear. Replace damaged parts.

replacing a showerhead

Ready to pamper yourself a bit? Replace a basic showerhead with one equipped with special features, such as a pulsating spray or adjustable spray patterns, or a large "rainfall" head. Pipe sizes for showerheads are typically the same (½ inch) from one installation to another. If you're unsure, take the old one with you to the store to make sure you get one that will fit the pipe.

TOOLS AND MATERIALS:
- **Wrench**
- **Groove-joint pliers**
- **Showerhead**
- **Rag**

1 Unscrew the old showerhead from the shower arm. Most can be removed by hand. If you find it to be stubborn, use a wrench or pliers.

2 Simply screw on the new showerhead. Hand-tighten. If you need to tighten further with a wrench or pliers, be careful. You don't want to scratch the finish.

3 Pamper yourself with a relaxing or invigorating shower!

WYNN TIP:
Wrap an old rag over the showerhead nut to protect it when using pliers or a wrench.

WYNN TIP:
Newer showerheads simply screw onto the shower arm, the chromed pipe that extends from the wall. This allows you to install virtually any new showerhead onto the existing arm. Older models may require a shower arm with a ball-shaped end that acts as a swivel. If you have an older model and are ready to upgrade, you can most likely replace the shower arm so you can choose from a wider range of new showerheads. Remove the old shower arm from the drop ell, the fitting the arm attaches to in the wall. Wrap plumber's tape around the male threads of the new shower arm before screwing it into place.

replacing a toilet

It may look daunting, but replacing a toilet is surprisingly easy. Be aware that toilets are made with ceramics, so handle gently. It's easy to crack a toilet by accidentally banging it or overtightening a hold-down nut.

TOOLS AND MATERIALS:
- **Wrenches**
- **Screwdriver**
- **Hacksaw**
- **Groove-joint pliers**
- **Putty knife**
- **Sponge**
- **Oil**
- **Wax ring**
- **Plumber's putty**
- **Drop cloth**
- **New toilet**

WYNN TIP:
Lighten the load of removing an old toilet by disconnecting the tank from the bowl. You'll find it a little easier to manage them separately.

REMOVE THE OLD TOILET

1 Shut off the water at the supply valve or the main water valve.

2 Flush the toilet until very little water remains in the tank and bowl. Use a sponge to soak up any remaining water in the tank and bowl—wear rubber gloves, an old long sleeve shirt, and protective eyewear because water in the bowl may present a biohazard.

3 Disconnect the water supply line from the supply valve.

4 Using a wrench, unscrew the hold-down nuts. Rust on the hold-down nuts may make them tight and difficult to remove. Try a squirt or two of penetrating oil to loosen them. If the oil doesn't work, you'll have cut the nuts off with a hacksaw.

5 Lift the toilet up and out. Be sure to have someone assist you; toilets are heavy and awkward to carry. Remember to lift with your legs, not your back.

6 Using a putty knife, remove and dispose of the old wax ring. Clean away any residual wax.

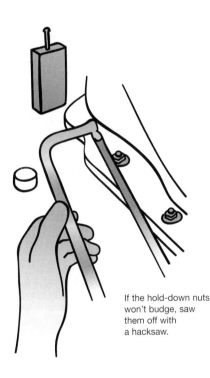

If the hold-down nuts won't budge, saw them off with a hacksaw.

WYNN TIP:
Most toilets sold today have their drains centered 12 inches from the wall. But some models are centered 10 inches from the wall. Before you buy, measure from the wall to the hold-down bolt of your current fixture to determine the model you need.

replacing a toilet *continued*

INSTALL THE NEW TOILET BOWL AND TANK

1 Use care and the assistance of a helper as you remove the new toilet bowl from its container. Turn the toilet upside down on a padded surface, such as an old rug remnant or folded drop cloth.

2 Roll a rope of plumber's putty about ¼ inch in diameter and press it around the perimeter of the bowl's base. Fit the wax ring (usually sold separately from the toilet) over the outlet opening.

3 Turn the bowl upright. With a helper, carefully set it in place, seating it in the closet flange drain opening. Be sure the hold-down bolts align with the holes in the base before you press the bowl into place.

4 Firmly press the bowl in place. Check again for proper alignment.

5 Slip a metal washer and a nut over each bolt. Tighten slowly, alternating from one bolt to the other. Don't overtighten the nuts; you might crack the bowl.

6 With the bowl in place, you're ready for the tank. Seat the spud gasket, beveled side down, in the bowl inlet opening.

7 With a helper, gently lower the tank onto the bowl. Make sure the tank holes align with those toward the rear of the bowl.

8 Install the tank hold-down bolts, washers, and nuts, and tighten using two wrenches. Do not overtighten. Make sure the rubber washer is installed inside the tank under the bolt.

9 If necessary, install the internal tank mechanics following the manufacturer's instructions. Connect the water supply to the tank fill valve. Turn on the supply valve. Test for leaks.

WYNN TIP:
Because toilets are large and awkward, you may want to have a helper to move the toilet into the bathroom and into position.

WYNN TIP:
In older homes, you may discover multiple layers of flooring. As a result, the closet flange often ends up below the floor surface. You may need to extend the ring upward with a special flange extender or double the wax ring.

spud gasket

bowl inlet

Step 6. The spud gasket should fit snugly into the inlet opening to provide a good seal.

Step 2. Install a rope of putty when the toilet is upside down.

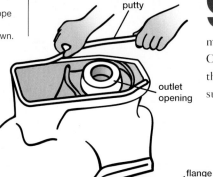

plumber's putty

outlet opening

flange

installing a stop valve

You probably don't think about stop valves until you need to shut off water to a fixture to make a repair. If you don't find a stop valve near the fixture, you'll have to search upstream until you find one, and that may take you all the way to the main shutoff valve for the whole house. Here's a typical installation on copper supply pipe.

TOOLS AND MATERIALS:
- **Hacksaw**
- **Groove-joint pliers**
- **Tubing cutter**
- **Adjustable wrench**
- **Propane torch (for copper)**
- **Plumber's tape**
- **Stop valve**

WYNN TIP:
Stop valves for sinks and toilets come with either ½- or ⅜-inch outlets. Make sure your flexible line is the same size.

1 Shut off the water supply and drain the line by opening a faucet at a lower location. Cut the copper supply pipe and clean the end. Leave enough pipe to hold a compression fitting.

2 Slide the nut and ferrule of the fitting onto the supply pipe. One end of the stop valve is threaded and sized to fit the pipe; the other receives the supply line for the fixture. Wrap the threads with plumber's tape. Install the stop valve by slipping the copper line into place, sliding the ferrule against the valve, and tightening the nut. Hold the stop valve in place with a second wrench as you tighten.

Step 2. An adjustable wrench used on each side of the fitting provides a sure grip without the danger of kinking the tubing.

WYNN TIP:
No matter what the material or size of your pipes, there's a stop valve made specifically to fit it. Copper lines use brass valves. Galvanized pipes typically use plated brass valves; plastic pipes, where allowed, use plastic valves. You can also use a transition fitting to change material just prior to the stop. If the valve will be in view, choose a chrome finish. If you're unsure of what to get when you visit the plumbing area of the home center, ask. Most sales associates will be happy to help.

Step 1. Using a tubing cutter makes quick work of cutting pipe and, more important, gives you a straight cut for the new fitting.

replacing a faucet

Wander into any home center and stroll down the plumbing fixture aisle and you will find hundreds of faucet styles. It can be mind-boggling how many you have to choose from. Yet there are few variations on the basic design. No matter the type you select, replacing a faucet is well within the reach of a do-it-yourselfer.

TOOLS AND MATERIALS:
- Groove-joint pliers
- Basin wrench
- Screwdriver
- Oil
- Putty knife
- Plumber's putty
- Plumber's tape
- Work light

WYNN TIP:
Try a squirt of penetrating oil to loosen old locknuts.

REMOVE THE OLD FAUCET

1 Shut off the water supply either at a stop valve or the main supply valve. If the faucet is downstream from others, open it to drain the line. Clear everything from under the sink so you have room to work.

2 Before you worm your way into the space below the sink, gather the tools you'll need, as well as some penetrating oil in case the mounting nuts are stuck. It helps to have someone to hand you tools as you work.

3 If your faucet has a sprayer, remove the nuts securing the hose to the faucet body and the spray head to the sink. Unhook the supply lines and move them out of the way.

4 Use the basin wrench to loosen and remove the mounting nuts holding the old faucet body to the sink.

5 Lift the faucet out from above. Scrape the sink top clean of old putty and mineral deposits.

INSTALL THE NEW FAUCET

1 Install a gasket or a rope of plumber's putty on the bottom of the faucet baseplate. Set the faucet in place. Make sure it is parallel to the backsplash.

2 Crawl under the sink. Have a helper hold the faucet in position while you work. Screw a washer and mounting nut onto each inlet.

WYNN TIP:

The hardest part of removing or installing a faucet is working in the cramped quarters of a cabinet. A basin wrench makes it easier to work on those hard-to-reach mounting nuts. A folded blanket will cushion your back. Set up a flashlight or work light.

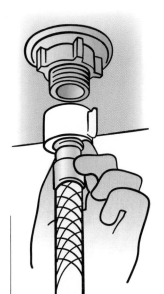

Step 4. Attach the mounting nut until it is hand-tight. Then tighten with a basin wrench until snug.

WYNN TIP:
Some faucets use flexible copper inlets for the water supply. Connect supply lines to them in the same way as you would regular inlets. Be careful not to kink them or the faucet will be ruined.

3 Tighten the mounting nuts with a basin wrench.

4 To connect the supply lines, brush the inlet threads with pipe joint compound or wrap them with plumber's tape. Twist the supply-line nut onto the inlet and tighten by hand. Finish tightening with a basin wrench.

5 Connect the other end of the supply line to the shutoff valve and tighten. Turn on the water and check for leaks.

INSTALL A SPRAYER

1 Make sure the water supply is shut off and the supply lines are drained.

2 Fasten the hose guide to the sink with a washer and mounting nut. Thread the spray hose down through the hole in the guide.

3 Apply pipe joint compound or plumber's tape to the threaded nipple at the end of the hose. Secure it to the spray outlet of the faucet.

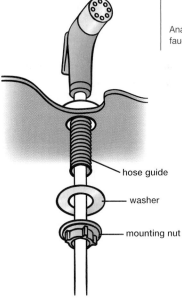

Anatomy of a faucet sprayer

hose guide

washer

mounting nut

The time to get started is now!

As a carpenter who does most of her work in front of a television camera, I am fortunate to have had a few opportunities that most carpenters don't. One of the most important to me is to inspire women to take on home repair and improvement projects. If you're just beginning, start small. That first success will lead to more projects. Soon you'll find that you've accomplished an entire house-full of repairs, and you'll be on to major improvements and creative projects.

I've heard from women whose husbands have had workshops in the garage or basement for 20 years, yet they had never ventured into the workshops. They said the tools and equipment intimidated them. But they've gone on to tell me that after watching me work, they've overcome the intimidation and found a new outlet. They've gone into the shop, used the tools and are getting things done in the house. They've shown me pictures of the projects they've completed and the furniture they've built. I never thought as a carpenter I would be able to play this sort of role, but I'm thrilled at the opportunity.

wynn insight

installing a hand shower

Pamper yourself by adding a hand shower to an existing shower or on a tub-only installation. It can be an economical alternative to a complete shower installation. A variety of showerheads are available, ranging from the simple to the exotic.

TOOLS AND MATERIALS:
- Groove-joint pliers
- Hammer
- Plumber's tape
- Old toothbrush
- Rag

ON AN EXISTING SHOWER

1 Remove the showerhead. Clean the threads with an old toothbrush and rag. If your shower arm does not have male threads, replace it with one that does. Wrap the threads with plumber's tape.

2 Attach the hand shower with pliers. The hand shower connector may have a diverter that allows you to choose either the fixed or the handheld head, a hanger bracket that the new head fits on, or a direct hose hookup—the hose attaches to the shower arm. For the latter, install a shower hanger.

3 Turn on the water, engage the diverter, and test the new hand shower. Check for leaks.

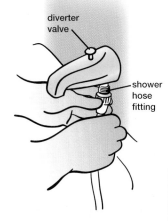

diverter valve

shower hose fitting

Step 4. Thread the fitting by hand, then tighten using a wrench.

ON A TUB-ONLY UNIT

1 Remove the old spout by inserting the handle of a hammer into the spout opening and turning counterclockwise.

2 Clean the exposed pipe threads with an old toothbrush and rag. You may need to remove the existing nipple and install one that is longer or shorter.

3 Apply plumber's tape and screw on the new spout with diverter valve.

4 Attach the hose to the shower-hose fitting. Turn on the water, test the sprayer, and check for leaks.

WYNN TIP:
Protect chrome parts from scratches by wrapping the jaws of the pliers with electrical tape.

WYNN TIP:
Some shower hangers have self-sticking backs. Just peel off the paper and stick the hanger in place. Others can be screwed to the wall. Mark for the screws. If you have ceramic tile on the wall, stick a piece of masking tape on the wall and mark it. Position the masonry bit on the spot and drill into the wall. Push plastic anchors in place and screw the hanger in place.

maintaining and fixing a water heater

Think of a water heater as an oversized coffee thermos with a heater—it's really not much more complicated than that. Cold water enters the tank. As the water cools below a set temperature, a heater—either a gas burner or an electric probe—turns on to heat the water.

CONDUCTING REGULAR MAINTENANCE

Sediment or rust buildup in the tank causes most water heater problems. Reduce the amount of buildup by flushing the tank at least once a year.

1 Turn off the water supply and the electric power or the gas supply.

2 Connect a hose to the drain valve and empty the tank into a floor drain or buckets.

3 Disconnect the hose and close the drain valve. Open the supply valve to fill the tank. Turn on the power or open the gas valve and light the pilot (page 243).

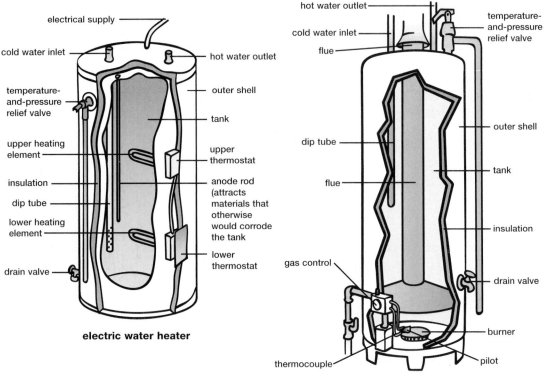

electric water heater

gas water heater

REPLACING A LEAKING DRAIN VALVE

Water leaking from the water heater drain valve means it's time to replace the valve.

1 Close the cold-water supply valve located on the top of the water heater. Shut off the gas or the electrical current to the water heater.

2 Attach a hose to the drain valve. Open the drain valve and drain the water heater into a floor drain or buckets. Unscrew the faulty valve.

3 Apply plumber's tape or pipe joint compound around the threads of a new valve. Screw in the valve by hand. Tighten using a pipe wrench.

4 Open the cold-water supply valve to fill the tank. Restore power or gas to the heater.

Step 3. Plumber's tape or joint compound will seal the pipe connection.

SYMPTOM	CAUSE	REPAIR
No hot water	No power to the heater (electric) Pilot light out (gas)	Check circuit breaker or fuse (electric) Relight pilot; replace thermocouple if pilot does not stay lit
Water not hot enough	Upper element burned out (electric)	Replace upper element
Not enough hot water— hot water runs out quickly	Thermostat set too low. Hot water must travel a long way to get to faucets Sediment buildup in tank Lower element burned out (electric) Burner blocked by dirt (gas) Leaking faucets	Turn thermostat up Insulate hot water pipes (see page 241) Drain and refill tank Replace lower element Clean burner or call gas company Repair faucets Replace with a larger tank
Tank makes noise	Tank not large enough for demand	Drain and refill tank
Leak from temperature-and-pressure-relief valve	Sediment in tank Thermostat set too high	Lower thermostat setting Replace valve
Leak around tank base	Defective temperature-and-pressure-relief valve Tank corrosion has created a leak	Replace water heater

maintaining and fixing a water heater
continued

Step 1. Testing the relief valve is one of your seasonal chores.

3 Open the drain valve and drain about one gallon of the water. Close the valve. Remove the drainpipe attached to the relief valve. Unscrew the valve using a pipe wrench or pliers.

4 Apply plumber's tape or pipe joint compound to the threads of the new valve. Screw on the valve. Tighten with a pipe wrench. Connect the overflow drainpipe.

5 Open the cold-water supply valve and fill the tank. Restore power.

TESTING AND REPLACING A RELIEF VALVE

1 Locate the pressure relief valve. It will either be on top or high on the side of the tank. Test it once a year by pulling on the handle. Water should rush out of the pipe attached to it. If it doesn't, it's time to replace the valve.

2 Shut off the cold-water supply valve to the tank. Turn off the power or the gas. Connect a hose to the drain valve. Place the opposite end either near a floor drain or in a bucket.

Step 3. Use a wrench or groove-joint pliers to unscrew the valve..

installing a kitchen faucet sprayer

Sometimes a small change can have a huge impact. Changing out that old, worn sink and faucet can rejuvenate and update any kitchen. While you're at it, make life easier by installing a kitchen faucet sprayer. Sprayers are available for most faucet styles, but make sure your sink can accommodate the sprayer. Otherwise you'll need to drill a hole in the sink or countertop.

TOOLS AND MATERIALS:
- **Adjustable wrench**
- **Basin wrench**
- **Adjustable wrench**
- **Flashlight**
- **Sprayer kit**
- **Silicone caulk or plumber's putty**
- **Sprayer kit**
- **Old cloth**

1 Turn off the water. If your sprayer does not have a plastic flange to seal it to the sink, apply a bead of silicone caulk or a rope of putty to the sprayer base. Insert the sprayer hose into the sink hole and press down to form a good seal.

2 From below, slip on the washer, then screw on and tighten the mounting nut using a basin wrench. From above, clean away any excess caulk or putty.

3 Screw the sprayer hose coupling onto the faucet's hose nipple and tighten with a wrench.

4 Connect and tighten the supply tubes. Seat the faucet. From below, make sure the sprayer's supply tube will not get tangled or caught on a stop valve when the sprayer is pulled out. Connect and tighten the supply tubing to the shutoff valves. Turn on the water supply and inspect for leaks.

Connect the sprayer coupling to the faucet nipple before mounting the faucet.

WYNN TIP:
You found the perfect sink, but it doesn't have a place for a sprayer. Before you invest in a knockout punch, consider purchasing a faucet with the sprayer in the spout. There are many styles and manufacturers to choose from.

Step 1. A properly seated base prevents future leaks.

maintaining a clothes washer

My clothes washer works hard, and I'm sure yours does too. Even though they're designed to last 10 to 15 years, they still need occasional maintenance. Sediment buildup from hard water can choke the supply lines over time. Give them a break by periodically cleaning the inlet screens.

TOOLS AND MATERIALS:
- Bucket
- Groove-joint pliers
- Tweezers or screwdriver
- White vinegar
- Old toothbrush or wire brush
- Needle-nose pliers
- Level
- Shims

1 Unplug the washer. Have someone help you move it away from the wall so you can work behind it.

2 Locate the hot- and cold-water valves and turn them off. Before you remove the hoses, get a bucket; they will most likely contain water and need to be drained.

3 Use groove-joint pliers to disconnect the hoses from the machine. This

WYNN TIP:
Inlet screens aren't very expensive. Rather than cleaning the old, replace them with new. It will save you time later since you won't have to clean them so often.

is a good time to replace the hose washers if sediment has built up.

4 Remove the inlet screens carefully; if punctured they will need to be replaced. They're important because they keep debris from getting inside the washer. Pry them out using tweezers, a screwdriver, or needle-nose pliers.

5 To clean old inlet screens, soak them overnight in a white vinegar solution. Remove stubborn deposits with an old toothbrush or a small wire brush. Rinse the screens and inspect them. If you still see deposits, soak them longer.

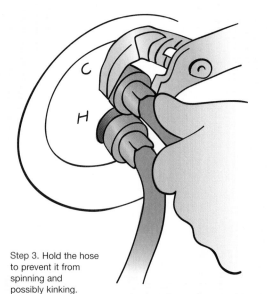

Step 3. Hold the hose to prevent it from spinning and possibly kinking.

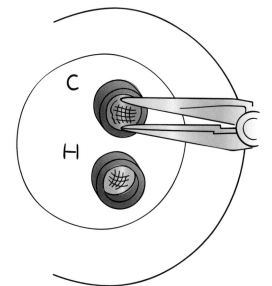

Step 6. Use a needle-nose pliers to help position the inlet screens.

7 Reattach the hot- and cold-water hoses. Connect only hand-tight. Using pliers, tighten an additional quarter turn.

8 With a helper, push the washer back into place. Since you've moved it, check to make sure it is level. Use either a bubble level or a carpenter's level. If using a carpenter's level, make sure to check not only front to back and side to side, but also along both diagonals. Adjust the washer's feet or place shims under the feet until it is level.

9 Turn the hot- and cold-water valves on and check for leaks.

6 Once the screens are clean, carefully reposition the inlet screens into the inlet openings. Make sure the dome-shaped side faces out. Hold them with tweezers or needle-nose pliers to help position them, but be careful not to damage them.

WYNN TIP:
Inspect the condition of the washer hoses. If they appear worn and cracked, now is the time to replace them.

WYNN TIP:
Before you start replacing the inlet filters on the supply hoses because your clothes washer fills slowly, check to make sure the supply valves are fully open. Someone may have partially closed them.

seasonal maintenance

Every change of season brings a change of weather in most parts of the country. You need to prepare your home for those transitions, which place new and different demands on structures, appliances, and mechanical systems.

Seasonal maintenance, as the name suggests, needs to be done regularly to keep your home in good working order. Even by doing minimal maintenance, you can probably avoid most major repairs.

Your home and the appliances in it wear out over time. But if you follow a regular maintenance schedule, as I outline in this chapter, you'll cut down on the frequency—and the expense—of those almost inevitable breakdowns and replacements. In addition to reading my recommendations, it's a good idea to check out the manufacturer's information regarding the upkeep of your heating and cooling systems. The company can provide detailed information specific to the make and model you have in your home.

Plan for change

When you set up your maintenance schedule, note it in your planner, calendar, or PDA. That way you're less likely to skip a project. It doesn't matter if you block out a weekend each season to take care of all the tasks or if you prefer, sprinkle them throughout the season. Just get them accomplished. Then move on to more fun activities.

identifying and sealing air leaks

You'd never leave a window open all winter, but you may be doing the equivalent if you haven't sealed air leaks in your home. Pass your hand around the perimeter of each exterior door and window. If you feel a draft, you've found a leak. Fix it and enjoy immediate cost savings on your heating and cooling bills.

TOOLS AND MATERIALS:
- Caulking gun
- Caulk
- Staple gun
- Scissors
- Plastic
- Duct tape
- Weather stripping
- Foam strips

SEAL A LEAK WITH CAULK

1 Be sure to use the right caulk for the job. If you have any questions, read the manufacturer's label or ask an expert at a home center or hardware store.

2 To load a caulking gun, invert the plunger handle and pull the plunger all the way back. Some guns have a tab that you push before you can pull the plunger back. Insert the caulk tube. Push the plunger forward until it stops.

3 Snip off the nozzle's tip. The closer the cut is to the tip, the narrower the bead will be. With some tubes, you need to puncture the inside seal with a wire or a long nail.

4 Pack ¾-inch or wider gaps with closed-cell foam backer strips first, then complete the seal by caulking.

5 Between perpendicular surfaces, such as a wall and the floor, bisect the angle with the gun's nozzle to make a smooth concave bead. Hold the gun at a 45-degree angle and pull it toward you in a smooth, steady stroke, maintaining an even pressure on the trigger.

6 Between flat surfaces, straddle the joint with the nozzle and pack the joint so the caulk bulges out of the joint slightly.

7 At the end of a stroke, lift the tip with a twist to catch caulk oozing from the nozzle. Quickly release the plunger. Remove any excess from the nozzle.

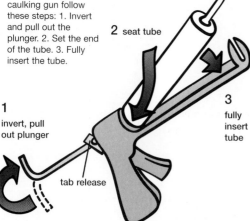

Step 2. To load a caulking gun follow these steps: 1. Invert and pull out the plunger. 2. Set the end of the tube. 3. Fully insert the tube.

2 seat tube

1
invert, pull out plunger

3
fully insert tube

tab release

WYNN TIP:
Unsure whether you have an air leak? Hold a sheet of plastic food wrap over the location. If the wrap moves, you've found an air leak.

8 Smooth the bead of caulk using a moist fingertip or a moist, tightly wadded rag. Try to smooth it in one stroke, applying even pressure. This takes some practice.

9 Save partial tubes of caulk by sealing them with a nail or screw. Or invert the cut-off tip of the nozzle and stuff it into the opening

FILL AROUND A VENT PIPE

In the attic, seal around vent pipes. First lay a generous bead of latex/silicone caulk. Cut a piece of plastic 4–5 inches wide and embed its bottom in the caulk as you wrap it around the pipe. Secure the top of the plastic with duct tape.

USE DUCT TAPE TO SEAL JOINTS IN DUCTS

Believe it or not, there is a reason duct tape has its name—it seals ductwork. Purchase professional-quality duct tape, which will last longer than the cheaper variety. Clean and dry the area before application. Press the duct tape into place carefully so there are no folds and few wrinkles.

FILL LARGE GAPS AROUND PIPES

Use foam weather stripping to fill large gaps around pipes. Find a type of foam that just fills the gap, without too much cramming. Complete the seal and give it a finished look by installing a pipe flange; fill the back of the flange with latex/silicone caulk. You can also fill large gaps around pipes with foam sealant. To add further protection, cover the sealant with plastic, using staples and duct tape.

CAULK SMALLER GAPS AROUND PIPES

Smaller gaps around pipes can be filled with either silicone or latex/silicone caulk.

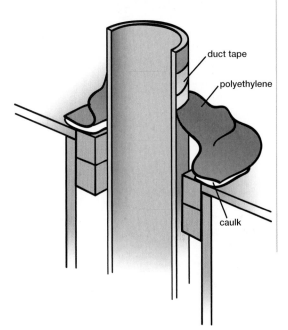

duct tape

polyethylene

caulk

Vent pipe. Seal a vent pipe with a layer of caulk, and then plastic secured with duct tape.

WYNN TIP:
Create a perfect line with masking tape. Press masking tape on each side of the joint. Caulk, wipe with your finger, and pull away the tape.

WYNN TIP:
Typically caulk should not be applied at temperatures below 50°F. Check the label.

CAULK AROUND ELECTRICAL CABLE

Seal, for example, where an electrical cable runs up from the basement into the living areas of your home. Use butyl, silicone, or latex/silicone caulk.

COVER AN ATTIC OPENING

If an interior wall opens to the attic, cut pieces of lumber or plywood to fit snugly. Caulk the pieces in place over the openings.

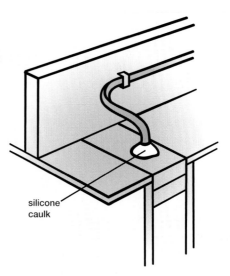

silicone caulk

Electrical cable. Check for gaps and seal anywhere an electrical cable penetrates a surface.

SEAL AROUND WINDOWS

Air leaks around interior sashes or storm windows cause condensation to form on the sash that's not leaking. The solution is to caulk the air leak. (For more about weatherizing windows see page 236–237).

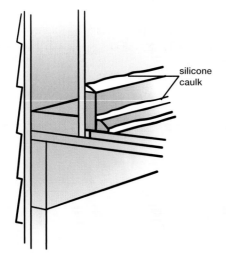

silicone caulk

Seal moldings. Apply latex/silicone caulk to seal moldings along exterior walls.

SEAL MOLDINGS

If there is a baseboard on an exterior wall, seal it with latex/silicone caulk. Smooth the caulk with a wet finger, then paint.

WYNN TIP:

An air leak from an electrical outlet or switch on the exterior accounts for less than 1 percent of home air leakage. That doesn't mean you shouldn't install outlet insulators, though. A lot of little leaks add up. You might want to address other issues, such as that drafty door, before you install insulating gaskets on electrical outlets and switches.

what if...

you'd like to reduce your heating and cooling costs?

With energy prices on the rise, most people are eager to reduce their monthly utility bills and conserve home energy.

Check if your utility company offers a free home energy inspection. Many will come to you to identify specific ways you can improve the energy efficiency of your home. Some even offer free or reduced cost energy-saving devices, such as outlet insulators, pipe insulators, and programmable thermostats.

Habits to conserve heat

Turn down your thermostat 8–10 degrees at night. You're probably curled up under a blanket or comforter anyway, so you won't feel the difference. You'll typically notice a cost savings of 8–15 percent.

Turn off bathroom or kitchen exhaust fans as soon as the humidity has cleared or you're finished cooking. Exhaust fans can draw heated air out of your home faster than you'd expect.

Lower the temperature of your water heater, but not to less than 120°F. This is a smart practice for both cost savings and protection against scalding. Wrap the water heater with an insulation blanket.

Habits to conserve cooling

Keep the thermostat set no lower than 78°F. On really hot days, turn it up. Your home should still feel comfortable and be cooler than outside.

If you have a programmable thermostat, set it warmer when you are gone and program it to turn down shortly before you typically return home.

Operate heat-producing appliances, such as washers, dryers, and dishwashers, at night or early morning.

adding spring metal weather stripping

You probably don't pay much attention to windows most of the time, but it's good to check their condition once a year. Many windows—and your utility bill—will benefit from the installation of spring metal weather stripping. Though it is more difficult to install than other types of weather stripping, it creates the tightest seal.

TOOLS AND MATERIALS:
- **Screwdriver**
- **Utility knife**
- **Tin snips**
- **Hammer**
- **Spring-metal kit or coiled spring metal and nails**

WYNN TIP:
Purchase spring-metal weather stripping with predrilled holes.

WYNN TIP:
Be sure the metal strip compresses when the window shuts so it provides a tight seal.

1 Plan to install the spring metal stripping in the sash channels, bottom of the lower sash, and where the sashes meet.

2 Before cutting and fitting the new weather stripping, fully open the sash. For double-hung windows, fit strips to completely fill the sash when it is fully closed.

3 Fasten a strip to the underside of the lower sash's bottom rail. Nail the strip with the open side facing the exterior. Drive all the nails securely. Gently pry the leaves of the stripping apart.

4 If the upper sash is not fixed in place, do the same to the top rail of the upper sash.

5 With the open side facing down, nail a strip to the bottom rail of the upper sash where the sashes meet when the window is closed. You may need to flatten the strip to make it fit.

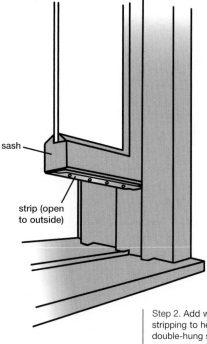

sash

strip (open to outside)

Step 2. Add weather stripping to help seal double-hung sashes.

WYNN TIP:
If you have casement windows, nail strips to the frame. Install strips spring-side-in so sashes open freely.

installing weather-stripping gaskets

To create a tight seal at the point where two surfaces on a window meet, install a gasket-type weather strip. Use self-adhesive strips, or drive nails or screws either directly through the strip or through a metal strip attached to the gasket. Thick, rounded gaskets provide a better seal.

TOOLS AND MATERIALS:
- **Scissors or utility knife**
- **Hammer**
- **Weather stripping**
- **Nails**

WYNN TIP:
Stretch the gasket material slightly as you attach it and make sure there are no gaps at the corners.

1 Seal the top and bottom sashes of double-hung windows by attaching strips to the outside of the upper sash's top rail and the outside of the lower sash's bottom rail. Make sure the weather stripping seals completely at all points but not so tightly as to make it difficult to close the sash.

2 Create a tight seal between the two sashes by attaching a strip to the bottom of the upper sash. The strip should completely cover the gap yet allow the window to close fully.

3 On a casement window, attach strips to the sash, or to the casing and the sill, whichever provides a tighter squeeze.

WYNN TIP:
Exterior gasket installation provides a tighter seal and is less noticeable than interior installation. But be careful if you're working on an upper-story window.

Step 2. Make sure to completely cover the gap between sashes with weather stripping, but allow the window to completely close.

INSTALLING FOAM WEATHER STRIPPING

For double-hung windows, use foam only on the top and bottom of the sashes, or attach it to the frame at the top and bottom. Foam can't handle friction.

On metal casement or awning windows, stick press-in-place foam tape onto the frame. You will probably need to use the thinnest material available. Apply the foam to all four sides of the opening.

sealing under doors

Drafty doors allow in chilling air during the winter and impact energy bills. Replacing an entire door can be an expensive upgrade. As long as the door itself is in good condition, insulate beneath it, as shown here, and around the door (see page 240) to eliminate drafts.

TOOLS AND MATERIALS:
- **Drill**
- **Screwdriver**
- **Tin snips**
- **Hammer**
- **Hacksaw**
- **Handsaw**
- **Saw or plane**
- **Tape measure**
- **Sweep**
- **Screws**
- **Primer**
- **Shoe trim**
- **Caulk**

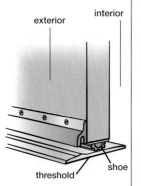

Door shoe. Before installing a door shoe, check to make sure there is enough clearance.

INSTALL A DOOR SWEEP

1 Check that the threshold is above the level of the carpet or flooring within the arc of the door. If not, there won't be clearance for the door sweep. Close the door and measure the width of the door.

2 Use tin snips or a hacksaw to carefully cut the sweep ⅛ inch shorter than the width of the door.

3 Position the sweep so its gasket just touches the threshold. Center it so there is ¹⁄₁₆-inch clearance on each side of the door.

4 Drive screws into the centers of the slots so you can adjust the sweep up or down as needed.

ADD A DOOR SHOE

A shoe fits to the bottom of the door to create a durable seal. Most have a drip cap mounted on the outside face of the door.

1 Remove the door. Measure and mark how much you will need to cut from the door.

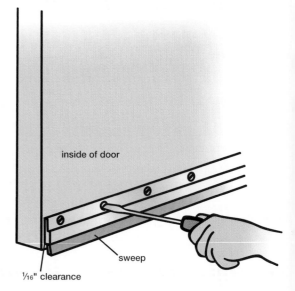

inside of door

sweep

¹⁄₁₆" clearance

2 Use a circular saw or a plane to cut or shave down the door. Apply primer to the bottom of the door to seal.

3 Mark the locations of the holes for the shoe trim on the door and predrill. Set the shoe trim in place, aligning the holes, and fasten with screws.

4 Insert the gasket into the trim and reset the door.

Step 4. After initially positioning the sweep, check if it needs to be repositioned slightly by adjusting the screw placement.

WYNN TIP:
Before installing any weather-stripping device, check that there is enough clearance for the door to swing open and to shut completely.

INSTALL A THRESHOLD WITH A GASKET

A threshold gasket works like a door shoe but fastens to the door threshold instead of the door.

1 Open the door as wide as possible and secure it so it doesn't get in the way. You don't have to remove the door unless the bottom needs to be trimmed to allow for the threshold gasket.

2 Measure and cut the new threshold gasket so it fits snugly within the door frame.

3 Thoroughly clean the area and apply a generous bead of caulk to the frame. This will form an airtight seal.

4 Remove the threshold rubber gasket from the trim and press the trim firmly into place. You may need to tap it with a hammer to form a good seal.

5 Drill pilot holes and drive screws to hold the trim. Feed the gasket into the trim and close the door to test for a snug fit.

ATTACH A DRIP CAP

1 Prevent water from seeping under a door and into the house by attaching a drip cap. First close the door and measure its width.

2 Use tin snips or a hacksaw to carefully cut the drip cap ⅛ inch shorter than the width of the door.

3 Center the drip cap on the bottom exterior of the door so that there is 1/16-inch clearance on each side of the drip cap.

4 Nail the drip cap onto the door.

WYNN TIP:
A badly worn threshold can be easily remedied by installing a metal or wood threshold with a replaceable gasket.

WYNN TIP:
Don't forget storm doors. You can buy replacement rubber or plastic sweeps that install on the outside of these. Drill pilot holes through the metal door before driving screws.

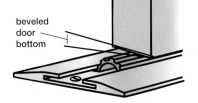

Gasket. The bottom of the door must be beveled slightly for a gasket threshold to work properly.

beveled door bottom

interior

adding weather stripping to doors

Entry doors are notorious sources of drafts and can leak twice as much air as windows. Doors have to withstand the abuse of constant traffic, and over time that wear and tear takes its toll on the weather stripping. Check the exterior doors of your home periodically.

TOOLS AND MATERIALS:
- Scissors
- Utility knife
- Tin snips
- Hacksaw
- Hammer
- Screwdriver
- Plastic wrap
- Foam tape
- Spring metal
- Metal-and-vinyl strip
- Nails

IDENTIFY POTENTIAL AIR GAPS

1 Close the door and look—first from the outside, then from the inside—for gaps in the weather stripping.

2 When the wind is blowing, hold a sheet of plastic food wrap near the door on the inside to detect leaks.

3 Check for crimped, flattened, or missing weather stripping at the top and sides. Feel along the threshold. Air infiltration means you need a bottom-of-the-door device (see pages 238–239).

SEALING A LEAK WITH FOAM TAPE

Foam tape installs easily but does not always do the trick. If the door closes tightly, the foam may tear off or prevent the door from latching. Use it when there is a gap between the door and the stop. Cut strips to length. Peel off the backing. Press the foam in place on the inside of the stops.

SEALING A LEAK WITH METAL-AND-VINYL STRIPS

1 This material is effective and durable and can be used in conjunction with spring metal. Close the door. Cut pieces to fit using tin snips or a hacksaw.

2 Press each piece so it just touches the door. Drive the screws provided into the center of each slot so you can adjust the position if needed.

SEALING A LEAK WITH SPRING METAL

1 Cut spring metal carefully to fit, using tin snips. Nail each strip to the jamb inside the stop, with the open end facing the exterior.

2 On the latch side, notch-cut the piece to fit around the strikeplate.

INSULATE BETWEEN DOUBLE DOORS

Apply foam tape to the inside of the half-round molding on older French doors. If the molding is damaged, replace it with insulated molding. Nail the molding to the face of the door that's more often closed.

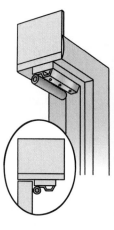

Metal and vinyl. Position the strips along the stop of the door frame.

WYNN TIP:
Don't forget to examine storm doors and doors that connect to a garage. The felt gasket around the frame and the sweep or gasket at the bottom of the door may need replacement.

preventing pipe freeze-ups

Ice-cold tap water may be a treat in the summer, but it's a potential problem in winter. If the tap water temperature fluctuates with the temperature outside, investigate. If pipes are exposed to a poorly insulated wall, they may freeze and burst. The best solution is to add insulation to the wall or ceiling. If this is not possible or practical, here are some other ways to prevent pipes from freezing.

TOOLS AND MATERIALS:
- Utility knife
- Flashlight
- Electrical tape
- Pipe jacket or insulation
- Heat tape

WYNN TIP:
Never double-wrap or overlap electric heat tape. Doing so can potentially create a fire hazard.

INSULATE PIPES

1 Purchase enough pipe jacket or insulation to cover every square inch of pipe—including connections.

2 Pipe jacketing comes in standard lengths. Cut it to fit with a utility knife. Secure the pipe jacket with electrical tape.

3 To install ordinary insulation, cut in strips and bundle it around pipes. Then secure the insulation with electrical tape.

WRAP PIPES WITH HEAT TAPE

Electric heat tape draws only modest amounts of current, so it is safe and inexpensive to use. Wrap tape around the pipe and plug the tape into a receptacle. A thermostat turns the tape on and off as needed. However the tape will not work during a power outage—the very time when the protection may be needed most.

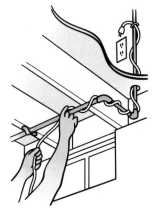

Heat tape. Remember that heat tape will not work during a power outage.

PROTECT OUTDOOR FAUCETS

Before winter, remove and drain garden hoses. Shut off the water leading to the outdoor faucet, allow it to drain, and leave it open. If there is no indoor shutoff, install one, or install a freeze-proof sill cock (the valve in an outdoor faucet).

PRECAUTIONS FOR COLD DAYS

On extremely cold days, turn on faucets that have vulnerable parts and let water trickle continuously. If there is a cabinet under the faucet, open its doors to let room heat warm the pipes.

WYNN TIP:
Consider insulating long hot-water runs, especially those that pass through unheated spaces. The added insulation will conserve water-heating energy.

thawing frozen pipes

If you're lucky enough to spot a frozen pipe before it bursts, you can thaw it.
Once thawed, insulate the pipe to prevent a repeat or worse, a ruptured pipe.

**TOOLS AND
MATERIALS:**
- **Hair dryer**
- **Old cloth**
- **Hot water, or
  space heater**

THAWING WITH A HAIR DRYER

Open the faucet the pipe
supplies so any steam can
escape. If the pipe is exposed,
apply heat directly with a hair
dryer or a heat gun turned to its
lowest setting. Move the dryer
or gun back and forth—don't
hold it in one spot.

THAWING WITH HOT WATER

Another solution for an exposed
frozen pipe is to wrap a cloth
around it, then pour boiling
water over the cloth. Allow the
water to cool, pour again, and
repeat until the pipe is thawed.
Be sure a faucet is open while
you do this so steam can
escape. Also make sure
you don't spill any water
on yourself.

THAWING CONCEALED PIPES

If the pipes are concealed,
thawing will take more time.
Open a faucet. Beam a heat
lamp or electric space heater at
the wall containing the pipe.
Monitor closely to make sure
the heat doesn't damage the
wall surface.

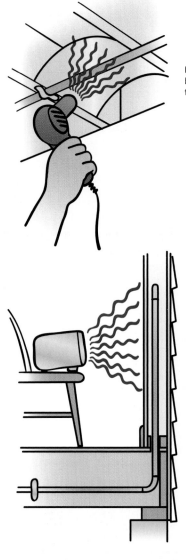

Move a hair dryer
back and forth to
thaw exposed pipes.

Keep a close watch
on a space heater
as you thaw
concealed pipes
to make sure the
heat doesn't
damage the wall.

lighting a pilot light

If your gas water heater or furnace isn't working, it's likely the gas pilot light has gone out. Lighting a pilot is not a difficult task, nor is it dangerous when you follow directions. Below are basic instructions for lighting a pilot. Check the directions on your furnace or water heater for specifics related to the make and model.

TOOLS:
• **Fireplace match or barbecue igniter**

1 Turn the control knob to the "pilot" position.

2 Hold down the pilot button as you extend a fireplace match or a long barbecue igniter to light the pilot.

3 Keep the button depressed for at least 45 seconds, then release. The pilot should stay lit; if not, you may need to adjust the thermocouple's position.

Step 2. Insert a long match through the access panel at the bottom of the panel.

reset button

gas cock

gas inlet valve

thermocouple

pilot

4 Turn the control knob to "on." The burners should ignite.

Step 3. Switch the gas cock to the "pilot" setting when lighting the pilot.

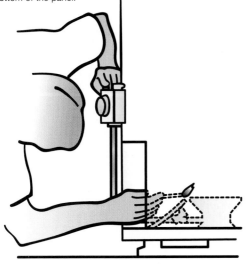

WYNN TIP:
Make sure the room is well ventilated. If you're having trouble lighting the pilot or keeping the pilot lit, allow the room to air out before retrying. If you don't feel comfortable working with gas, contact a pro.

maintaining a heating/cooling system

Extend the life of your heating and cooling systems with seasonal maintenance. There are many types and configurations of systems. I've picked a few standard systems and have included maintenance tips here. In addition to reviewing this information, follow the maintenance instructions that came with your system. It's also a good idea to have a professional complete an annual maintenance test.

WYNN TIP:
To reduce energy costs and get the most out of your heating-and-cooling system, keep air registers, base-board heaters and radiators clean. Also make sure they aren't blocked by furniture or drapes.

OUTDOOR NATURAL GAS OR PROPANE HEAT PUMPS AND AIR-CONDITIONERS

- Inspect the unit and pad to make sure it's level.
- Remove debris from the inside of the unit.
- Clean the coil and cabinet with a dry-vac if needed.
- Inspect the fan motor and blades for wear and damage.
- Visually inspect switch equipment; test to make sure it's in working order.
- Check the compressor and tubing for damage and kinks.

INDOOR NATURAL GAS OR PROPANE FURNACES OR AIR HANDLERS

- Lubricate the motor on older models.
- Inspect the fan belt for slack, cracks, and slippage.
- Clean debris from the unit.
- Visually inspect the coil, drain pan, and drain lines for debris and damage.
- Sniff around the lines. If you detect gas, open all windows and call a professional.

- Check to see if the burner assembly requires cleaning.
- Replace the air filter.

EVAPORATIVE COOLERS

- Always turn off the power at the service panel before maintaining the system.
- Check the belt for slack and cracks.
- Remove debris from the unit.

OIL FURNACES

- Clean soot and debris off the chimney, flue, and draft regulator.
- Check the combustion chamber for cracks and holes.
- Replace filters.
- Remove the burner tray and clean the electrodes.
- Oil all motors and bearings per the manufacturer's recommendations.

RADIATORS

- Check the air vents.
- Test the steam trap.
- Bleed the radiator starting with units on the upper floor working down.

balancing a forced-air system

Have you noticed that some rooms in your home just aren't as comfortable as others? You can solve this problem by rebalancing the air system. Adjustments to ductwork can increase or reduce the air supply to a particular room so that warm or cool air reaches rooms far from the furnace or cooling system.

TOOLS AND MATERIALS:
- **Outdoor/indoor thermometers**
- **Wrench or pliers**
- **Masking tape**

WYNN TIP:
If you have central cooling, you may have to rebalance the ducts every summer and winter. Mark seasonal settings on the ducts.

REDIRECT AIR FLOW

Partially closing registers will cool off a room but won't redirect the air. Instead, adjust dampers (flaps) in the ductwork. A handle or locknut on the side of the duct controls the airflow, so fine-tuning a system is easy. You may be tempted to adjust the dampers for only one or two rooms that have airflow problems, but you'll get better results by tuning the entire system.

1 Open the dampers. Loosen the locknut and turn the handle parallel to the duct. To identify which ducts serve each room, close them one at a time to determine which room isn't getting air. Label the dampers. Open the registers in all rooms, and open all the dampers in the ducts.

2 Synchronize several thermometers by laying them together for 30 minutes and noting any differences in the readings. Tape a thermometer on a wall in each room, about 3 feet above the floor but not directly above a supply register.

3 Adjust dampers to the rooms, starting with the one where your home's thermostat is located. For example, in the winter open dampers to send more heat to cooler rooms; close dampers to warmer areas.

4 Recheck the temperatures. Note any increase in air delivery to other rooms. Recheck the temperatures and continue adjusting dampers until you achieve the balance.

Step 1. To open a damper, turn the handle clockwise until it is parallel with the duct.

replacing a thermocouple

If you're having a problem keeping the pilot light lit in a gas furnace, boiler, or water heater, the thermocouple may be the source of the problem. It is like a thermostat that controls the burner. Replacing one is fairly easy.

TOOLS AND MATERIALS:
- **Flashlight**
- **Adjustable wrench**
- **Long matches**
- **Thermocouple**

1 Shut off the gas inlet valve and remove the access cover so you can see the burners.

2 Disconnect the thermocouple from the control by unscrewing a hold-down nut. The other end may be held in place with a nut or it may simply pull out.

3 Purchase a new thermocouple of the same length. Install the replacement, taking care not to kink the tube. Make sure the bulbous end is positioned so it will touch the pilot flame.

4 Turn on the gas inlet valve and relight the pilot (see page 243). Replace the access cover.

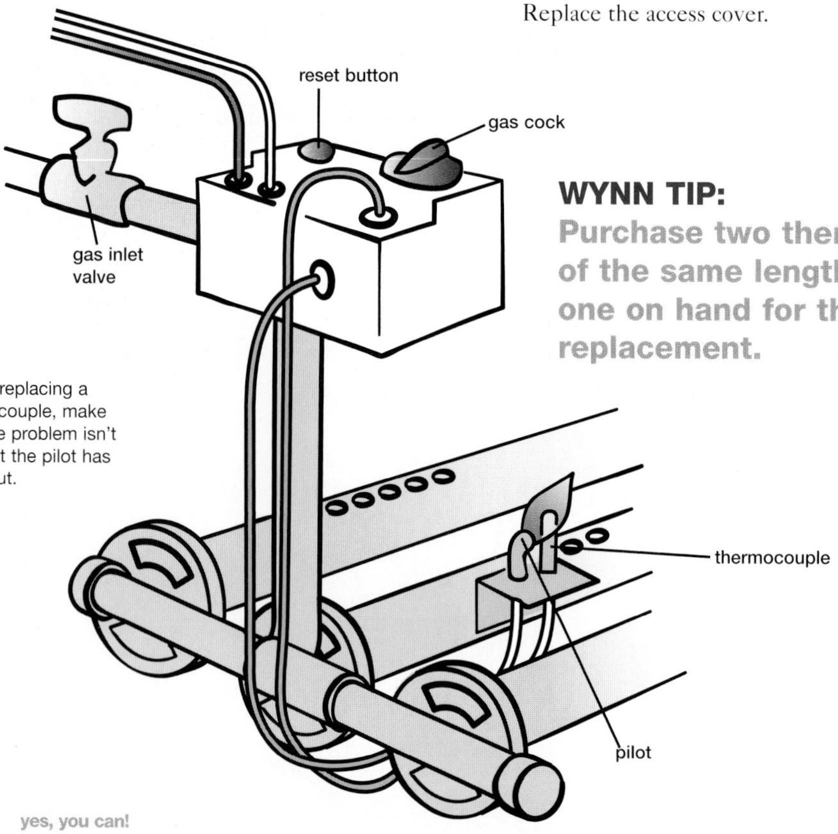

WYNN TIP:
Purchase two thermocouples of the same length so you have one on hand for the next replacement.

Before replacing a thermocouple, make sure the problem isn't just that the pilot has gone out.

reset button

gas cock

gas inlet valve

thermocouple

pilot

checking oil-burning furnaces

The first time your oil-burning heating system shuts down, reset the safety switch and try again. If the burner kicks off again, shut off all power. The burner motor and ignition may be protected by separate fuses or breakers.

TOOLS AND MATERIALS:
- **Screwdriver**
- **Clean rag or tissue**

1 There may be one burner disconnect switch on the side of the furnace and another outside the furnace room. Switch both off before attempting any repairs.

2 If the primary safety or stack switch shuts off, wait 5 minutes, then press the reset lever or button. Combustion air blowers usually are protected by an overload device. Restart by pressing the reset button.

IF THE BURNER HAS AN ELECTRIC-EYE PRIMARY SAFETY

Look for an access cover that lets you get to its photocell. Wipe the photocell with a clean rag or tissue to remove soot. Reassemble it, turn on the burner, and see if the furnace fires.

IF THE FURNACE HAS A STACK SWITCH SAFETY ON THE FLUE

Remove the screw holding the unit to the stack. Slide it out and wipe off the sensor. Reassemble the unit.

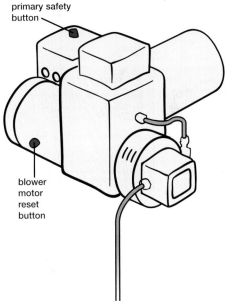

primary safety button

blower motor reset button

WYNN TIP:
Don't continually restart a stubborn oil burner. Unburned oil could accumulate in the combustion chamber and "flash back." If the furnace won't fire after three attempts, call for professional service.

replacing a furnace filter

Blowing air from a furnace stirs up dust and pollen. A high-quality filter catches most of these particles. If you neglect to change the filter according to the manufacturer's recommendation, the dirty filter chokes airflow and makes the unit work harder, thus wasting energy. In fact, a severely clogged filter can cause a furnace to overheat and shut down. Most filters can be cleaned, while others must be replaced.

TOOLS AND MATERIALS:
- **Vacuum**
- **Furnace filter**

1 Most blower doors lift or swing open. On some models, the door will be at the top of the furnace. Purchase an exact replacement filter designed for your furnace make and model.

2 Many filters slide out. Look for dirt on or around the blower too. Vacuum, if necessary. A hammock-type filter wraps around the base of the blower; it is also easy to replace.

WYNN TIP:
To effectively remove pollen, mold, and bacteria as well as nearly all dust, have a contractor install an electrostatic filter.

WYNN TIP:
Inexpensive filters trap only larger particles. To keep your air even cleaner, purchase the highest-quality filter available for your furnace.

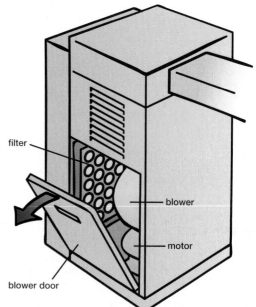

filter

blower

motor

blower door

Step 1. Access the filter by opening the blower door. The filter is typically located on the side next to the blower and motor.

glossary

Know it by name? Find it here

A–B

Access panel. A removable panel in a tub surround, wall, or ceiling that permits repair or replacement of concealed items, such as whirlpool pumps or faucet bodies.

Actual dimension. True size (exact measurement) of a piece of lumber, after milling and drying. *See also* Nominal dimension.

Aerator. A device screwed into the spout outlet of most sink faucets that mixes air with the water to achieve less water splash and smoother flow.

Air chamber. A short, enclosed tube on water lines that provides a cushion of air to control sudden surges in water pressure that sometimes result in noisy pipes.

Amp (A). A measurement of the electrical current in a circuit at any moment. *See also* Volt and Watt.

Auger. A flexible metal cable fished into traps and drain lines to dislodge obstructions.

Awl. A sharp-pointed tool used to make starter holes for screws or to scribe lines.

Backerboard. A ready-made surface for setting tile. Also called cement board. Can be cement-based or gypsum-based.

Backsplash. Typically a 3- to 4-inch-high length of material at the back edge of a countertop extending the full length.

Ballast. Transformer that steps up the voltage in a fluorescent lamp.

Ballcock. The assembly inside a toilet tank that, when activated, releases water into the bowl to start the flushing action. It also prepares the toilet for subsequent flushes.

Balusters. Spindles that help support a staircase handrail.

Bridging. Boards nailed between joists to add rigidity and keep the joists from warping. Often used to quiet squeaking floors.

Building code. Local ordinance governing the manner in which a home may be constructed or modified. Most codes are concerned with fire and health, with separate sections relating to electrical, plumbing, and structural work.

Bullnose tile. Flat tile with at least one rounded edge, used to trim edges of a tile installation.

Butt joint. The joint formed by two pieces of material when fastened end to end, end to face, or end to edge.

Butter. To apply mortar on bricks or blocks with a trowel before laying them.

C–D

Cable. Two or more insulated conductors wrapped in metal or plastic sheathing.

Casing. Trimwork around a door, window, or other opening.

Caulk. Any compound used to seal seams and joints against infiltration of water and air.

Circuit. The path of electrical flow from a power source through an outlet and back to ground.

Circuit breaker. A safety switch that automatically interrupts electrical flow in a circuit in the event of an overload or a short.

Cleanout. A removable plug in a trap or a drainpipe that allows easier access to blockages inside.

Closet bend. The elbow-shaped fitting beneath toilets that carries waste to the main drain.

Conduit. Rigid or flexible tubing through which wires are run for protection.

Continuity tester. A device that tells whether a circuit is capable of carrying electricity.

Coped cut. A profile cut made in the face of a piece of molding that allows for butting it against another piece at an inside corner.

Crosscut. To saw a piece of lumber perpendicular to its length or its grain.

glossary
Know it by name? Find it here.

Dado joint. A joint formed when the end of one member fits into a groove cut partway through the face of another.

Damper. A valve inside a duct or flue that can be used to slow or stop the flow of air or smoke.

Deadbolt. A locking device activated only with a key or thumb turn. Unlike a latch's beveled tongue, deadbolts have squared-off ends.

Dimension lumber. A piece of lumber that is at least 2 inches thick and at least 2 inches wide.

Dimmer. A specialty switch that lets you vary the intensity of a light.

Double cylinder. A type of lock that must be operated with a key from inside and outside.

Drain-waste-vent (DWV) system. The network of pipes and fittings that carries liquid and solid wastes out of a building to a public sewer, a septic tank, or a cesspool. It also allows for the passage of sewer gases up through the roof.

Drywall. A basic interior building material consisting of sheets of pressed gypsum faced with heavy paper on both sides. Also known as wallboard, gypsum board, plasterboard, and Sheetrock®.

E–G

Elbow. A fitting used to change the direction of a water supply line. Also known as an ell. Bends do the same thing with drain-waste-vent lines.

Face frame. The front structure of a cabinet or chest of drawers made of stiles and rails; it surrounds the door panels or drawers.

Field tiles. Flat tiles, in contrast to trim tiles that are shaped to turn corners or define surface edges.

Fixture. (1) Any electrical device permanently attached to a home's wiring. (2) Any of several plumbing devices that provide a supply of water or sanitary disposal of liquid or solid wastes.

Flue. A pipe or other channel that carries off smoke and combustion gases to the outside air.

Flush. On the same plane as, or level with, a surrounding surface.

Framing. The skeletal or structural support of a home. Sometimes called framework.

Fuse. A safety device designed to stop electrical flow if a circuit shorts or is overloaded. Like a circuit breaker, a fuse protects against fire from overheated wiring.

Glazing. (1) A protective and decorative coating that is fired onto the surface of some tiles. (2) The process of installing glass by securing it with glazier's points and glazing compound.

Grain. The direction of fibers in a piece of wood; also refers to the pattern of the fibers.

Graphite. A soft, black carbon powder used to lubricate working metal parts such as those found in a doorknob or lock.

Green board. Similar to regular drywall, this material is moisture resistant, though not waterproof. Also referred to as blue board.

Grit. The abrasive material bonded to sandpaper. Grit is designated by numbers, such as 120-grit. The higher the number, the finer the abrasive.

Ground. Refers to the fact that electricity always seeks the shortest possible path to the earth. Neutral wires carry electricity to ground in all circuits. An additional grounding wire, or the sheathing of metal-clad cable or conduit, protects against shock from a malfunctioning device.

Ground-fault circuit interrupter (GFCI). A safety device that senses any shock hazard and shuts down a circuit or receptacle.

Grout. A thin mortar mixture. Also, the process of applying grout.

H–N

Heat loss. Heat escaping from a home. Heat gains and losses are expressed in Btu per hour.

Hot wire. The conductor that carries current to a receptacle or other outlet. *See also* Ground and Neutral wire.

Incandescent bulb. Light source with an electrically charged metal filament that burns at white heat.

Insulation. A nonconductive covering that protects wires and other electricity carriers.

Jamb. The top and side frames of a door, window, or other opening.

Joint compound. A formula used with paper tape to conceal joints between drywall panels.

Joists. Horizontal framing members that support a floor and/or ceiling.

Junction box. An enclosure used for splitting circuits into different branches. In a junction box, wires connect only to each other, never to a switch, receptacle, or fixture.

Knockouts. Tabs that can be removed to make openings in an electrical box. They accommodate cable and conduit connectors.

Level. When a surface is at true horizontal. Also a tool used to determine level.

MDF (Medium Density Fiberboard). Made of fine wood chips, this material is available in 12- and 16-inch-wide pieces often used for shelving.

Main drain. That portion of the drainage system between the fixture drains and the sewer drain.

Miter joint. The joint formed when two members meet that have been cut at the same angle.

Molding. A strip of wood, usually small-dimensioned, used to cover exposed edges or as decoration.

Mortise. A shallow cutout in a board usually used to recess hardware.

Neon (voltage) tester. A device with two leads and a small bulb that determines whether a circuit is carrying current.

Neutral wire. A conductor that carries current from an outlet back to ground. It is clad in white insulation. *See also* Ground and Hot wire.

Nominal dimension. The stated size of a tile (usually including a standard grout joint) or a piece of lumber, such as a 2×4 or a 1×12. The actual dimension is somewhat smaller.

O–P

O-ring. A round rubber washer used to create a watertight seal, chiefly around valve stems.

On-center (OC). The distance from the center of one regularly spaced framing member or hole to the center of the next.

1-by (2-by). Refers to nominal one- or two-inch thick lumber of any width, length, or type of wood. Actual thicknesses are ¾ inch and 1½ inch, respectively.

Outlet. Any potential point of use in a circuit, including receptacles, switches, and light fixtures.

Overload. When a circuit is carrying more amperage than it is designed to handle. Overloading causes wires to heat up, which in turn blows fuses or trips circuit breakers.

Particleboard. Panels made from compressed wood chips and glue.

Partition wall. Unlike a load-bearing wall, a partition supports no structure above it and can therefore be removed.

Pilot hole. A small hole drilled into a board to avoid splitting the wood when driving a screw or nail.

Pipe joint compound. A material applied to pipe threads to ensure a watertight seal. Also called pipe dope. *See also* Plumber's tape.

Plumb. The condition that exists when a surface is at true vertical.

glossary

Know it by name? Find it here

Plumb bob. Tool used to align vertical points.

Plumber's putty. A doughlike material used as a sealant. Often a bead of it is around the underside of toilets and sinks.

Plumber's tape. A synthetic material wrapped around pipe threads to seal a joint. Often called pipe tape. *See also* Pipe joint compound.

Plunger. A suction-action tool used to dislodge obstructions from drain lines. Also called a force cup and a plumber's friend.

Polarized plugs. Electric plugs designed with asymmetrical prongs so the hot and neutral prongs cannot be inserted into a receptacle incorrectly.

Primer. A first coating formulated to seal raw surfaces and hold succeeding finish coats.

R–S

R-value. A measure of the resistance to heat transfer that an insulating material provides. The higher the R-value, the more effective the insulation.

Rafters. Parallel framing members that support a roof.

Receptacle. An outlet that supplies power for lamps and other plug-in devices.

Relief valve. A device designed to open if it senses excess temperature or pressure.

Rip. To saw lumber or sheet goods parallel to the grain pattern.

Romex. A trade name for nonmetallic-sheathed cable.

Sash. The part of a window that can be opened, consisting of a frame and glass.

Service entrance (service head). The point where power enters a home.

Service panel. The main fuse or circuit-breaker box in a home.

Shim. A thin strip or wedge of wood or other material used to fill a gap between two adjoining components or to help establish level or plumb.

Short circuit. A condition that occurs when hot and neutral wires contact each other. Fuses and breakers protect against fire, which can result from a short.

Sill. The lowest horizontal piece of a window, door, or wall framework.

Sill cock. The valve of an outdoor faucet. Building codes frequently require sill cocks to be frost-proof so that they are not damaged by ice produced by cold weather.

Spline. A thin piece of wood fitted into slots on the edges of two joined boards to strengthen the joint.

Square. The condition that exists when two surfaces are at 90 degrees to each other. Also, a tool used to determine square.

Stiles. Vertical members of a door assembly or cabinet facing.

Stop valve. A device installed in a water supply line, usually near a fixture, that lets you shut off the flow to one fixture without interrupting service to the rest of the system.

Straightedge. An improvised tool, usually a 1×4 or 2×4 with a straight edge, used to mark a line on material or to determine if a surface is even.

Stud. Vertical 2×4 or 2×6 framing members spaced at regular intervals within a wall.

Stud finder. Electronic or magnetic tool that locates studs within a finished wall.

Subfloor. Usually plywood or another sheet material covering the floor joists.

Sweep. A flexible strip placed on the bottom edge of a door for insulation and to prevent drafts.

T

Taping. The process of covering drywall joints with tape and joint compound.

Tee. A T-shaped fitting used to tap into a length of pipe at a 90-degree angle for the purposes of beginning a branch line.

Template. A pattern to follow when re-creating a precise shape.

Thermocouple. An electric device for measuring temperature.

Thin-set mortar. A setting adhesive for tiles.

Three-four-five method. A way to check for square. Measure 3 feet along one side and 4 feet along the other. If the corner is square, the diagonal distance between those two points will equal 5 feet.

Three-way switch. Operates a light fixture from two locations.

Threshold. The plate at the bottom of some—usually exterior—door openings. Sometimes called a saddle.

Time-delay fuse. A fuse that does not break the circuit during the momentary overload that can happen when an electric motor starts up. If the overload continues, this fuse will blow.

Tread. The level part of a staircase.

Trim tile. Tiles that are shaped to turn corners or define the edges of an installation. Includes, cove trim, bullnose, V-cap, quarter round, inside corner, and outside corner.

Trowel. Any of several flat and oblong or flat and pointed metal tools used for handling and/or finishing concrete and mortar.

U–V

Underwriters knot. A knot used to secure wires in a lamp socket.

Vapor barrier. A waterproof membrane in a floor, wall, or ceiling that blocks the transfer of condensation to the inner surface.

Veneer. A thin layer of decorative wood.

Volt (V). A measure of electrical pressure. Volts × amps = watts.

Voltmeter. A device that measures voltage and performs other tests.

W–Z

Wall anchor. A fastener such as the toggle bolt or Molly that is used to secure objects to hollow walls, or a concrete anchor used to secure objects to concrete or masonry walls.

Wall box. A rectangular enclosure for receptacles and switches.

Warp. Any of several lumber defects caused by uneven shrinkage of wood cells.

Watt (W). A measure of the power an electrical device consumes. See also Amp and Volt.

Wet wall. A strategically placed cavity (usually a 2×6 wall) in which the main drain/vent stack and a cluster of supply and drain-waste-vent lines are housed.

METRIC CONVERSIONS

U.S. Units to Metric Equivalents			Metric Units to U.S. Equivalents		
To Convert From	Multiply By	To Get	To Convert From	Multiply By	To Get
Inches	25.4	Millimeters	Millimeters	0.0394	Inches
Inches	2.54	Centimeters	Centimeters	0.3937	Inches
Feet	30.48	Centimeters	Centimeters	0.0328	Feet
Feet	0.3048	Meters	Meters	3.2808	Feet
Yards	0.9144	Meters	Meters	1.0936	Yards

To convert from degrees Fahrenheit (F) to degrees Celsius (C), first subtract 32, then multiply by $\frac{5}{9}$.

To convert from degrees Celsius to degrees Fahrenheit, multiply by $\frac{9}{5}$, then add 32.

index

Know what needs to be fixed? Find it here.